NEGOTIATION

NEGOTIATION

Inns of Court School of Law

BLACKSTONE PRESS LIMITED

First published in Great Britain 1996 by Blackstone Press Limited, Aldine Place, London W12 8AA. Telephone: (020) 8740 2277
www.blackstonepress.com

© Inns of Court School of Law, 1996

First edition 1996
Second edition 1997
Third edition 1998
Fourth edition 1999
Fifth edition 2000

ISBN: 1 84174 057 8

British Library Cataloguing in Publication Data
A CIP catalogue record for this book is available from the British Library.

Typeset by Montage Studios Ltd, Horsmonden, Kent
Printed by Ashford Colour Press, Gosport, Hampshire

All rights reserved. No part of this book may be reproduced or transmitted in any form or by any means, electronic or mechanical, including photocopying, recording, or any information storage or retrieval system without prior permission from the publisher.

FOREWORD

These manuals are designed primarily to support training on the Bar Vocational Course, though they are also intended to provide a useful resource for legal practitioners and for anyone undertaking training in legal skills.

The Bar Vocational Course was designed by staff at the Inns of Court School of Law, where it was introduced in 1989. This course is intended to equip students with the practical skills and the procedural and evidential knowledge that they will need to start their legal professional careers. These manuals are written by staff at the Inns of Court School of Law who have helped to develop the course, and by a range of legal practitioners and others involved in legal skills training. The authors of the manuals are very well aware of the practical and professional approach that is central to the Bar Vocational Course.

The range and coverage of the manuals have grown steadily. All the manuals are updated annually, and regular reviews and revisions of the manuals are carried out to ensure that developments in legal skills training and the experience of our staff are fully reflected in them.

This updating and revision is a constant process and we very much value the comments of practitioners, staff and students. Legal vocational training is advancing rapidly, and it is important that all those concerned work together to achieve and maintain high standards. Please address any comments to the Bar Vocational Course Director at the Inns of Court School of Law.

With the validation of other providers for the Bar Vocational Course it is very much our intention that these manuals will be of equal value to all students wherever they take the course, and we would very much value comments from tutors and students at other validated institutions.

The enthusiasm of the staff at Blackstone Press Ltd and their efficiency in arranging production and publication of the manuals is much appreciated.

The Hon. Mr Justice Elias
Chairman of the Board of Governors
Inns of Court School of Law
August 2000

CONTENTS

Foreword	**v**
Preface	**ix**

1 Introduction to Negotiation — **1**
1.1 The importance of negotiation skills — 1
1.2 Learning negotiation skills — 2

2 The Essentials of Negotiation — **7**
2.1 What does negotiation mean? — 7
2.2 Types of negotiation — 8
2.3 Issues to be negotiated — 11
2.4 The negotiation process — 13

3 Legal Negotiations — **15**
3.1 Generally — 15
3.2 Why cases settle — 15
3.3 Negotiations by solicitors and barristers — 18
3.4 The role and influence of the lay client — 22
3.5 'Without prejudice' negotiations — 23
3.6 Effective legal negotiators — 24

4 Strategy and Style — **29**
4.1 Introduction — 29
4.2 Strategy overview — 30
4.3 Competitive strategy — 33
4.4 Cooperative — 37
4.5 Collaborative/principled/problem-solving — 40
4.6 Choosing a strategy — 47
4.7 The big questions — 48
4.8 Summary — 51

5 Tactics and Techniques — **53**
5.1 Introduction — 53
5.2 Specific tactics — 53
5.3 Dubious tactics — 63
5.4 General attitude/preparation for tactics — 64
5.5 Dealing with deadlock/failure to move — 64
5.6 Other problems — 65
5.7 Techniques for getting past no — 66

6 Cognitive Influences — **69**
6.1 Introduction — 69

6.2	Human influence and the role of emotion	69
6.3	Expectations and perceptions	69
6.4	The self-fulfilling prophecy	70
6.5	Selective perception	71
6.6	Concessions and psychological influences	71
6.7	Reciprocal behaviour	72
6.8	Not coping	73
6.9	Communication skills	73

7 Persuasion — 77
7.1	Introduction	77
7.2	The use of argument	77
7.3	Other persuasion techniques	83
7.4	Conclusion	85

8 Ethics of Negotiation — 87
8.1	Introduction	87
8.2	The opponent	87
8.3	The lay client	89
8.4	The professional client	90
8.5	The court	90
8.6	Problems	90

9 Preparation and Strategic Planning — 93
9.1	What should preparation and strategic planning cover?	93
9.2	Analysis	94
9.3	Planning the presentation of the case	101
9.4	Planning concessions	104
9.5	Strategy, structure and tactics	107
9.6	Your written plan	108
9.7	Sample written plans	109
9.8	Checklist for preparation	124

10 Conducting a Negotiation — Making the Most Effective Use of the Process — 127
10.1	Working to achieve the client's objectives and acting within instructions	127
10.2	General factors regarding the negotiation process	128
10.3	The stages in the negotiating process	130
10.4	Reviewing your conduct of a negotiation	141

11 Recording and Enforcing a Negotiated Agreement — 143
11.1	The vital role of client acceptance	143
11.2	General elements of a final agreement	144
11.3	Forms for an enforceable agreement	145
11.4	Enforcement of negotiated agreements	154

12 Appropriate Dispute Resolution — 157
12.1	Appropriate not alternative	157
12.2	What is wrong with litigation?	157
12.3	The alternatives	158
12.4	Arbitration	160
12.5	Mediation	161

13 Assessing Negotiation Skills — 165
13.1	Learning lawyers' negotiation skills	165
13.2	The negotiation course	166
13.3	The negotiation criteria	167

14 Sample Exercise — 173

15 Suggested Reading — 193

Index — 195

PREFACE

Although we have all been negotiating since birth, it is widely accepted that negotiation skills can be learned and developed and negotiation is now part of legal professional training in many jurisdictions. This training recognises that to improve your skill as a negotiator, you need to understand what influences peoples' behaviour in a negotiation, to know how to prepare properly for the negotiation and, to practise negotiating using this understanding and knowledge.

The purpose of this Manual is to provide a theoretical background and give practical advice on preparing for and conducting a negotiation. It is also designed to assist those learning or developing their skills as a negotiator within the legal context, particularly barristers.

A substantial amount has been written about negotiation in recent years, particularly about different types of strategy, some of which is prescriptive in that it recommends adopting a particular strategy. This Manual does not prescribe any particular strategy, as different situations may call for different strategies. The Manual tries to assist understanding of the underlying ethos, particular characteristics and advantages and disadvantages of the different strategies so that you are able to consciously choose an appropriate strategy and deal with that adopted by your opponent.

Effective negotiation is based on proper preparation which includes: a clear idea of what is being sought in the negotiation by the client and the opponent; a thorough understanding of the law and facts; and careful consideration of what you will seek and are prepared to offer in the negotiation and the factual or legal arguments or reasoning which may be used to support this. On this, the Manual is more prescriptive, in that we believe that negotiation is about persuasion. While strategy may be an effective tool against an unenlightened opponent, thorough understanding of the case and proper use of persuasive argument can be effectively used whatever the opponent's strategy.

ONE

INTRODUCTION TO NEGOTIATION

1.1 The Importance of Negotiation Skills

1.1.1 IS COURT ROOM ADVOCACY THE PRIME SKILL?

The word 'barrister' produces for most people the picture of an advocate in court on his or her feet either addressing the court or questioning a witness. It is generally recognised that this work is highly skilled and that the skill lies in being able to put the case persuasively. We have all seen it either in the courtroom or on the screen, just the right question asked of the witness, just the right phrase used to convince the jury.

However, a barrister's role extends well beyond this scene of courtroom drama. One could say it only represents the tip of the iceberg. Most cases never get to trial. A very high percentage of civil cases settle (estimates differ but it is probably around 80 to 90%) and these settlements are achieved by negotiation. Many cases settle at the court door. For most people trial is the last resort. Thus any barrister who has been briefed for trial will frequently find himself or herself negotiating the case to try to reach a settlement outside the courtroom. Lawyers, barristers and solicitors, spend a substantial part of their time negotiating.

Most civil cases settle. Negotiation skills are therefore used more in the determination of civil cases than courtroom advocacy.

1.1.2 HOW DOES NEGOTIATION DIFFER FROM COURTROOM ADVOCACY?

Trials occur because two parties cannot agree. There is a dispute and they cannot agree how to resolve it aside from taking the case to a third party (i.e., to court) to determine the dispute for them. There are two basic aspects of good courtroom advocacy. First, there is the ability to address the court using argument to persuade the court to see the case your way. Secondly, there is the ability to ask the right questions of witnesses to elicit information which strengthens your case or weakens your opponent's in the eyes of the court. While there are differing levels of sophistication in the use of these two abilities, basically these are the two tasks of an advocate in court. In both circumstances the advocates on both sides of the case are seeking to persuade a third party, the court, to see the facts and law from their point of view — i.e., to find in their favour.

Although not all negotiations are about matters which are actually disputed, for example, two people may negotiate the terms on which they will operate a partnership, negotiation is a process by which people try to reach agreement or settlement where there are differences either real or perceived. Negotiation could be said to include any situation where a decision is sought which takes into account more than one person's point of view. Unlike courtroom advocacy, where the advocates are trying to persuade a third party who will make a final determination of any differences, in negotiation the negotiators are trying to persuade each other about how they can, between them, resolve differences. Like advocacy, negotiation is about the use of information and persuasion. Negotiations involve questioning and discussion. In questioning, each negotiator will be seeking information to assess what the differences are and how best they can be resolved in a way that he or she wants. In discussing the case, each negotiator will be attempting to persuade the other negotiator to resolve the differences in the manner that he or she wants.

Persuasion can be defined as causing a person to have a belief of fact or that a thing is so or inducing a person to do something. The word 'persuade' is used in this broad sense and, as you will see when considering strategies and tactics in negotiation, there are a variety of methods of 'persuading' used in negotiations. The ability to persuade is an essential skill of a good advocate and a good negotiator. The prime difference is that advocates are seeking to persuade a third party and negotiators are seeking to persuade each other.

1.2 Learning Negotiation Skills

1.2.1 CAN NEGOTIATION SKILLS BE LEARNED?

'Can we discuss this case and see if we can settle it?' may be the first thing which is said to you on your first day at court. The frequency with which court cases settle means that when you are briefed for a hearing you will take on two roles, as negotiator and courtroom advocate. There will almost invariably be discussion between counsel of any case prior to a hearing, even if this discussion is not to settle the whole case. You have arrived fully prepared to present the case in court but are you prepared for this discussion which may obviate the need for trial (the very thing you have prepared for)?

Can you learn to negotiate outside the courtroom in the same way you can learn to present a case in court effectively?

- There are set procedures and rules for the conduct of court hearings which you can find out by reading books on advocacy or asking colleagues so that you go into court at least understanding the process and your role in it. What procedures apply to negotiations and where can you find out about them? How do you decide the order in which matters should be discussed? How do you learn to structure and take control of the proceedings and what is covered?

- In a trial the court determines the outcome on its assessment of the merits of the parties' cases. In a negotiation you have to decide whether the settlement suggested is a good one for your client. How do you judge it? What standards do you use? You are not an impartial judge weighing up both sides. Your duty is owed to the client. On the other hand, in preparing for trial, you should have assessed the merits of the case. How do you use this assessment?

- In court there are rules of evidence and procedure which determine what information is made available to the court. Again you can look these up in a book or find out from colleagues so you know what is expected. What information should you exchange in a negotiation?

- Court etiquette sets certain standards of behaviour for the various parts played in a courtroom trial. Although personality still does play a part in this, to a degree courtroom behaviour has been ritualised and you can learn the conventions by watching others in court or reading books on advocacy. Are there any rules of etiquette in negotiation? How much does behaviour and personality influence what happens in a negotiation and the ultimate settlement reached?

It is now well accepted that legal skills such as legal research, interviewing, drafting, etc. can be learned. The concept that some skills used by lawyers are innate and cannot be learned clings more heavily to advocacy and negotiation than to others. This myth is perhaps being eroded more quickly in respect of courtroom advocacy than negotiation.

Advocacy in the courtroom is done according to set rules with both the process and the result being observed and open to analysis and assessment by a variety of people including the decision makers (judge, magistrate or jury), the advocates, the parties, the witnesses and members of the public (where the case is heard in public). It is therefore possible for there to be discussion and possible consensus about what constitutes good advocacy. For obvious reasons, e.g., the main players are lawyers, the characteristics of a good advocate have largely been defined from a legal point of view (although there is huge cross-over with general presentation skills). Courtroom advocacy has been the province of lawyers until recently. However, the monopoly of lawyers in providing this service is breaking down and much time and resources are being spent on analysing both the elements of good advocacy and how these can be learned.

Negotiation, on the other hand, is done privately; only those participating know what happened in the course of the negotiation and the terms of the settlement. Any later discussion about the negotiation will usually be confined to the outcome and whether or not it was what was sought. Although people know what they need to achieve in a negotiation (i.e., get a good outcome), they are much less clear about how to do it. How does negotiation work? What is the process and how can one do it to achieve a good outcome?

While courtroom advocacy is seen as the province of lawyers, everyone negotiates. Thus, our concepts of both the process of negotiation and the characteristics of a good negotiator and a good settlement come from a much broader range of transactions and participants than our concepts about advocacy.

We have all been negotiating since infancy when our main task was to try to control the feeding schedule. As adults we negotiate in a more sophisticated way using a broader range of tactics (hopefully!). We negotiate every day both in our working lives, e.g., seeking a pay rise, and in our personal lives, e.g., deciding what movie to see, what to have for dinner, etc. through a vast list of everyday situations. As a skill used by professionals, however, we probably associate negotiation more with trade union negotiations or commercial transactions and salespeople than with the legal profession. This has influenced the concepts of what good negotiation is all about. Two classic pictures of successful negotiators are, first, the brash hard-nosed born negotiator who basically gets what he or she wants by bullying and, secondly, the golden-tongued, charming negotiator who gets what he or she wants by clever manipulation. People who see negotiation in these terms tend to think that negotiation is a skill which comes naturally to some and cannot be learned by others. They think that being a good negotiator depends on your personality. While personality does play a part, good negotiation skills can be learned.

1.2.2 HOW CAN NEGOTIATION SKILLS BE LEARNED?

Given the number of interactions you have each day, you frequently 'negotiate' without being conscious of doing so. In many interactions which are in fact negotiations, you do not analyse what you are doing and why. You may be conscious that you are being more successful in getting what you want sometimes than others and you will already have some individuality in how you negotiate and the tactics you use. However, you need to learn to build on the skills you have and adapt them to negotiating in a legal context. To do this you need to understand the process, your part in it and to know what is and what is not effective.

Lawyers have come later than some professions to skills training. Until very recently they 'learned' their skills 'sitting with Nelly', i.e., watching others on the assumption that they would be able to distinguish the good from the bad habits, the effective from the ineffective techniques and then somehow adopt the good and effective and reject the bad and ineffective. Much of the learning for barristers was focused on courtroom advocacy, and the experience of observing negotiations in process was very limited both in time and in the range of people observed as it would be restricted to one's pupil master or pupil mistress (or others in chambers to whom one might from time to time be assigned). What one observed about negotiation was therefore completely arbitrary and done without any context of what one should be looking for, what, if any, research or theories existed about the process, effective and ineffective strategies, tactics, behaviour, etc. or how to judge a settlement or a negotiator's performance.

Sales people are taught how to sell and part of the training is learning how to negotiate within the commercial context. They have training programmes and there are scores of books written on successful negotiation techniques for sales people.

There is a large body of literature on negotiation in a variety of contexts beyond those of the world of commercial selling. These include the more general business environment and the world of international relations. Some of this work draws on theories which have been debated for much longer: for example, dispute theory (how disputes arise, are dealt with and settled) and game theory (what people do in highly structured games which require them to decide a strategy against an opponent). There is a smaller but growing body of literature on negotiation in the legal context which draws on some of the other disciplines and covers a wide variety of issues including: attempts to categorise the different types of negotiations; discussion of different strategies and tactics and the factors which influence the effectiveness and choice of strategy; analysis of the process of negotiation; factors which influence whether people settle a case or take it to trial; and where negotiation fits in the judicial system, particularly given the development of alternatives to litigation. There is some empirical research on negotiation but it is limited both in the number of research projects done and in the manner in which they were done.

Negotiation is now part of legal professional skills training in many jurisdictions. There appears to be a similar basis to the training across jurisdictions which has been heavily influenced by some of the literature and theories which focus on analysis of negotiation, strategy and tactics.

Learning negotiation is about learning to understand the process and theories and how to apply these to your situation *not* about learning a formula or rules which will guarantee a perfect negotiation. To learn to negotiate effectively you need to understand the process, the strategies and tactics used and have some criteria against which to judge in what ways a performance is and is not effective and determine whether and why an outcome is a good or a bad settlement. With this understanding you are able to assess and critique your own and others' performance in negotiations.

1.2.3 THE PURPOSE OF THE MANUAL

1.2.3.1 The theoretical framework

Negotiation is an intellectual skill. It combines thinking and doing. The more you understand about the skill, the more you will understand how you and others operate and see the ways in which you can become more skilled. Just practising negotiation without any understanding of the theory means you merely reinforce your existing methods of negotiating, probably ingrained from childhood. You do not extend your range of techniques and may well reinforce bad habits.

Chapters 1 to **8** of this Manual therefore set out a theoretical framework to enable you to understand the different types of negotiation, what happens in any negotiation, the peculiar characteristics of legal negotiations, the different strategies and tactics which are often used and some of the cognitive influences and ethical considerations in negotiations.

1.2.3.2 Practical steps

Negotiating effectively in a legal context, in particular within the civil justice system, requires detailed practical preparation, planning and control of the conduct of the negotiation and ensuring that the negotiation is properly concluded. **Chapters 9** to **11** deal with these practical considerations using a worked example of a civil case.

INTRODUCTION TO NEGOTIATION

1.2.3.3 **Civil dispute resolution**

Chapter 12 sets negotiation in the context of civil dispute resolution generally. The current training for a barrister is focused on learning to operate within a litigation framework, i.e., resolving disputes through the court. However, there is increasing concern about the faults of this system and alternatives are being promoted more and more vigorously. ADR, originally an acronym for Alternative Dispute Resolution and fast becoming an acronym for Appropriate Dispute Resolution, is expanding. A variety of dispute resolution methods are being developed, the most common methods aside from litigation being arbitration and mediation. This chapter outlines the differences between the methods and where negotiation fits within the whole dispute resolution scene.

TWO

THE ESSENTIALS OF NEGOTIATION

2.1 What Does Negotiation Mean?

The term 'negotiation' can cover a wide range of activities. It is difficult to give a single definition. The *Concise Oxford Dictionary* (1982) defines negotiate as 'confer (with another) with view to compromise or agreement'.

2.1.1 COMPROMISE/CONCESSIONS

Negotiation is about communication and compromise. However, just conferring with a view to compromise will not necessarily get you to agreement. Negotiation is also about movement, making and seeking concessions.

Many people consider negotiation to be the same as simple bargaining. The classic example is haggling in a market over the price of an item. The only issue is how much will be paid and both the buyer and the seller have a figure in mind which differs. The 'bargaining' process is about how far each side will move toward the other to reach an agreed price. While such bargaining is a form of negotiation, the term negotiation includes much more complex scenarios, e.g. international negotiations or a divorce settlement, and involves more sophisticated considerations.

2.1.2 SHARED, COMPATIBLE AND CONFLICTING INTERESTS

Two definitions by writers on legal negotiation take on board that it is more complex than just simple bargaining:

- Donald G. Gifford in his book *Legal Negotiation Theory and Applications* defines negotiation in the introduction as '... a process in which two or more participants attempt to reach a joint decision on matters of common concern in situations where they are in actual or potential disagreement or conflict.'

- Roger Fisher and William Ury (Harvard Negotiation Project) define negotiation in the preface to their book *Getting to Yes: Negotiating Agreement Without Giving In.* 'Negotiation is a basic means of getting what you want from others. It is back-and-forth communication designed to reach an agreement when you and the other side have some interests that are shared and others that are opposed.'

These definitions recognise that negotiations can include a broad range of issues including shared interests or common concerns together with those on which there may be disagreement, opposition or conflict. The first of these definitions also recognises that the disagreement may be actual or potential.

2.1.3 EXCHANGE OF INFORMATION

Although the principal purpose of a negotiation is for both parties to accept something different from what they *ideally* want in order to reach agreement on what each will get, it is also about exchanging information on a variety of matters including what the parties want, the facts they allege, the evidence they have, etc.

2.1.4 PERSUADING BY ARGUMENT

Negotiation is not just haggling or arguing in the sense of exchanging rhetoric. However, argument is a fundamental part of negotiating. Negotiation is about persuading the other side to your view by the use of reasoned argument based on rational analysis. Most books and articles on negotiation fail to address this aspect of negotiation. Those who see negotiation as a battle or a straight competition, focus on manipulative tactics which involve coercion rather than rational persuasive argument. Those who see negotiation as a more collaborative process with both parties working together to reach settlement, tend to duck the issue with a slight tendency to treat the use of argument as 'impolite'. Good argument is about advancing reasons to persuade and persuasion is an important part of negotiation.

2.1.5 DYNAMIC INTERACTIVE PROCESS

Any negotiation is a dynamic, interactive process. The negotiators' behaviour, expectations and analysis of what is possible are all influenced by the process and by each other's behaviour, expectations and statements of what is possible. During the negotiation, both parties' perceptions and judgments, strategy and tactics will change. Negotiation can be compared to a game of chess where the move of one party influences how the other moves, where one is looking several moves ahead all the time.

2.1.6 GETTING WHAT YOU WANT

Finally and most importantly, negotiation is about getting what you want. For a lawyer this means achieving the client's objectives as far as possible. While it may involve a variety of issues, shared or conflicting, exchange of information, the use of argument, etc. the focus of the negotiation, the reason for the discussion, argument, etc. is to achieve the parties' goals as far as possible.

2.1.7 WHY IS THE DEFINITION IMPORTANT?

How you define negotiation may influence how you negotiate. If you see it as simple bargaining then you will tend to use simple bargaining strategies. If you see it as a more complex process with a greater range of possibilities you will extend your strategies to include more sophisticated analysis and behaviour and use a much wider range of methods to achieve compromise.

Negotiation could be described as a process of trying to find a positive, realistic and wide-ranging solution to a problem which offers as much as possible to both sides. At its best it is a creative process in which both sides look as objectively as possible at a whole problem and try to find a joint solution.

2.2 Types of Negotiation

The study of negotiation involves consideration of how people seek to and do reach agreement in a huge range of contexts on a wide variety of issues from simple sales transactions, through more complex business deals and legal transactions (e.g., agreeing a lease or settling a claim), to resolving international disputes. Analysing negotiations to see how they differ and whether and how these differences influence the negotiation and the negotiators assists people to understand the process of negotiation. Understanding how the process works is one of the steps in learning how to do it effectively.

Although there is an infinite variety of contexts and issues negotiated, they can be classified in different ways. There is some overlap in the classifications and you may

THE ESSENTIALS OF NEGOTIATION

find that some books classify them differently. Set out below are some different contrasting types of negotiation which are relevant to the work of a barrister.

2.2.1 DISPUTE RESOLUTION VERSUS TRANSACTIONAL

The principal purpose of a negotiation can be to resolve a dispute (i.e. to deal with events which have already happened) or to regulate future transactions (i.e. be forward looking, setting out the rules for an envisaged future relationship between the parties).

- In a dispute settlement, such as a personal injury claim, the purpose of the negotiation is to reach agreement on how the parties should resolve differences resulting from past behaviour, e.g. an accident. The parties are not negotiating out of choice. They must deal with each other to resolve the dispute which has arisen, either through the courts or some other process of dispute resolution, e.g. negotiation. They probably have little if any interest in future dealings with each other. Their behaviour in the negotiation may reflect this in that they will feel no real need to be conciliatory.

- In a transactional negotiation (also called deal-making or rule-making), such as negotiating a lease or partnership agreement, the principal objective is to agree on rules for regulating the future dealings between the parties within that context. Unless one party has a monopoly, the parties are not compelled to negotiate. They have chosen to do business together. They are negotiating together by choice because they wish to set up an agreement by which they can operate in the future. Their behaviour in the negotiation will reflect a consciousness that they will have to build a working relationship.

Not all negotiations fall neatly into one or other of these two categories. Thus, for example, you may be asked to negotiate a settlement for breach of contract where both parties wish to continue their contractual relationship. Principally a dispute resolving negotiation, it includes a transactional element.

2.2.2 SINGLE ISSUE VERSUS MULTIPLE ISSUE

A negotiation can be about a single issue, for example the price of an item in a market, or about a number of issues, for example the terms a of divorce settlement. Clearly a negotiation involving a number of issues is a more sophisticated interaction and has much greater scope for imaginative problem-solving or trade-offs than one in which only a single issue is at stake. However, few negotiations are genuinely about a single issue. Even a dispute which may appear to be a single issue, e.g. a claim for a debt, contains several issues such as: whether it is due at all, how much is to be paid, when payment will be made, whether instalment payments are possible, whether interest was or should be payable, etc.

2.2.3 DISTRIBUTIVE/ZERO-SUM VERSUS INTEGRATIVE

This classification overlaps with the one at **2.2.2**.

- In a distributive or 'zero-sum' negotiation, one party always gains at the expense of the other party. It is a 'win/lose' situation on the assumption that both parties want equally and exclusively the subject matter being negotiated, usually money. In a genuinely distributive or 'zero-sum' negotiation, the parties are likely to be more competitive as they really are 'competing' to achieve gains.

- In an integrative negotiation, one party's gain is not necessarily at the expense of the other party. It is potentially a 'win/win' situation based on the assumption that the parties have some underlying interests which are not in conflict, either because they are shared or because they put differing values on different aspects of the subject matter. An integrative negotiation gives more scope for trade-offs which benefit both parties. There is therefore much more incentive for the parties to be more cooperative and conciliatory in an attempt to find the compatible interests.

NEGOTIATION

The classification is not rigid. Although a case may at first sight appear to be a single issue, distributive negotiation, careful analysis of the facts, law and objectives will usually reveal a variety of issues and potential underlying interests where parties are not in direct conflict. A negotiation which appears initially to be distributive or 'zero-sum' may have integrative elements. Thus, for example, if the claimant in an action puts more value on the actual sum received and the defendant on the period over which payments can be made, the settlement can reflect these differing priorities.

2.2.4 IMPERSONAL VERSUS PERSONAL MATTERS

The subject matter of a negotiation can range from a contract which is 'strictly business', e.g., between two large corporations, to one which affects the whole of a person's life, e.g., a divorce settlement with children involved or a personal injury claim where the person has been permanently disabled. The issues being negotiated can therefore be quite impersonal, for example, resolving the matter of delivery dates or level of interest on a commercial contract. Alternatively, they can be very personal with high emotional content, for example, who has custody of the children. The arguments used to support one's position in the negotiation will reflect the issues being negotiated. Clearly, where the issues are more personal, there is much more possibility of the negotiation becoming personalised and emotion-charged and descending into an argument about rights and wrongs rather than a negotiation to resolve the matter.

The issues in any negotiation can range through the spectrum, e.g., in a divorce the parties may have no personal attachment to certain assets and be able to divide them in a very impersonal manner but feel very strongly over other assets which have high sentimental value. A negotiation which appears to be quite impersonal on the face of it may in fact be highly personal, e.g., a person may feel that his or her job depends on the outcome of a negotiation of a very commercial matter.

2.2.5 REPEAT PLAYERS VERSUS ONE-OFF PLAYERS

Any single negotiation is ostensibly only about those issues on which settlement is being sought in that negotiation and we generally therefore assume that the negotiators are only concerned with the factors affecting those issues and this negotiation. However, in some cases the parties are repeat players and see any individual negotiation within the wider context. Thus, for example, insurance companies negotiate huge numbers of claims. The way in which they deal with any one claim, e.g., one for personal injury, will take on board their experience of dealing with these claims, the fact that they can spread the cost of any individual claim over a huge number of claims and the effect of settlement of this claim on other claims they may have. They will be less anxious about losses in any one claim than about their losses overall. Their overall strategy will be to maximise their profits over the whole of their business. They often adopt a highly competitive stance or 'hardballing' in which they just refuse to budge in the knowledge that they have leaway on each individual negotiation which the claimant (who is almost invariably a one-off player) does not. The repeat player uses the fact that the psychological and financial costs of litigation often push the claimant into settling at a lower value.

2.2.6 REPRESENTATIVE VERSUS FOR ONESELF

A person can negotiate on their own behalf or on behalf of another person, e.g., a client, or on behalf of a group of people, e.g., a trade union. Negotiating on behalf of others introduces a whole new set of dynamics into the negotiation.

(a) The person or persons on whose behalf the negotiation is undertaken will know what they want out of the negotiation and have expectations about the outcome and what can be achieved.

(b) They will also have their own ideas about how the negotiation should be conducted.

(c) The relationship between the party represented and the negotiator may affect the negotiation. The involvement of the party represented in the negotiation may be substantial or minimal depending on the degree of trust placed in the negotiator, the relative positions of power and the personalities involved.

(d) The negotiator will be seeking approval from the party represented both in the outcome and the process. Some studies show that when people negotiate as representatives for someone else, they tend to be more competitive, particularly when they negotiate where the represented party can see them.

2.2.7 MULTIPLE PARTY VERSUS TWO PARTY

Much of the literature and discussion about negotiation considers it in the context of interaction between two parties. However, a negotiation may involve a number of parties, for example, a company reorganisation or insolvency will involve a variety of types of creditors and shareholders all with slightly different interests. In litigation, there may be several defendants who may in turn add third parties.

Negotiations involving a number of different parties are more complex. They are likely to involve more issues and more possibilities for settlement including settling with some but not all the other parties. It also alters the dynamics by allowing the development of coalitions by which some of the parties band together to attain their own goals or block those of others. This Manual does not attempt to cover the complications produced by additional parties. However there is a good section in the book by Gifford, Donald G., *Legal Negotiation Theory and Practice*, West Publishing, St Paul MN, 1989, Chapter 10, pp. 174–183.

2.2.8 OTHER TYPES OF NEGOTIATION

Negotiations can be categorised in a number of other ways to distinguish factors which may affect the negotiation process. Thus, for example, there has been quite a lot written on the dynamics of international negotiations, on cross-cultural negotiations and on negotiations within the field of labour relations. These are quite specialist areas and not covered here. However, should your practice develop to include any of these areas you should be aware of the impact this may have on the negotiations you do and be conscious that there are books and articles which can give you an insight into the additional factors involved.

2.2.9 WHICH CATEGORIES CONCERN BARRISTERS?

The work of a litigation advocate involves principally dispute resolution negotiations in which the number of issues and the scope for integrative solutions varies enormously. Barristers conduct negotiations as representatives across the spectrum from the very impersonal to the highly personal and may be acting for a repeat player (e.g., an insurance company) or a one-off player (e.g., the injured party). The negotiation may be two-party (just claimant and defendant) or multi-party (where there are a number of defendants and/or third parties are joined in proceedings).

2.3 Issues to be Negotiated

Negotiation is about dealing with the substantive issues on which agreement is sought. However, it is also about procedural matters. Both parties to a negotiation will be seeking agreement not only on the issues they are concerned with but also how the negotiation is actually conducted. There are a variety of procedural or non-substantive issues which form part of the negotiation.

2.3.1 HOW, WHERE, WHEN AND WHO

Negotiations can take place in a variety of ways, by letter or fax, telephone or face-to-face discussion. The way in which the negotiation is conducted clearly has influences on the negotiation.

NEGOTIATION

Negotiating by letter or fax means that the information, offers and responses are written down and can be reviewed in detail. Although it removes the need for instanteous responses it means that it is more important to be careful in the wording of what is proposed. Some of the behavioural aspects of negotiation such as tone of voice, ability to think quickly, use of silence, which are part of oral negotiations (by phone or face-to-face discussions), are absent. While this may mean it is less stressful for the participants it also means they get less information about each other.

Face-to-face negotiations give the negotiators much more information about each other in that they can assess the personality and feelings of the other side better and use this knowledge in the negotiation, either to build rapport or against their opponent.

The timing, location and participants in a face-to-face negotiation may be factors which influence the process. Many international negotiations have pre-negotiations to determine where the negotiations will be held to avoid the power imbalance which might result from one party controlling the location. Everyone recognises the psychological impact of playing a home game as opposed to an away game and similar considerations apply to negotiations. In addition, the person on whose premises the negotiation takes place can control the physical layout of the location and put the opponent in a disadvantageous position, e.g., by sitting oneself at the head of the table (in the position of power).

Finally, the number and status of those attending the negotiation can affect the process and will often be discussed to ensure equality of power.

2.3.2 THE AGENDA

Deciding what will be discussed, the order in which matters will be considered and who starts the negotiation are all matters which themselves are subject to negotiation as they can influence both the conduct and the outcome of the negotiation.

2.3.3 EXCHANGE OF INFORMATION

Although the aim of the negotiation is to reach agreement on the issues being negotiated, much of the process of negotiation involves exchanging information. Some people use negotiations purely as a method of getting information, a fishing expedition to find out the strengths and weaknesses of their opponent's position to then use that information in another context, e.g., to plan their case for the trial. The amount of information the negotiators seek and are prepared to disclose will have a real impact on the negotiation process and much is written about this element of negotiation in the literature about different strategies and in many 'how to do it' guides for commercial negotiations.

2.3.4 INTERPRETATION OF FACTS/RULES/NORMS/LAW

In a negotiation, each party puts his or her case, what is being sought and the arguments for that, from his or her own perspective. But this is just one person's perception of what happened, the facts and any relevant rule, norm or law being used to support their argument. No two people see an event in the same way. Perception and reality are different. Disagreement or conflict can stem from different interpretations of events or circumstances. Discussion about these different interpretations or perceptions to see whether any agreement can be reached will form part of the negotiation.

2.3.5 SETTLEMENT STANDARD

The purpose of the negotiation is to reach agreement. But the need for negotiation has arisen at least partially because the parties have not been able to agree. Against what criteria do the negotiators measure the proposals and decide to settle? Do they each have their own criteria or do they discuss the criteria to be used and try to reach agreement on it? What kind of criteria are appropriate to consider? There are a great variety of potential criteria, e.g., social norms, legal standards, the concept of 'fairness'.

In considering the criteria one needs to be clear about what one means. Thus, for example, if the concept of 'fairness' is invoked, what does this mean: fair to whom? Is one speaking of equity (to each according to the contribution made) or equality (split it down the middle)?

2.3.6 STRATEGIES/TACTICS/BEHAVIOUR

There is a large and growing body of literature on the different strategies and tactics used in negotiation, some directed specifically at legal negotiations. This is covered in detail in **Chapters 4** and **5** and it is raised here only to highlight the fact that the strategy and tactics which the negotiators use can also be subject to negotiation. Any negotiation invariably involves the use of strategy and tactics. Those involved in the negotiation will recognise this and deal with it without expressly commenting on it. Discussion expressly about strategy and tactics in a negotiation is rare. However, the strategy, tactics and behaviour of the negotiators can be negotiated implicitly, by the response to the strategy or tactic, or expressly, by labelling the behaviour and insisting on discussing its use in the negotiation.

2.4 The Negotiation Process

Consideration of the process of negotiation involves looking at what happens and in what order from the very beginning of the negotiation to the very end.

Although there are no set rules for the order in which a negotiation should be conducted, a number of people who have studied negotiation have found a recognisable pattern which most negotiations follow, a series of developmental stages through which most pass. As with most research on human behaviour, the writers do not use exactly the same terminology nor do they take a completely uniform approach, some dividing it into more phases than others. However, there is a great degree of similarity in their descriptions.

It is important, however, to understand that the following fairly simplistic division into four basic phases is merely a description of a general pattern which has been identified and not a rigid structure which all negotiations must follow or necessarily will follow. Each negotiation is unique. Many involve a number of issues and discussion of the different issues may fall in different phases. The phases of any negotiation may overlap and may in fact be repeated. Understanding the process helps one to recognise what may be happening at any particular stage and why certain behaviour may be more prevalent at some stages than others.

2.4.1 OPENING/ORIENTATION/POSITIONING

In this phase the negotiators set the scene. They assess each other's style and approach and set out their positions, how they expect the negotiation to proceed, their view of the merits of the case and what they are seeking out of the negotiation.

Both negotiators will use this phase to assess the opponent's style and strategy. The behaviour of the two negotiators in this phase will 'set the tone' and have a strong impact on the overall orientation of the negotiation, e.g., whether it is cooperative or competitive. The exchanges enable the negotiators to learn to interpret the words, language and non-verbal cues of their opponent before the dynamics of negotiation become more intense.

The negotiators are also likely to set out their 'opening positions', i.e., what they want out of the negotiation. Exactly what that 'opening position' is will depend on the strategy which the negotiator is adopting (see **Chapter 4**).

In this phase the negotiators will generally be fairly guarded and more competitive than cooperative, unless one or other of the negotiators is specifically setting out to put the negotiation on a very collaborative path.

NEGOTIATION

2.4.2 EXPLORATION/DISCUSSION

In this phase the negotiators exchange information, explore the legal and factual issues, try to determine the strengths and weaknesses of the two sides and see how the differences in the positions initially stated can be resolved. There will also be some attempt to narrow the differences by making and/or encouraging concessions. As in the initial stage, unless consciously adopting a collaborative approach, the negotiators are likely to be wary of each other. They are likely to be relatively selective in the information they reveal and concessions they make, really using this stage to gather and assimilate information from the other side to enable them to reassess the case.

2.4.3 BARGAINING/CONVERGENCE

In this phase the parties realise that movement is essential to reach agreement and serious efforts are made to resolve differences. This stage may be precipitated by an approaching deadline. The negotiators are likely to be more cooperative in this stage than in the previous two stages. A number of experiments have shown that concession-making increases as the deadline approaches.

2.4.4 SETTLEMENT OR BREAKDOWN

This final phase is the one in which the negotiators either reach settlement or end the negotiation. If they do reach agreement, the details of it must be agreed including the mechanics for ensuring it is fulfilled. Alternatively, the negotiation may break down for a variety of reasons and, for example, in a legal case the matter proceeds to trial.

2.4.5 CONCLUSION

Recognising the phases of a negotiation and that competitive behaviour is more likely at the start and cooperative later, can assist you both to understand your opponent's behaviour and to adapt your own. Cooperative behaviour at the start may be met by competitive behaviour. However, it is worth reiterating that the above pattern is not one which is religiously followed in all negotiations. While many negotiations will move from a basically competitive phase to a more cooperative or collaborative one, this is not always so. Do not assume that all negotiators will become more cooperative over time.

Many negotiations take place over a period of time with different parts of the process involving different people. It is important to be conscious of what has happened previously. This will enable you to at least attempt to assess what stage the negotiation has reached at the point you become involved.

THREE

LEGAL NEGOTIATIONS

3.1 Generally

The amount of time spent negotiating and the type of negotiations in which any lawyer tends to get involved will depend on the area of law in which he or she works. Many solicitors spend a large part of their time negotiating. This is particularly true of those who practise in certain areas, for example, commercial or property, where the bulk of their work is negotiating terms of contracts or leases, i.e., transaction or deal-making negotiations. Solicitors who specialise in litigation also spend a lot of their time negotiating. Roughly 90% of cases settle and many of these disputes are resolved by negotiations between solicitors.

The concept of dispute resolution is generally applied to civil cases on the basis that civil cases are disputes between the parties. Criminal cases can also be resolved without trial. However the underlying concept here is different in that, in a criminal case, a person is prosecuted for an offence against the state, with the prosecution almost invariably being brought by the state or a body with delegated powers, such as a local authority. It is not uncommon for the prosecution and defence to negotiate or 'plea bargain' to resolve a criminal case without going to trial. The main issues involved in such a negotiation are the number and seriousness of the charges which will be considered by the court when sentencing, the defence seeking to get the prosecution to drop or reduce the charges, the prosecution seeking to get guilty pleas on sufficient charges to represent the seriousness of the behaviour for which the defendant is charged. While 'plea bargaining' does take place, the recognition given to it in the system is far from clear and there are very different ethical and strategic considerations from those which apply to civil cases. This Manual focuses on negotiation in the context of civil dispute resolutions and does not attempt to deal with the dynamics, ethics and considerations of plea bargaining (see *Professional Conduct Manual*).

Most barristers specialise as advocates within the litigation process. Like litigation solicitors they too will be involved largely in dispute resolution negotiations. Negotiation within the context of civil disputes will take place throughout the various stages of the process from the time the dispute is identified to its ultimate conclusion. Exactly what is involved in the negotiation and how it is conducted will vary depending on the stage reached in the litigation process and the incentives to settle.

3.2 Why Cases Settle

People who have a civil dispute have some choice in how to resolve it. The principal choices have in the past been litigation or negotiation but mediation (really a facilitated negotiation, see **12.5**) is gaining ground as an alternative to litigation. There has been some work done, both theoretical and empirical, to attempt to understand why some cases settle and others proceed to trial.

An overview of the position is well set out in the following quote from Gary Goodpaster in the introduction to his article 'Lawsuits as Negotiations', *Negotiation Journal* (July 1992), pp. 222–239:

Litigating a dispute is both a major alternative to negotiating it and a way to force its negotiation. Litigation arises when the parties to a 'mature' dispute have attempted to negotiate it and failed, or have ignored, or refused, the possibility of negotiating it. If the dispute goes to trial, the parties will, through the cases they present, importantly influence the result. Nevertheless, a judge or jury, rather than the parties will decide the outcome. On the other hand, parties settle most lawsuits rather than try them. Indeed, it is the deadline that a pending trial imposes on the possibilities of a negotiated settlement, the risk of loss at trial, and possibly the added expense of trial that motivates many lawsuit settlements.

Since most lawsuits settle before trial, it is useful to view litigation not solely as a way to reach an adjudicated result, but also as a highly structured negotiation game, a refined and constrained version of competitive bargaining. Litigation is, in effect, a 'branched track' mode of dispute resolution. Although apparently heading for an adjudicated result, the parties can, and usually do, shunt their dispute away from the trial station and onto a negotiation siding. It is therefore important to consider how and why parties progress toward a litigated result while at the same time moving toward settlement, and to understand why the process works as it does.

3.2.1 WHY LITIGATE IN THE FIRST PLACE?

In his article cited above, Goodpaster sets out six principal reasons why people litigate (i.e., issue proceedings) rather than negotiate a settlement:

(a) 'Refusal to deal': one party refuses to negotiate and the other party has no power to compel them to do so aside from issuing proceedings.

(b) 'Negotiation failures': negotiation between the parties fails for some reason, e.g., lack of negotiation skills. One of the parties thinks that litigation will give them leverage or a better result.

(c) 'Zero-sum situations': the parties see the dispute as zero-sum which puts them in a win/lose situation. Litigation will force the other side to do something and bear the costs. The dispute has usually arisen from a one-time past transaction (e.g., an accident) and the parties are adversaries, hostile to one another, see no benefit in cooperating and litigation offers a better result.

(d) 'The litigator-negotiator's role': lawyers work in a litigation context, may fail to see alternatives and advise litigation as a way to get leverage in any negotiation.

(e) 'Lawyer-client relationships in lawsuits': issuing proceedings transfers much of the power to decide and shape the negotiation away from the client to the lawyer who manages the case within a litigation context which is itself adversarial.

(f) 'The litigator-negotiator's bias': the lawyer is a representative negotiator which increases the competitive element (see **2.2.6**). This effect is strengthened by the requirement in the lawyers' professional code to, in the case of the Bar (para. 203) '... promote and protect fearlessly and by all proper and lawful means his lay client's best interests'.

3.2.2 WHY CASES SETTLE AFTER ISSUE OF PROCEEDINGS

The two principal theories discussed by Goodpaster on what influences people to settle or proceed to trial once they are into the litigation process are the selection theory and the strategic bargaining theory. In addition, he identified a variety of factors which are influential.

3.2.2.1 The selection theory
Developed by George Priest and Benjamin Klein and set out in their paper 'The Selection of Disputes for Litigation' (1984) 13 *Journal of Legal Studies* 1–55, the selection theory is that trials are most likely to occur in close cases.

The parties negotiating stances are determined by their assessment of the likely outcome at trial. They know that the court will apply a standard against which it will judge the case (e.g., in a negligence case) and then find for one or other party (i.e., the decision is all or nothing, in that the defendant will lose regardless of the distance below the standard he falls). Both the claimant and defendant assess their case against this standard by considering the likely size of award multiplied by the probability of judgment in their favour. (The formula also deals with costs but, given the different treatment of costs in the US — each party usually bears his or her own regardless of outcome — this is not relevant to UK cases.) Both claimant and defendant base their offers and demands on their assessment of the case on the above analysis. If the case falls close to the standard (e.g., of care in a negligence case), the parties are far more likely to have very different assessments of the outcome and much less likely to have offers and demands that meet and are more likely to see trial as giving them more than a negotiated settlement.

Thus in this theory predictability of outcome is the determining factor. The closer the case is to the standard which the court will apply (i.e., the more uncertain the outcome) the more likely it will go to trial because the parties cannot accurately weigh up what is a fair risk or settlement.

3.2.2.2 The strategic bargaining theory

Developed by Robert Cooter, Stephen Marks and Robert Mnookin and set out in their paper 'Bargaining in the Shadow of the Law: A Testable Model of Strategic Behaviour' (1983) 11 *Journal of Legal Studies* 225–251, the strategic bargaining theory is that the obstacle to agreement is the strategic nature of the bargaining. Trials can occur, even where neither negotiator is optimistic about the outcome or where outcomes may be relatively easy to predict, because of the uncertainty about the opponent's behaviour and how much he or she is prepared to concede. A variety of factors influence the parties' expectations and both adopt strategies to increase their potential gain. Thus a negotiator even with a weak case may weigh up the opponent as being averse to risk and therefore consider that he or she will concede more if there is a real risk of trial.

3.2.2.3 The variables

From a variety of studies, Goodpaster has identified a number of variables which influence whether or not a case goes to trial including:

(a) The parties' ability to predict trial outcome. The litigation process enables the parties to assess the law and facts. Cases where the law and facts are contested are more likely to go to trial.

(b) The benefits and costs of settlement now against those of continued litigation.

(c) How the litigation is financed. A party not liable for costs is more likely to run the risk of trial.

(d) Whether the parties are 'repeat' or 'one-off' players. A repeat player is more likely to run the risk of trial in any individual case.

(e) Whether the parties have differential stakes in trial or settlement. The parties may be seeking different things through litigation with 'asymmetrical' stakes in the outcome. Thus a party sued for professional negligence may really want a trial to clear his or her name whereas the party suing just wants to recoup losses suffered. What each wants will affect their strategy and approach to settlement.

3.2.3 THE BENEFITS OF SETTLING FOR THE CLIENT

While some cases clearly merit a full trial, it can often be in the client's best interests to avoid going to court. Settling a dispute can:

(a) Reduce the friction between the parties. This is particularly important where there is an existing relationship or the prospect of an on-going relationship, either business or personal.

NEGOTIATION

(b) Reduce the costs by obviating the need for steps in the litigation process, the most obvious and expensive one being the trial.

(c) Reduce the delay in resolving the dispute.

(d) Reduce the anxiety and stress for the client caused both by having to live with the uncertainty of the outcome until trial and worrying about the whole trial process, e.g., having to give evidence, having to relive a particularly traumatic experience (such as an accident).

(e) Avoid the 'winner take all' outcome, which is inevitable in a trial where the court can only decide in favour of one party, and enable a more flexible compromise.

(f) Increase the range of possible outcomes for the client. The court has limited powers in what it can order which are circumscribed by the case as pleaded by the parties. A negotiated settlement can include elements which are beyond the court's powers to order.

3.2.4 WHAT CASES SHOULD GO TO TRIAL?

Although most cases do settle and there are great benefits for the client in settling in almost any case, provided it is done on satisfactory terms, there are some cases where trial may be more appropriate.

(a) A case may be litigated to seek clarification of the law. Only a judgment of the court will give this. Some cases are run as 'test cases' to establish a principle. While part of the purpose of running the case is to 'test the law', the lawyer should never lose sight of the fact that it is being tested on the back of a client. While the lawyer must balance the benefits which can be achieved for a wider group by establishing a principle against the needs of the client whose case is being run, the ultimate decision as to whether to settle or go to trial remains that of the client.

(b) A client may have a real need for his or her 'day in court'. This is an objective and it is the client's right to use the civil justice system to achieve this. While the lawyer's role includes talking through the pros and cons of trial versus settlement with the client and getting the client to see it in perspective, the decision whether or not to settle is that of the client.

3.3 Negotiations by Solicitors and Barristers

The role of the solicitor and barrister in the conduct of a case differs. The solicitor has the overall conduct of the case seeing it from beginning to end and instructs or briefs a barrister for certain aspects of it. (The *Case Preparation Manual* sets out the stages of a civil case and the differing roles of the solicitor and barrister in more detail.)

Civil disputes cover a broad range of cases including those conducted through tribunals and courts. Whatever the type of adjudication, a case can be divided into the following stages:

- pre-action (initial consideration by the client and lawyers as to whether adjudication is appropriate),

- initiating proceedings (issue and service of relevant documents to start relevant proceedings),

- interim (exchange of documents and information, collection and preparation of the evidence for trial),

- trial,

- appeal,
- enforcement.

A case can be settled at any of these stages.

Although there is nothing to prevent the parties themselves from negotiating a settlement, once lawyers have been instructed negotiations are usually conducted through the lawyers, with most of this being done by the solicitors (see **3.3.1**). Generally the solicitor prepares the case for trial (or appeal, etc. where relevant) in tandem with negotiating a settlement. While settling early in the litigation process does save the costs of these processes, negotiating a settlement is not an excuse for failing to observe time limits in litigation.

A number of factors will influence when negotiations take place, for example, having sufficient information to assess the case properly and strategic considerations of how the various stages in the litigation process affect the case. Certain aspects of the procedure are specifically aimed at exchange of information between the parties (e.g., disclosure whereby the parties are entitled to mutual inspection of relevant documents, mutual exchange of witness statements and expert reports) and this may affect the timing or conduct of any negotiation. There are a number of devices available to the claimant and defendant to put pressure on the other party to settle (e.g., a payment into court by the defendant which restricts the claimant's rights to costs if he or she does not obtain more at trial).

At whatever stage a case is settled, relevant procedural requirements must be considered. Settlement before proceedings have begun will be recorded and enforced as a contract. Settlements on behalf of a minor require court approval even if done before a case is issued. Once proceedings have been initiated, any settlement must deal with the existence of the proceedings, e.g., by obtaining the appropriate court order or discontinuing the case (see the *Civil Litigation Manual*).

3.3.1 SOLICITORS' NEGOTIATIONS

A whole variety of factors gives solicitors more flexibility in what they can do in a negotiation than is available to barristers in most cases. Solicitors see their clients through the case, develop relationships with them and get to know them to a degree. They have opportunities to discuss the case with the other side over a period of time through a variety of methods using a combination of exchange of letter, phone calls and/or meetings with the other side. Although less and less true with increasing control of cases by the courts, they are, to a degree, able to control the speed of the litigation, e.g., maintaining a slow pace to enable greater time for negotiation or speeding it up to put pressure on the other side to settle. Solicitors are in a position (subject to costs) to obtain whatever information from the client or others they consider to be relevant to the case. They can investigate alternatives to trial, including options which no court could order.

3.3.2 COURT-DOOR NEGOTIATIONS

A barrister's involvement in a case is controlled by the solicitor who instructs or briefs counsel as and when the solicitor considers it necessary. Barristers' principal functions are advising on merit, quantum and evidence, drafting court documents, and advocacy at hearings. While they may be instructed to advise on whether or not an offer of settlement is appropriate, their role as negotiators is usually, at least in their first few years, confined mostly to court-door negotiations. Negotiating in this context is much less flexible.

(a) Negotiating at the court door puts terrific time pressure on the negotiators. Frequently they have very little time (maybe 20 to 25 minutes), in which to reach a settlement prior to the case being called on.

(b) Being a referral profession, barristers have limited access to information. Frequently they arrive at the court never having met the client with only the information the solicitor has chosen to include in the papers. Where counsel is involved in a interlocutory hearing (e.g., summary judgment) at an early stage of the proceedings (a frequent role for junior counsel), the solicitor will have been conscious of not taking any steps which might cost the client and be wasted because the case did not proceed to trial. Thus the brief may not contain full information (e.g., expert reports), all the necessary documentation, or much in the way of evidence (e.g., proofs from witnesses).

The circumstances at court mean counsel also have limited opportunity to get more information from the solicitor or client, both because of lack of time and lack of attendance by those with the information. Those attending court may include the solicitor and the lay client. However, often the solicitor will not attend but send an 'outdoor clerk', i.e., a file-carrier from the solicitor's office who may be extremely bright and *au fait* with the client and his or her case or may be a part-timer who has no idea about the case and very little, if any, legal knowledge. In addition, on an interim hearing which relies on affidavit evidence, although it is wise for the client to attend in case something unexpected happens, provided the affidavit has been sworn there is, strictly, no need for the client to attend as he or she will have no role to play (the evidence being that contained in the sworn affidavit). Thus the barrister may have access to fairly comprehensive information where both the solicitor and lay client attend or have to rely solely on information from the brief. However, there may be little space to separate the parties or discuss the matter with the solicitor or client out of earshot of the opponent.

(c) Barristers generally do not have an on-going relationship with their lay clients. Their involvement with their lay client is short-lived. Generally, particularly in cases of small financial value, their contact is limited to discussions immediately before going into court when the clients are focused on what will happen in court. These factors make it more difficult for barristers to ascertain and understand lay clients' underlying concerns and interests.

(d) Barristers have limited opportunities to give proper consideration to a wide range of options. They act in very limited circumstances, i.e., at the court door, with limited time. They have two clients, the lay and the professional, and have a duty to both. These two factors put the following limitations on their ability to create options in any negotiation:

   (i) There are a limited range of options which the court can ratify. This need not necessarily always limit counsel to ratifiable solutions. However, the court's power and interest in ratifying the solution will vary from case to case and barristers negotiate with this as a consideration.

   (ii) There is no time or opportunity to investigate the viability, practicality and enforceability of options not already envisaged by the papers and court hearing.

   (iii) There is pressure to find a solution which satisfies the lay and professional client and, in some cases, the court.

   (iv) Going outside the solicitor's instructions raises issues of professional conduct where the barrister is acting on instructions from solicitors who, given the financial value of the case, have sent a 'file carrier' who knows nothing about the case.

(e) Barristers negotiating at the court door are doing so at least part way into the litigation process if not at the very end (i.e., trial) and this will be reflected in the parties' and professional clients' mindsets and views of the case.

(i) The clients, lay and professional, may have adopted fairly entrenched positions for a variety of reasons, e.g., their investment in time, finances and emotion in fighting the case or purely as a matter of strategy.

(ii) At the door of the court of trial, the bulk of the costs will already have been incurred and the client may consider that settling at this point will make little difference to the costs.

(f) The facilities in which the negotiation takes place are usually very limited (possibly standing in a crowded corridor), and the whole physical environment may have an effect on the behaviour of those negotiating. Finding a sideroom in which to negotiate may alter this behaviour.

(g) Finally two other factors might influence the conduct of court-door negotiations.

(i) The type of case. The fact that the case is at the court door may mean that it is one in which there is greater uncertainty as to the outcome at trial and this is why settlement has not been reached before and is more difficult (see **3.2.2.1**).

(ii) Barristers at this stage may be taking over part-way through the negotiation process, the solicitor having gone through much of the process, leaving only part for the barrister to do.

3.3.3 OTHER CONTEXTS

While many of the negotiations which barristers, particularly junior barristers, conduct take place outside the court door, barristers do negotiate in other contexts. For example, negotiations may take place between counsel early in the process some time before the hearing date. Alternatively, a barrister may receive a phone call from counsel for the other side seeking information, e.g., about cases that he or she will be relying on at the hearing. The conversation becomes a discussion about resolving the case through negotiation.

Be conscious of the impact that the different modes of communication have on a negotiation. In particular, ensure that you do not attempt to negotiate a case when your mind is not focused on it (for example, if you have just returned from or are just going to court on another case). Do not be afraid to say, 'I'll phone you back' and give yourself the space to consider carefully how you are going to deal with the matter before speaking to the other side.

3.3.4 OTHER PEOPLE

Negotiating with the lawyer for the other side (whether barrister or solicitor) is clearly an important aspect of the work of barristers. However, barristers also spend a fair amount of time negotiating with others.

More and more people are undertaking cases themselves without the assistance of lawyers. Litigants in person are more personally involved with the case and generally (but not always) have limited knowledge of the law. Negotiating with them requires a more complex balancing act than negotiating with another lawyer as, although one is still seeking the best for one's client, one must not take unfair advantage of the litigant in person.

The need to 'negotiate' with a judge does arise: for example, it may be necessary to persuade the judge to give counsel more time to negotiate a settlement when the case should have been called on or to persuade the judge to endorse a consent order where he or she has the power to withhold that consent. This form of negotiation clearly shows the overlap between advocacy and negotiation skills.

There are a huge variety of people who become involved in cases with whom barristers 'negotiate' in one form or another, from court officials (from whom additional time is more frequently sought than directly from the judge), through various witnesses who may be experts (e.g., social workers or doctors), or lay witnesses (e.g., friends or relations of the client).

Finally, barristers negotiate with both their professional and lay clients. The barrister and solicitor may see the case differently and 'negotiate' over whose view or tactics prevail. The lay client will also have views about the case. Although the client is in the driving seat in that he or she instructs the lawyers to conduct the case and ultimately makes many of the decisions about the case, the lawyers owe the client professional duties to ensure the case is conducted in the best possible way and this gives rise to rather complex considerations.

3.4 The Role and Influence of the Lay Client

Legal negotiations in a split profession can involve a complex variety of relationships, i.e., between barrister and solicitor, solicitor and client and barrister and client, because of the differing roles and views of the case each player has. Both the lawyers have professional duties to the client and to each other. This gives rise to different areas of consideration: the different roles of the lay client and the lawyers, and how the different roles of the lawyer and the client influence the negotiation.

3.4.1 IT'S THE CLIENT'S CASE

A lawyer is negotiating for the client. It is the client's case. The lawyer is the expert, the professional adviser and representative acting on behalf of the client. This gives rise to four basic factors to remember when so acting.

3.4.1.1 The client's objectives

A lawyer negotiating for a client must ensure that he or she really does understand the client's objectives, interests and needs and pursue these in the negotiation. What the client wants should be fully explored with a wide view taken of the various needs or interests which may be included. The client may have short and long term interests. While money may be an objective there may be other matters such as a need for vindication or an apology. While the client may express the objectives in money terms, it is important also to find out the interests and needs behind the objectives. It may be that what the client is seeking is financial security, which may come from reinstatement in a job rather than a large money settlement.

The lawyer must also understand the client's priorities. What are the relative values placed on the different interests and needs?

3.4.1.2 Act only with authority

A lawyer acts as his or her client's agent in a negotiation and general agency rules apply. The lawyer has actual authority to act only within the client's instructions and should never settle outside this actual authority. However, from the other party's point of view, a lawyer is acting for the client and has the apparent or ostensible authority to settle a case after proceedings have been issued. The extent of this apparent authority can of course be cut down by giving the other side notice of any limit on it. A lawyer who acts outside his or her actual authority but binds the client because the agreement comes within the apparent authority will be liable to the client.

A barrister's brief will normally contain a lot of information which makes it clear what the client will or will not accept, i.e., set the parameters of the actual authority of counsel in negotiating a settlement. However, there may well be matters of detail on which it is not clear exactly what the client wants. Making it apparent to the other side that any negotiation is subject to the authorisation or approval of the client, leaves counsel open to agree detail on condition that the client does approve (i.e., giving notice of the limited authority). By setting this parameter, it leaves counsel free to try to tie up the detail in the best way possible without binding the client.

3.4.1.3 The lawyer's professional role

The lawyer's role in any civil case is to deal with matters of law, procedure and evidence. It is the lawyer's professional duty to the client. The lawyer must advise the client both of his or her view of the case and of what, in his or her judgment, is the best course of action. This means ensuring the client understands how the strengths and weaknesses of the case or any procedural or evidential matters affect the chances of achieving the objectives that he or she is seeking. It is the lawyer's job to ensure that when the client decides whether or not to accept an offer or agree to settle, the decision is a fully informed one. The terms of the settlement must be fully explained as must the effect, in particular that settlement will mean the end of the matter and there will normally be no possibility of reopening it or seeking more.

Failing to advise the client properly or just accepting a decision where the client clearly does not understand his or her legal position or consequences of the decision is a breach of duty to the client. (See the **Conference Skills Manual** on the subject of advising the client.)

3.4.1.4 The client must decide

Decisions about substantive matters, e.g., whether or not to negotiate, what issues are open to negotiation and whether or not an offer should be accepted, must be made by the client. It is the client's case and the lawyer must ensure that any decision about whether to settle or not is that of the client and not of the lawyer. Whether the settlement is acceptable must be measured against the client's objectives, needs and interests. Having advised fully (see above), the lawyer must then accept the client's decision and abide by it. If the client is not prepared to accept a settlement, that is his or her perogative. The only exception to this may arise if the client is legally aided and the lawyer has to advise on the merits of pursuing the claim.

3.4.2 INFLUENCE OF CLIENT AND LAWYER ON NEGOTATION

The fact that the lawyer is acting as a representative and not on his or her own behalf can mean that he or she tends to be more competitive (see **2.2.6**). In addition, the lawyer's role in the litigation process and their resulting bias may produce a more competitive stance. It may also influence the way the client sees the case, reframing it by the words used and advice given on the possible options so the client alters his or her objectives to reflect the litigation process and what is available within it (see **3.2.1**).

3.4.3 LAWYERS AS REPEAT PLAYERS

Although lawyers may negotiate for clients who are one-off players, they themselves are repeat players (i.e., they will probably be negotiating against the same lawyers over time). This is particularly true of a small profession like the Bar. The lawyer owes a duty to the client in any single negotiation to achieve the best for that client. On the other hand he or she will have to maintain a working relationship with what are in effect his or her colleagues. This may produce tensions. For example taking a very competitive stance in one case may produce the best for that client. However, this may make it more difficult to negotiate for future clients because the previous behaviour may colour later negotiations. Alternatively, there may be a temptation to settle a case because of peer pressure when in fact the offer does not achieve the best for the client. A possible middle ground is to develop a reputation as a firm but fair negotiator.

3.5 'Without Prejudice' Negotiations

Negotiations with a view to settlement should be conducted 'without prejudice' whether by letter, fax, phone or face-to-face meeting. This basically means that the contents of the negotiation cannot be revealed to the court to assist it to determine the case. While any negotiation with a view to compromise is impliedly without prejudice, the position is also frequently expressly stated, e.g., by putting the words 'without prejudice' on a letter.

NEGOTIATION

More detailed guidance on the evidential position of 'without prejudice' communications is contained in the **Evidence Manual** and on the ethics in **Chapter 8** of this Manual.

3.6 Effective Legal Negotiators

3.6.1 DO WE KNOW WHAT IS EFFECTIVE?

The reaction of some students to negotiating is immediate enthusiasm. They have always liked debating and arguing and are keen to start winning negotiations. Other students are immediately wary; they do not like arguing and are rather apprehensive of their chances against an aggressive opponent. In fact, both reactions are based on a quite common misconception that people are successful negotiators because they can be aggressive, state their views forcefully and believe wholeheartedly in winning or, the reverse side of the coin, that people who wish to avoid conflict, appear fair and reasonable and reach a good compromise are not good negotiators.

While there is much discussion in the literature about effective negotiation techniques, there is little empirical data about what lawyers do in negotiations. Carrie Menkel-Meadow summarised in her paper 'Lawyer Negotiations: Theories and Realities — What We Learn From Mediation' (1993) 56(3) *Maryland Law Review* 361–379, '... empirical work on negotiation in a variety of legal contexts remains relatively paltry, but is depressingly consistent'. She then reviews several studies which show that lawyers settle quickly, with few exchanges of offers, use conventional patterns of negotiation behaviour and seek standardised solutions.

That there clearly are varying degrees of effectiveness in negotiations between lawyers is demonstrated by an experiment by Gerald Williams, Professor of Law at Brigham Young University in which he got 40 experienced practising lawyers to prepare and conduct a negotiation to settle the same personal injury case and compare results. The settlements varied from $15,000 to $95,000 (average $47,318), with a number of pairs not settling.

Clearly this shows that different lawyers get very different results with exactly the same case. The fact that some lawyers get far better results than others (e.g., for the claimant obtaining $95,000 and for the defendant $15,000 are both well away from the average) leads one to assume that they are more effective negotiators (although they may in fact just be less ineffective than their opponents).

There are few empirical studies of actual legal negotiations in which behaviour is observed and considered to see what is and is not effective. Much of the literature is based on experiments in game theory (i.e., people playing highly structured games which require them to decide a strategy against an opponent) or observations of students doing simulated negotiations.

One study which has been discussed in much of the literature was done by Gerald Williams. Using questionnaires, interviews and videotaped performances, lawyers were rated on a huge number of traits to determine whether they were effective, average or ineffective and whether they were competitive or cooperative. He concluded that:

- 49% were rated as effective, 38% as average and 12% ineffective.

- 65% of negotiators could be categorised as cooperative and 24% as competitive (11% had insufficiently consistent patterns to be categorised).

- Neither approach guaranteed effectiveness. However, 59% of cooperative and only 25% of competitive were rated as effective and 3% of cooperative and 33% of competitive were rated as ineffective.

LEGAL NEGOTIATIONS

Williams also analysed the traits which people associated with effective, average and ineffective cooperative and competitive negotiators. While there are differences in the characteristics for the two approaches, some of the characteristics which were shared by effective 'cooperatives' and 'competitives' are:

(a) Rational, analytical, intelligent.

(b) Realistic.

(c) Thoroughly prepared on the facts and law, legally astute.

(d) Convincing.

(e) Perceptive, skilful in reading opponent's cues.

(f) Honest, ethical, trustworthy, adhered to customs and courtesies of the Bar.

(g) Creative, versatile, adaptable.

(h) Self-controlled, poised.

(i) Took satisfaction in using legal skills.

William's study is not the definitive answer on effectiveness and can be criticised, e.g., he does not distinguish between strategy and style (see Condlin 'Bargaining in the Dark: The Normative Incoherence of Lawyer Dispute Bargaining Role' (1992) 51 *Maryland Law Review* 1–104 at 17–22 in particular). However, his study and results have been used in many discussions about different strategies as it does give some insight into how legal negotiators are perceived and what is and is not seen as effective. It counters the misconception that all lawyers are tough, aggressive, hard-nosed negotiators. It also confirms what a number of writers on negotiation state: that competitive negotiators are not frequently seen as effective. It would appear that it is easier to be an effective cooperative negotiator than an effective competitive one.

There is scope for all students to become effective negotiators, by building on many of the skills they already possess, e.g., by being rational, analytical, perceptive, creative. Effectiveness also comes from understanding how these skills are used in a negotiation and from being thoroughly prepared.

3.6.2 UNDERSTANDING THE THEORY AND PRACTICE

Doing something skilfully generally means that it appears to be done effortlessly. While there is little overt recognition of the skill being exercised there is an underlying understanding of the component parts of the skill, the overall context in which it is used and how and when to use various techniques. Skilled advocates are more effective partly because they are very familiar with the context in which they work, e.g., know instinctively when they can and cannot interrupt or what they can and cannot say to the judge. This is equally true of negotiation. Understanding the mechanics and subtleties of the negotiation process allows you to see more clearly what is happening and what may be influencing the negotiation. This enables you to control what happens more effectively. Understanding the different strategies, styles and tactics which you can use and may be used by your opponent enables you to identify and deal with them more effectively. Rarely an express part of the negotiation, all these factors underpin the activity and a real understanding of them will help you to be an effective negotiator.

3.6.3 PROPER PREPARATION AND PLANNING

While understanding the more amorphous aspects of negotiation mechanics and behaviour will increase your confidence and effectiveness, it is of no use unless you go to the negotiation equipped with the proper tools. To be effective in the negotiation you

NEGOTIATION

must be properly prepared: thoroughly understand the client's objectives, have analysed the facts and law of both your own and your opponent's case, assessed the strengths and weaknesses of your and your opponent's case, considered the arguments which may be used by and against you and planned how you are going to make and seek concessions.

3.6.3.1 Analysis of the papers

The brief from the solicitor should contain sufficient information to give you an overview of the case. It should enable you to sort out who the parties are, what the case is about, what stage it has reached, who the solicitors and counsel for the other side are (have you any experience of them?), where and when the negotiation is to be held, what issues are involved and what type of negotiation it is. All this helps you to put your role and the negotiation in context.

3.6.3.2 Client's objectives

The solicitor may have summarised in the brief what the client is seeking. The client's statement will contain not only information about what happened but also about what he or she wants. Other documents, e.g., correspondence between solicitors, may also give you information about the client's objectives.

It is important that you consider carefully the full range of potential objectives of the client. Many people think of negotiations as being just about money. How much does the client want? While many negotiations do include a financial element, some do not and most will include non-financial objectives as well. There is a huge range of potential objectives and it is important that you enter the negotiation properly aware of the full range and the varying importance which the client attaches to the different objectives. Thus a client who has been wrongfully dismissed may put obtaining an apology from the employer high on the list of objectives. You must be aware of this and give it its proper weight in the negotiation. Although financial objectives will frequently be important do not always assume they are exclusively sought or the most important objective.

It is also important to try to get behind the stated objectives of the client to see what the real interests or needs are. For example, if your client is seeking damages for personal injury, what needs does he or she have both immediately (e.g., medical expenses), and in the future (payment of a housekeeper to undertake work he or she can no longer do). Are there alternatives to a money payment which might better satisfy your client's objectives or be an equally viable alternative?

You also need to consider carefully matters which far too many lawyers consider 'mere detail'. What are the tax implications of payment of a sum? When should it be paid? Should it be paid as a lump sum or in instalments? What about interest? What about costs?

Having identified all the client's objectives, you need to prioritise them.

In considering both what the client's interests are and the priorities given to them, you need to be conscious that the interests identified and the priorities given are those which accord with the client's values, needs and interests and not your own. A client from a different cultural or ethnic background or of a different sex may well have very different views from you as to what he or she wishes to achieve in the case. However, just because someone is of the same sex, ethnic and class background as you, do not assume they view the case the same way you do.

3.6.3.3 Opponent's objectives

In most cases there will have been a fair amount of communication between the parties and their solicitors about the case prior to you being briefed. There will therefore be some information in the brief about the case for the other side from which you can at least get some idea of what he or she might be seeking. Although this information will be less complete than for your client, you should undertake the same exercise in considering the opponent's objectives as you have done for your client.

3.6.3.4 Matching objectives

Once you have identified and attempted to prioritise the objectives of both sides, you should consider whether there are any which are shared (i.e., that both parties want), compatible (i.e., where the parties value things differently), or whether they genuinely conflict. This assists in a variety of ways. It enables you to see exactly what is genuinely in dispute (i.e., really needs to be negotiated as opposed to merely agreed) and enables you to formulate possible offers which are almost certain to appeal to the other side while also achieving your client's objectives.

One example of a shared objective is where both parties want a continuing relationship, either personal or business. Thus, for example, two parties may have fallen out over a past business deal but both have good reasons for wishing to trade with each other in future. They may not agree fully on the terms for this future dealing which have to be negotiated but a strong common factor is the desire to continue the relationship.

3.6.3.5 The issues

The most important skill of any lawyer is the ability to analyse a case, determine what the issues are, put the facts, law, evidence and procedure together and identify the strengths and weaknesses from both sides. This ability involves a number of different tasks which are dealt with in some detail in the *Case Preparation Manual*. This aspect of preparing for a negotiation is not dissimilar to preparing to conduct a case in court.

Taking on board the client's objectives, you must identify the facts alleged by each side, distinguishing between those which are agreed, disputed or ambiguous. You must also be aware of the factual gaps. What information do you not have which might be important and/or held by the other side?

You must also consider the relevant law. What supports or undermines your and your case opponent's case? How does the law apply to the alleged facts to strengthen or weaken the two sides of the case?

In any negotiation the parties involved will have constructed their views on the basis of the facts as they see them with little regard to the evidence which supports their view. Depending on the stage the case has reached there may be little formal evidence in the papers, e.g., there may be no expert's report or witness statements. However, you must analyse the papers to identify what if any evidence there is for the allegations made which can be used for or against you.

Finally, negotiating within the litigation process means that there may well be procedural points which must be considered as they could be used for or against you. For example your client may have obtained judgment in default (of the opponent filing a defence). While the opponent may consider that the chances are very high that the court will set judgment aside, clearly, when discussing any settlement which alters what your client is getting from that contained in the judgment, you must take this procedural point on board.

3.6.3.6 Planning your concessions

Negotiation is about moving towards agreement which means both sides have to plan how they are going to move, i.e., what concessions they are going to make. A 'concession' is defined by Donald G. Gifford in *Legal Negotiations Theory and Application*, West Publishing, St Paul MN, 1989, p. 141 as 'any modification of a negotiator's bargaining proposal making it less advantageous to his or her client'. Planning what you are going to concede, and when and how you will do it is a vital part of the preparation for a negotiation.

What is conceded in any negotiation must involve both consideration of the client's objectives including his or her priorities and the strengths and weaknesses of the case which are apparent from the analysis of the issues. *When* and *how* you make the concessions forms part of your negotiation strategy and must also be planned as much as possible. The concept of concessions and when and how they are used in the different strategies is covered in more detail in **Chapter 4** and the planning of them in the context of a real case in **Chapter 9**.

3.6.3.7 Planning the negotiation

Finally you must consider how you want the negotiation to proceed. In what order do you wish to cover the issues or the claims by your client? What information do you want to get from your opponent? What information are you prepared to give your opponent? Will you make concessions before or after getting or giving certain pieces of information? What strategy and tactics are you going to use? How are you going to start the negotiation?

You also need to consider the overall structure you want the negotiation to take. However, planning a negotiation is not like planning in the other interpersonal skills of advocacy and conference skills. Although those skills are also 'interpersonal' in that they involve interacting with others, in those skills you can set a structure which you then largely follow or adapt because you are in charge. You are conducting it. Although you must take on board the other person(s) involved, this need not alter your fundamental structure. Thus, in making a submission there may be interventions from the judge which alter part of the structure of what you will say; in examining a witness, you may have to rethink some questions because you are not getting the answers you expected or, in interviewing a client, you may find you have to adjust to take on board the concerns which he or she is raising. In planning a conference you can set an agenda, explain this to the client and then conduct the conference according to the agenda.

A negotiation is a much more dynamic interactive process. Although there are some identifiable phases through which many negotiations pass, no negotiation can be forced into a rigid structure which one or other parties controls. Every negotiation is unique and you need to be flexible. Planning the overall structure of a negotiation means considering generally the order in which you want to deal with things. Are there basic issues you feel need to be resolved before you move on to others? Are there matters which need clarification before there is any discussion of concessions?

Whatever your plan you must ensure that you have prepared so that you do cover all the relevant issues, claims and objectives of your client. The agreement reached will bind the parties and it is essential that no aspect is left out through inadvertence. One important aspect which is frequently overlooked by students is the form which the agreement will take. You need to consider what is the most appropriate form, given the stage of the case and your client's objectives, and plan to negotiate this if necessary (do not assume that it will just be agreed).

3.6.3.8 Summary

Proper preparation and planning is essential to ensure effective negotiation. If you are someone who takes naturally to negotiation, you still need the proper tools to do it well. If you are someone who is nervous about negotiating, having the tools honed will increase your confidence and ability to control your behaviour in the negotiation. Like good advocacy, good negotiation depends on proper preparation.

More detailed guidance on preparation and planning is given in **Chapter 9** which include consideration of strategy and tactics and use of concessions, etc., in the context of a case.

FOUR

STRATEGY AND STYLE

4.1 Introduction

4.1.1 DEALING WITH DIFFERENCES

Negotiating is about resolving differences, real or perceived. The parties are apart and want to come together, to reach agreement.

People cope with differences in a variety of ways and their manner of coping is related to their personality (e.g., how assertive or conciliatory they are), and their self-image (e.g., whether they pride themselves on being leaders, fighters, sharp and tough or being facilitators, problem-solvers, reasonable and fair-minded). Although there is a wide range of ways of coping with difference or conflict, the following attempts to categorise them into five different basic reactions.

4.1.1.1 Avoiding
'Avoiding' is to withdraw, not deal with it, ignore it in the hope it will go away. It is a 'lose/lose' reaction. The person cannot cope with dealing with differences and tries to avoid doing so by denying the differences or withdrawing from the discussion. As negotiation is all about discussing and resolving differences, avoidance is totally ineffective.

4.1.1.2 Accommodating
'Accommodating' does not deny the existence of the disagreement or conflict but resolves it by giving in completely to what the other side wants. It is a 'lose/win' reaction which leads to capitulation by the accommodator. As negotiation is about reconciling differences for both parties, this reaction is totally ineffective.

4.1.1.3 Competing
'Competing' involves dealing with the differences head on by 'fighting' it out on the basis that the strongest competitor wins. It is a 'win/lose' reaction which leads to confrontation. While it is useful in some circumstances, e.g., our civil justice system is an adversarial one in which advocates are expected to compete, it has its drawbacks, e.g., where there is no independent judge of who wins it can produce deadlock.

4.1.1.4 Cooperative/compromising
The 'cooperative/compromising' reaction is to deal with differences on the basis that they can be resolved by cooperating with the other person on the understanding that both sides will compromise equally to resolve the differences. It is a 'win/win' reaction which does not produce the best results. If both parties react this way it does mean that agreement will be reached but it will not necessarily be one which adequately or genuinely resolves the underlying differences.

4.1.1.5 Collaborative/problem-solving
The 'collaborative/problem-solving' reaction is to deal with differences as if they were a joint problem which can be solved by analysis and pooling of information and resources. It is a 'win/win' reaction which can lead to optimum results.

NEGOTIATION

4.1.1.6 Know your reactions

Nobody has just one reaction to dealing with differences. We all react in a much more complex way which mixes these reactions in differing degrees in different situations. The reactions to any one situation may come from basic personality type, from feeling unconfident because of lack of expertise, or from being unprepared. You cannot plan your personality type, nor can you do much to change it. You also, probably, cannot alter some of your basic instincts and ways of coping which you have used since childhood. Thus if you are a naturally cooperative person you cannot change overnight into a competitive one, or *vice versa*. However, you can try to become more conscious of your own tendencies and basic ways of dealing with differences and learn to control and adapt them to assist you to become a good negotiator.

You can also ensure you are properly prepared for a negotiation. The better prepared you are the less 're-active' and the more 'pro-active' you will be.

4.1.2 STRATEGY AND STYLE DISTINGUISHED

Any negotiation involves not only the substance of what is said, i.e., the content of any discussion about the differences, but also how it is said, i.e., the person's behaviour or demeanour. It is important to be able to distinguish between these two, to be able to identify and understand the different strategies and styles being used.

Strategy is the overall approach taken to achieve a good settlement. It involves decisions about how to open, what concessions to make and seek and when and how to make or seek them, what information will be sought and given, the order in which matters will be discussed, any tactics to be used, etc. It is important to understand the component elements of the different strategies to be able to plan and use them consciously — and recognise when they are being used against you. The different strategies are therefore covered in some detail later in this chapter.

Style is the manner of delivery, a person's attitude and demeanour. A person's style includes a whole range of factors including the particular language used, tone and volume of voice and physical presence, e.g., the way he or she sits or stands. Style can extend to particular types of statements, e.g., making personal remarks about the opponent or being sarcastic or condescending are hallmarks of a competitive style.

While people's styles vary enormously, two types which can be relatively readily categorised and identified are the competitive and the cooperative styles. A competitive style is argumentative, using emphatic language and attempts to wear the opponent down. It could include bullying or demeaning the opponent to undermine him or her. A cooperative style is friendly, courteous, tactful, conciliatory and attempts to gain trust by using good manners and charm. These two describe styles at either ends of the spectrum and many people will fall in the middle, e.g., speak fairly forcefully without bullying or demeaning or be very friendly but also very assertive.

A person's style does not always match his or her strategy. A person with a very cooperative style, who is charm itself, may be employing a highly competitive strategy. It is important therefore to separate the substance of what is being said about the negotiation from the way in which it is delivered: to separate style from strategy and deal with both.

4.2 Strategy Overview

4.2.1 INTRODUCTION

A negotiation strategy is the way in which the negotiator plans to manage the interaction in the negotiation including the exchange of information, the making and seeking of concessions and the overall structure of the negotiation to achieve his or her objectives. Strategic behaviour is complex and varies from person to person and case to case. However, specific patterns of strategic behaviour have been identified and labelled as comprising particular negotiation strategies. There are three strategies most frequently identified in books which form the basis of many legal professional training courses. While there is general consensus about what the different strategies involve, there is not total agreement on terminology. The three classifications are:

(a) The 'competitive' strategy (which is the term almost universally used for this strategy).

(b) The 'cooperative' strategy (alternatively called 'compromising').

(c) What is sometimes termed the 'collaborative' strategy which is derived from two similar but differing strategies promulgated by different schools of thought, namely:

   (i) the 'principled' approach developed by Roger Fisher and William Ury of the Harvard Negotiation Project, and

   (ii) the 'problem-solving' approach which Carrie Menkel-Meadow of UCLA set out in her paper 'Toward Another View of Legal Negotiation: The Structure of Problem-Solving' (1984) 31 *UCLA Law Review* 905–937.

Some writers only distinguish two strategies; the competitive (as we describe it) and the cooperative (in which they collapse the two which we have labelled 'cooperative' and 'collaborative' into one which generally leans more towards the 'collaborative').

4.2.2 THE UNDERLYING THEORIES

Basically the underlying theories of the strategies are as follows:

(a) Competitive strategy: seeks to maximise one's own gains by taking a strong stance (e.g., high opening demands, making few concessions, giving little information) on the basis that this will force the opponent to move towards one. The goal is victory.

(b) Cooperative strategy: assumes that there must be concessions on both sides and seeks, by demonstrably being 'reasonable' in the demands and concessions made and sharing information, to engender trust and reciprocal behaviour in the opponent. The goal is agreement.

(c) Collaborative strategy: assumes the parties can work together (i.e., collaborate) to reach agreement by exploring the underlying interests of the parties, sharing information, being creative in the options considered and judging any settlement against some agreed test or criteria. The goal of the problem-solving and principled approaches differ:

   (i) In problem-solving strategy the goal is to achieve a settlement which is fair and reflects both party's real needs or interests with the lowest transaction costs relative to desirability of the result.

   (ii) In principled strategy the goal is to achieve a settlement which is objectively fair by some external authoritative norm.

One could categorise the three strategies as 'hard bargaining' (competitive negotiator who is after victory and cares little about the relationship), 'soft bargaining' (cooperative negotiator who seeks agreement and does care about the relationship) and 'rationale bargaining' (principled or problem-solving negotiator whose approach is more complex, who seeks an agreement which is based on rational assessment).

4.2.3 SIMILARITIES OF COMPETITIVE AND COOPERATIVE

The competitive and cooperative strategies are based to a degree on the same analysis and some shared assumptions about what happens in a negotiation. These are that

NEGOTIATION

the two parties (e.g., claimant and defendant and their lawyers) have analysed the case and determined:

(a) the most they can get (their opening position);

(b) the least they will accept (their bottom line);

(c) the size and frequency of the steps they are prepared to make to get from their opening position to settlement (their concessions).

There will be settlement if there is an 'area of agreement', i.e., overlap between the two. Thus in the following situation:

Claimant's opening position: £4,000   bottom line: £2,000

Defendant's opening position: £1,000   bottom line: £3,000

The area of agreement is:

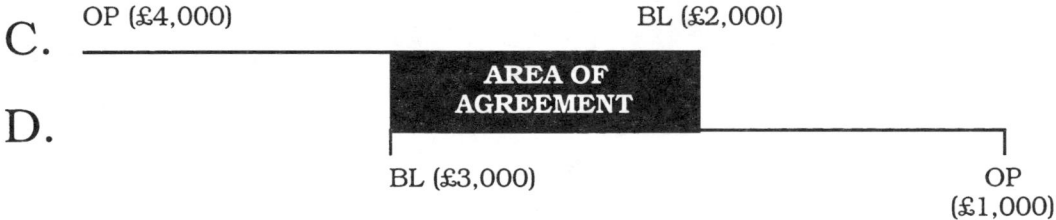

OP = opening position

BL = bottom line

There is an 'area of agreement' or overlap here of £1,000 so they should reach settlement. Both will probably assume that they will not get what they state in their opening position. The big question is where along the line will the settlement be? Will it be closer to the claimant's or the defendant's bottom line? Both will try during the negotiation to ascertain what the other's bottom line is so they can aim for that. Both use the concession-making process to seek agreement.

4.2.4 DISTINGUISHING FACTORS OF COMPETITIVE AND COOPERATIVE

The basic distinguishing factors, at least of the competitive and cooperative strategies, are:

(a) general underlying ethos and assumptions;

(b) opening position/demands;

(c) how they deal with concessions;

(d) how they deal with information;

(e) general stance;

(f) possibly, matching style;

(g) how success is measured.

While these factors do distinguish the two strategies, any particular negotiator will not necessarily use one strategy on all these factors nor throughout the whole negotiation. A negotiator may take a predominantly competitive or predominantly cooperative

32

approach. Alternatively, he or she might be competitive on concessions but cooperative on information or start out being competitive and move to being cooperative. The following analysis is done purely to try to give you some understanding of the basic characteristics of the strategies.

4.2.5 HOW COLLABORATIVE STRATEGIES DIFFER

There is a different underlying ethos to both the principled and problem-solving strategies. While the above two tend to see negotiation as swapping concessions and exchanging information largely to determine the opponent's position, these 'collaborative' strategies view it as a more complex interaction in which interests are explored and solutions sought jointly. They tend to use different language and concepts from competitive or cooperative ones and it is therefore difficult to compare them on these particular factors and we have not attempted to do so.

4.3 Competitive Strategy

Sometimes called positional bargaining or hard bargaining because of the extreme position and tough stance taken, this is perhaps the most identifiable strategy. It is the one promoted in most commercial 'How To Do It Guides' for business or sales people. It is also the one most people expect a lawyer to adopt. It is basically adversarial and the barrister works in an adversarial system.

4.3.1 UNDERLYING ASSUMPTIONS AND ETHOS

The competitive strategy is based on the assumption that all negotiations are distributive, zero-sum, i.e., each side wants equally and exclusively what the other side wants. By definition, one side's gains are the other's losses. The competitive negotiator genuinely sees the other party as his or her 'competitor' or 'opponent' with a similar mind set (i.e., out to compete, to win).

The competitive negotiator has high expectations and the overall aim is to maximise his or her own gain, to come out ahead, to do better than the opponent, to claim victory. It is a win/lose approach. The underlying theory of the strategy is that taking a firm stance, fairly extreme positions, making few and small concessions and withholding information will reduce the opponent's expectations or cause loss of confidence, thereby manipulating him or her into moving towards the competitive negotiator.

4.3.2 OPENING/DEMANDS

An integral part of a competitive strategy is to open high (i.e., to open at the most extreme position maintainable), stay high and sometimes increase. Throughout the negotiation the demands will remain near the best possible outcome. The demands made may be inflated, i.e., above what the negotiator really considers to be the best possible outcome.

4.3.3 CONCESSIONS/OFFERS

Another intregal part of a competitive strategy is to make as few concessions as possible while obtaining as many as possible from opponent. Thus a competitive negotiator:

- makes few concessions
- makes small concessions
- makes unimportant concessions
- makes false concessions (i.e., suggests a particular point is important and makes a concession on it when in fact it is of little importance)

NEGOTIATION

- is slow to make concessions (i.e., does not make them early in the negotiation).

The competitive negotiator demands concessions from his or her opponent and:

- may impose it as a condition of the relationship
- focuses on concessions from the opponent
- may require a concession from his or her opponent before considering making one himself or herself.

4.3.4 INFORMATION

Exchanging information gives negotiators insight into each other's positions. What really is the opponent's 'bottom line'? What are the real strengths and weaknesses of the opponent's case? The competitive negotiator uses information exchange as a tool to win. The strategy is to disclose as little information as possible while getting as much information from the opponent as possible. The competitive negotiator:

- reveals as little information as possible
- is selective in the information disclosed
- may give inaccurate information (which raises an ethical issue on exactly what the information is and how inaccurate it is).

On the other hand the competitive negotiator presses the opponent for information.

4.3.5 GENERAL STANCE

Competitive negotiators take a strong stance, want to be seen as tough, determined, unyielding. They are on the offensive, single-minded, out to win and not bothered with doubts or indecision that may produce a more reconciling approach. They want to control the negotiation and will therefore generally take the initiative at the start, the aim being to gain the upper hand. They will maintain pressure throughout by stressing the sense of urgency, the need for rapid progress, to 'deal with this issue now' often leaving the opponent little space to exert pressure back. They may use additional tactics to increase this pressure, e.g., using 'the deadline' (real or fictitious) and the 'walkout' (see **Chapter 5**).

Competitive negotiators seek to take every advantage and concentrate on achieving their objectives. The objectives of the opponent has little or no relevance to them. They are slow to express sympathy for or even acknowledge the opponent's position. They are not interested in any rationale or fair analysis of the case. Their discussion about the two sides will be done in an attempt to exaggerate the strength of their own case and stress the weakness of the opponent's case.

Competitive negotiators will use a variety of techniques to confuse or divert the opponent away from obtaining information or discussing issues they find difficult (e.g., because it exposes a weakness in their case). They may stick to one point tenaciously refusing to discuss any other issue. Alternatively, they may jump to another issue when discussing the current one gets too difficult.

Competitive negotiators generally distrust their opponent and assume all effective negotiators are competitive. They see cooperative negotiators as weak, naive and deserving of exploitation. They interpret cooperative behaviour as a sign of weakness and seek to exploit it.

4.3.6 MATCHING STYLE

A person using a competitive strategy may also use a competitive style which tends to be argumentative rather than conciliatory, using emphatic language, tone of voice, etc., to appear tough and uncompromising. A competitive negotiator presents from the basic standpoint that he or she is always right and/or superior and the opponent wrong and/or inferior. A competitive negotiator may use blame as a tool in creating this impression, i.e., the problems are caused by the opponent or his or her client. While not always intended to be so by the competitive negotiator, many of the aspects of the style are experienced by the recipient as aggression towards him or her. Some competitive negotiators positively seek to cause discomfort to the opponent, for example by being sarcastic, ridiculing the opponent, making accusations and threats (within ethical limits), and by using intimidation in an attempt to wear down the opponent on the basis that some people have real difficulty coping with aggression and will adopt avoiding behaviour to stop it.

Few people using a competitive strategy with a competitive style will use all the stylistic techniques above as it would result in belligerent and obvious behaviour. They are more likely to use different aspects of the style at different times throughout the negotiation. It is also worth mentioning again that a person with a competitive strategy may well *not* adopt a competitive style. Competitive negotiators are as able to be charming and friendly as cooperative ones.

4.3.7 MEASURING SUCCESS

A competitive negotiator usually defines success by reference to how much he or she has won, possibly by comparison with how well the other side has done, i.e., has he or she come out ahead. Thus success is defined fairly narrowly and may well disregard a variety of important aspects such as whether any shared interests have been identified, what the outcome might do to future relationships between the parties, etc.

4.3.8 ADVANTAGES/WHEN USED EFFECTIVELY

Competitive strategy is more like simple bargaining than any of the other strategies and as such is used most successfully in those type of situations, i.e., where there really is only a single issue, a distributive, 'zero-sum' negotiation.

It may also be used, where there is an imbalance of power, by the person with the power. Power imbalance can stem from a variety of sources, e.g., having a very strong case or being a repeat player negotiating against a one-off player (an insurance company negotiating against a claimant). The person with the power adopts a competitive strategy because he or she risks less if there is no settlement.

The use of pressure, hard stances, etc., in this strategy does increase the tension and stress level. The overall strategy of giving little either by way of concessions or information, maintaining control and pressure which may be coupled with a competitive style, attempts to undermine the opponent and cause him or her to 'give in'. Clearly this will work if the opponent is susceptible to such manipulative behaviour and it may result in winning more concessions, gaining more and a better outcome. It can be particularly effective with opponents who are inexperienced or have difficulty coping with aggression and conflict.

There is little chance of exploitation by the opponent because of the competitive negotiator's basic attitude of distrust for the opponent and approach of few concessions and selective, limited disclosure.

This strategy is relatively easy to understand and use provided one's personality allows it. It has very limited objectives and keeps consideration of issues to the minimum. It has a simpler and more obvious behaviour pattern and is less intellectually taxing because of the limited range of issues under discussion.

4.3.9 RISKS AND LIMITATIONS/WHEN NOT USED EFFECTIVELY

A competitive strategy is not the most effective one in a multiple issue, integrative negotiation where there are a variety of issues, needs and interests on which agreement

NEGOTIATION

is sought. The hard stances, limited disclosure, tension-creating behaviour means that far less information is exchanged. Both negotiators tend to become more rigid, retreat into their stated positions and 'play their cards close to their chest'. Communication is distorted. The exchange between negotiators is limited and unimaginative. They will probably fail to explore the full range of issues or options available with the result that the clients get a less good deal than they might. Any common or compatible interests of the clients may never be explored let alone form part of the settlement.

Even in a negotiation with limited issues to be negotiated, a competitive strategy tends to emphasise differences rather than common ground. It generally increases misunderstanding between the parties and makes them think they are farther apart than they really are.

Many people are not susceptible to the manipulative behaviour of a competitive negotiator. They do not react to the increased tension, don't 'play the game', are not undermined, do not lose confidence and do not give in. Indeed, a fairly common reaction to the behaviour is to do quite the reverse of the assumption of the competitive negotiatior — to 'dig one's heels in'. This can be done either by avoiding behaviour (just refusing to discuss the issue) or by retaliation (mirror the behaviour of the competitor). In either case deadlock is the result.

There is a real risk that a competitive strategy will escalate into really aggressive behaviour which irritates and frustrates the other side. The client's interests are lost sight of and the negotiation becomes a real battle rather than an attempt to settle. The parties may get stuck battling over trivial issues and fail to recognise the main issues which should be discussed. It may take longer to reach agreement as both sides jockey for position and do not deal with the issues or need for exchange of information.

A competitive strategy is not effective if there is an on-going relationship. Such a strategy can easily destroy it. Even where the actual negotiation is not carried out by the parties, e.g., done by the lawyers, some of the stance of the negotiators may be carried back to the client who may be affected by it. The outcome may reflect the strategy (i.e., really be win/lose) or be described by the lawyer or the other party in competitive terms (i.e., in win/lose language) which may undermine any on-going relationship.

People who negotiate regularly, particularly within a set community, e.g., the Bar, develop a reputation based on their behaviour and what is relayed about their behaviour. Someone who uses a competitive strategy or style will become known as a competitive negotiator. There are studies which show that people confronted by a competitive negotiator respond competitively. Thus one could get onto a treadmill of competitive negotiations with less flexibility in choice of strategies.

Finally, some unprepared negotiators have a tendency to use the competitive strategy in an attempt to cover up their lack of preparation. As the strategy involves limited disclosure and strong positional stances which reveal little about the analysis and real position, it is tempting to take a competitive stance where in fact you have done insufficient analysis or do not know the real position. However, a competitive strategy does depend on credibility. The negotiator using it must be able to carry it through. Using it to mask lack of preparation runs the real risk of blowing your cover and losing all credibility.

4.3.10 HOW TO DEAL WITH COMPETITIVE NEGOTIATORS

Competitive negotiator's strategy is based on appearing to be inflexible to manipulate the opponent into moving. However, in fact they are prepared to make some concessions and to give limited information. Be aware of the strategy, refuse to be manipulated, possibly label the behaviour, be proactive and not reactive, do not get emotional and take a firm but conciliatory stance. Point out the limitations and risks of their strategy. For more detail see **5.7**.

Ignore the style used, focus on the objective merits of the arguments used. Try to see why they are acting like this — are they naturally aggressive personality? Are they in a position of power? Are they just unprepared and bluffing? Are they responding to you — i.e., are you using a competitive strategy?

4.4 Cooperative

Cooperative strategy can also be called soft bargaining or 'cordial' bargaining (see Robert Condlin, 'Bargaining in the Dark: The Normative Incoherence of Lawyer Dispute Bargaining Role' (1992) 51 *Maryland Law Review* 1–104 at pp. 16–22). Most discussions of this particular strategy are in the context of comparing the effectiveness of the different techniques used in competitive and cooperative strategies. Many articles, books and materials for negotiation courses tend to mix characteristics of pure cooperative strategy with those of the more 'collaborative' (principled and problem-solving), some not really distinguishing between the two (e.g., Williams' research on effective negotiators compared only competitive and cooperative without distinguishing the additional 'collaborative' techniques as a separate strategy). While use of some of the techniques is effective, few people would recommend a purely cooperative strategy.

4.4.1 UNDERLYING ASSUMPTIONS AND ETHOS

The underlying assumption is that a negotiator can create an open, trusting atmosphere by making concessions, sharing information, etc. and that the other negotiator will respond to this by being open and trusting too, i.e., reciprocating concessions and information-exchange. A cooperative negotiator focuses on the principle that to reach agreement, both sides must give. The main goal is agreement not victory; cooperative negotiators are more concerned with reaching agreement than precisely what they get out of the agreement. They are concerned with both sides, either genuinely or because they have to be to get something from them. They compromise as a matter of principle or necessity.

Cooperative negotiators believe that their own compromising behaviour will produce similar behaviour in the other negotiator. One could say they are trying to create an atmosphere of 'mutual' compromise, to manipulate their opponent into coming towards them by introducing a moral element of 'fair play' based on joint compromise.

4.4.2 OPENING/DEMANDS

Cooperative negotiators open in a way which shows they are trustworthy and see the negotiation as a compromise. Their opening proposals will be at a reasonable level and during the negotiation they will make reasonable suggestions, frequently explaining the basis for what they are seeking.

4.4.3 INFORMATION

Cooperative negotiators share information freely. Seeking to build trust, they do not exaggerate or make false statements but make fair statements of facts. In the same way that competitive negotiators use the exchange of information as a technique to achieve their goal (victory), cooperative negotiators use exchange of information to achieve their goal (agreement). They may assume that the other side will automatically give information freely or that, by being open and honest themselves, making fair statements, etc., they can create a trusting atmosphere which will produce open and honest behaviour in the other side who will be equally forthcoming.

Cooperative negotiators are genuinely interested in exchanging information to assist them to assess what is a fair settlement. They give information and listen to what the other side has to say. They explain their positions and give reasons for their proposals.

NEGOTIATION

4.4.4 CONCESSIONS/OFFERS

Cooperative negotiators make unilateral concessions based on the assumption that this will encourage the other side to reciprocate. On the basis that both parties want to reach agreement, they assume this means movement by both. They focus on this aspect of the negotiation (i.e., a fair amount of movement by both sides). They make concessions on the assumption that the other side also sees the negotiation as mutual movement towards agreement or that they can encourage the other negotiator to see it this way. The cooperative negotiator hopes that the other side will 'follow their example' and will reciprocate to make the negotiation 'fair'.

4.4.5 GENERAL STANCE

Cooperative negotiators take a conciliatory stance, want to be seen as trustworthy, open, honest, ethical and fair. They probably also want to be liked. They want to be seen as being concerned about both their own client and the other side and reaching a fair agreement. They possibly care more about reaching agreement than what the agreement actually gives the client, and are concerned more about maintaining the relationship than getting the best result.

Cooperative negotiators focus on building and maintaining an open, honest and trusting environment and avoiding generating conflict. They do not want to be seen as taking advantage, using questionable tactics to achieve their ends or being aggressive. They want to trust the other side and have the other side trust them.

4.4.6 MATCHING STYLE

Cooperative negotiators generally match their style to the strategy. They are courteous and pleasant. They seek to deal with the opponent on an equal footing — they do not try to undermine or intimidate. They use non-threatening language and present in a manner which is 'reasonable' rather than emphatic or forceful.

4.4.7 MEASURING SUCCESS

Cooperative negotiators usually measure success by whether or not the negotiation 'feels fair' which may take into account not only the ultimate agreement and what the client gets out of it but whether the process was fair: roughly how much did each side compromise, did the negotiators treat each other 'fairly', was there 'equal treatment' in exchange of information and concession-making?

4.4.8 ADVANTAGES/WHEN USED EFFECTIVELY

A cooperative strategy can be effective in situations where the continuing relationship is in fact more important than what exactly was achieved for each of the parties in this particular settlement. This continuing relationship could be either business (e.g., two parties really do wish to continue trading despite a past dispute) or personal (e.g., in a divorce where the parties really do not want to affect continued relationships by both parents with the children). It is unlikely to damage the relationship as the whole strategy emphasises the importance of reaching agreement while building and maintaining a relationship.

Given the main focus is on agreement, a cooperative strategy means there are fewer risks that the negotiation will break down. Using a cooperative strategy may result in the parties reaching agreement faster than in a competitive situation, particularly where both sides are cooperative.

Where both sides use a cooperative strategy, it is likely to result in the parties reaching an agreement which is seen as 'fair', as they will feel not only that the terms of the agreement are fair but that they have been fairly treated in the negotiation. Provided both parties use a cooperative strategy, it can be much less stressful than a competitive one.

4.4.9 RISKS AND LIMITATIONS/WHEN NOT USED EFFECTIVELY

Making unilateral concessions is risky as the behaviour may well not be reciprocated. It is very difficult if not impossible to retract a concession once made. The negotiator may have reached the 'bottom line' and have nothing left to trade in the negotiation.

A strategy which relies on making concessions to create an open, trusting atmosphere means that too much may be conceded too early in the negotiation. The negotiator gets too close to the bottom line too early and is then left with very little room to manoeuvre over the rest of the negotiation.

Making concessions is interpreted as a sign of weakness by competitive negotiators. It is seen as soft, done only because of lack of ability to compete. It also reinforces for competitive negotiators the belief that their strategy works, i.e., they are getting movement towards themselves. They will continue to use their strategy, possibly pressing harder for concessions. They will take advantage of what they preceive as the lack of ability of the opponent on the basis that they will get what they deserve.

It is fairly clear from the above that a cooperative strategy is vulnerable to exploitation. Surprisingly many cooperative negotiators do not recognise when they are being exploited. They continue using their strategy (i.e., making concessions and volunteering information) even though they are getting nothing in return. Many cooperative negotiators continue working on the assumption that their behaviour is being or will be reciprocated when it is clear that this is not the case. Because they fail to check whether or not their strategy is actually working, they are open to real exploitation.

The underlying ethos of cooperative strategy is to create an open, trusting atmosphere and reduce any sense of conflict or aggression. This means that cooperative negotiators tend to avoid the confrontational or challenging aspects of a negotiation. They may try to deal with competitive techniques by being conciliatory and open, rather than recognising and possibly drawing attention to the disruptive competitive technique used. They are also less likely to really test the opponent's statements, or to probe for reasons for proposals or for evidence to back up statements of fact. Clearly this leaves them open to exploitation.

Cooperative negotiators' main aim is to reach agreement. There is therefore a real risk that they will focus too much on reaching agreement and concede too much to achieve it. They may lose sight of obtaining the client's objectives. They may undervalue the strengths of their own case and hence not pursue them. Alternatively they may mistake an easy option (i.e., one easily agreed) for the correct one (i.e., in the client's interests). This is a risk and a weakness even where there are two cooperative negotiators; where a cooperative negotiator is against a competitive one he or she may lose quite a lot.

Cooperative negotiation strategy is based on mutuality of concessions and shared information. Cooperative negotiators may react emotionally to competitive ones. The moral element of the cooperative strategy (both negotiators reciprocating and having a sense of 'fair play') means that there is real room for cooperative negotiators to see competitive ones as unfair and selfish. The cooperative may react to this with a sense, even if not a strong one, of moral indignation which is introduced into the negotiation. They may then misread the situation and assume there is more disagreement than in fact exists.

From the above it is clear that using a cooperative strategy against a competitive negotiator is highly risky. While one cannot tell exactly what strategy will be used against one prior to a negotiation, there are some situations where it is more likely than others, e.g., where one is negotiating against someone who has much more power — someone with a much stonger case or a repeat player or where the negotiation really is zero-sum.

NEGOTIATION

4.5 Collaborative/Principled/Problem-solving

4.5.1 INTRODUCTION

Writing and discussion about the above two strategies, competitive and cooperative, tend to be descriptive rather than prescriptive. People have tried to analyse what people do in negotiations, label the behaviour and categorise it as competitive or cooperative. Some 'How To Do It Guides' are also 'prescriptive' in that they recommend the use of the competitive strategy. However, the bulk of the writing merely attempts to assist people to understand what has long been behaviour patterns in negotiations and to see what is and is not effective.

There are three main differences which require a different approach to this third strategy. First, it encompasses the thinking behind two similar strategies which have relatively recently formed part of the discussion on strategies, the 'principled' approach as set out in the book *Getting to Yes: Negotiating Agreement Without Giving In* published in 1981 by Roger Fisher and William Ury of the Harvard Negotiation Project and the 'problem-solving' approach proposed by Carrie Menkel-Meadow of UCLA in her paper about it (see **4.2.1**) in 1984.

Secondly, writing on these approaches tends to be more prescriptive than descriptive. The writing on these two approaches goes beyond describing what people do. Taking on board what negotiation is all about, different behaviours in negotiation, etc., they formulate strategies (i.e., prescribe behaviour) which they consider result in better settlements and more effective negotiations. The authors, particularly Fisher and Ury and Menkel-Meadows, argue strongly that their approaches should be used.

Thirdly, in both strategies the two negotiators seek to work together to further both parties' interests and aims, maximise the gain for both, to come up with a 'win/win' settlement. They assume that negotiation is not about each side just stating their position, that it is more complex than each side simply determining the best they can get, the worst they will accept (bottom line) and then doing an information exchange and 'concession dance' to meet somewhere between the two opposing sides' bottom lines. This behaviour (i.e., that used in both competitive and cooperative) they label 'positional'. The principled and problem-solving approaches have specific techniques to enable the parties to look more closely at the substance of the negotiation and the standard against which the settlement will be judged and to do this jointly. They assume that few negotiations are about a single issue or zero-sum.

The two approaches are covered under the single name of 'collaborative' because, along with many other characteristics, they share this fundamental approach of working together (collaborating) to reach settlement. They are similar to the cooperative strategy in that they aim to create an open, cooperative atmosphere. However, both take a more reasoned, intellectual approach to negotiation than the fairly basic 'sharing' approach of cooperative negotiation or the 'fighting' approach of competitive negotiation.

The 'principled' approach is much more widely known and discussed and we therefore set out the basic characteristics of this one before the problem-solving approach.

4.5.2 PRINCIPLED NEGOTIATION

4.5.2.1 Introduction

This strategy is based on the research and experience of Roger Fisher and William Ury, Directors of the Harvard Negotiation Project at Harvard Law School which runs courses and publishes a substantial amount of material on negotiation, including the *Negotiation Journal*. The work done on negotiation covers a huge range of areas including trade unions, international peace treaties, large commercial transactions and legal negotiations. The strategy is set out in their book *Getting to Yes: Negotiating Agreement Without Giving In* (1991), a small paperback. We set out below a brief summary of the main characteristics of the strategy based on the main elements:

(a) separate the people from the problem (**4.5.2.2**);

(b) focus on interests not positions (**4.5.2.3**);

(c) invent options for mutual gain (**4.5.2.4**);

(d) insist on objective criteria (**4.5.2.5**);

(e) develop a best alternative rather than a bottom line (**4.5.2.6**).

4.5.2.2 Separate the people from the problem

Negotiations can centre on the interpersonal relationship rather than the substantive issues which require settlement. This is inefficient, reduces the effectiveness of the negotiators and can result in a less good settlement for the parties. To avoid emotion and personalities interfering in the negotiation separate people's feelings from the substance being negotiated. 'People' problems may stem from:

(a) Different perceptions: the different parties will almost invariably have different perceptions of the problem.

- Try to see it from the other side's point of view.

- You need not agree with it but try to understand their point of view.

- Do not assume they intend to do what you fear.

- Do not blame them for your problem.

- Discuss the perceptions held by each side.

- Allow the other side to save face wherever possible. People often hold out because they do not want to be seen to be backing down. So make your proposals as consistent with their principles, past words and deeds as possible.

(b) Emotions: we all have them and they can get in the way.

- Recognise and acknowledge the emotional aspect of any negotiation. Allow the other side to let off steam if necessary. Learn to listen without responding to attack or emotional outbursts.

(c) Communication: good communication is essential.

- Do not be so busy thinking about what you have to say that you do not listen. Check with them that you do understand correctly what they have said.

- Try to use phraseology which builds a working relationship. If you repeat what they say, try to do so in a positive way and from their point of view. Speak about yourself not them, e.g., 'my client feels let down' not 'your client broke his word'.

4.5.2.3 Focus on interests not positions

Negotiations can focus on the negotiators' statements of their positions rather than on the real interests or needs of the parties. The example given is of two people working in a library. One wants the window open to get fresh air, the other does not want to sit in a draft and wants it closed. Each states their position on whether the window be open or closed. They limit the negotiation to simply arguing about how much it should be open, a quarter, half, two-thirds, etc., none of which satisfies either of them. Focusing on interests, i.e., a solution which provides fresh air without a draft, may produce more alternatives to consider which may in the end satisfy both, e.g., opening a window in an adjoining room which brings in fresh air without a draft.

NEGOTIATION

Negotiators must differentiate between:

(a) Issues: the matters on which the parties disagree, e.g., in a personal injury case, there are the issues of liability, possible contributory negligence and quantum.

(b) Positions: stances or proposals put forward on the issues, e.g., the defendant is liable, there is no contributory negligence and the claimant will accept nothing less than £x.

(c) Interests/needs: the real wants or concerns of the parties which underlie the positions, e.g., the claimant has suffered substantial injuries, has had to pay substantial medical expenses, has had to take a less taxing job with less income, has had social and recreational activities curtailed because of the injuries, etc., feels very aggrieved about what has happened, feels a loss of self-image because of reduced mobility and job status, etc.

Positional bargaining occurs where negotiators lock themselves into exchanging stances or proposals without finding out what the underlying interest are. Using the principled approach, negotiators try to identify and explore the underlying interests on the basis that there may be some which are shared (i.e., both want the same thing, such as a continuing relationship), or, if not shared, compatible (as in the window example above) as well as those which conflict. The techniques suggested for focusing on interests are:

(a) Identify them:

  (i) Ask 'why?': seek an understanding of the needs, fears, and desires which underlie their position.

  (ii) Ask 'why not?' — try to analyse why an opponent will not agree to what you want; what would be the effect for them?

  (iii) Be conscious that both sides are likely to have a variety of interests that motivate them.

  (iv) Do not overlook the most powerful interests (basic human needs — security, economic well-being, etc.).

  (v) Write down the interests to help you to remember them and possibly stimulate ideas about how to meet them.

(b) Discuss them:

  (i) Describe your client's interests as clearly as possible. Be specific, make the interests 'come alive'.

  (ii) Acknowledge that their interests are part of the problem. Be sympathetic where appropriate.

  (iii) Tell them what your client's interests and needs are first and then tell them your proposals for how those needs can be met (i.e., put your reasons *before* your proposals so they hear the reasons).

  (iv) Look forward for solutions, not back to where the problem came from.

  (v) Identify your options but be flexible in your approach to each option.

  (vi) Be hard in your approach to the problem but soft on the people.

4.5.2.4 Invent options for mutual gain

Many negotiations are seen as single issue, i.e., existing along a single dimension such as the sale of a piece of land where the single issue appears to be the price. If the price is viewed as the single issue one party's gain is the other party's loss. The more the seller is forced to compromise on price, the more the buyer gains. By inventing options for mutual gain this part of the strategy seeks to avoid the win/lose dynamic by inventing options that can bring gains to both sides. For this reason some writers refer to this part of the principled strategy as 'expanding the pie'.

Central to the concept is the ability to reconsider the issues in the negotiation and view them not as single issue and zero-sum, but multiple issue and integrative. The concept is best illustrated by the well-known example of two sisters arguing over an orange. Having finally agreed to split the orange into two, one sister took off all the peel and ate the fruit, whilst the other discarded the fruit and saved the peel for a cake she was making. Neither had stopped to consider the other's underlying reasons for wanting the orange so they missed the opportunity for both to have more of what they wanted.

Consider the following example as an illustration of pie-expanding:

> An owner of a vineyard and exclusive resort property is in financial difficulty. A local financier is looking to invest capital. A few of the options available are:
>
> - **Sale**:
>   sale of the resort property and the vineyard;
>   sale of the vineyard whilst retaining the resort property;
>   sale of the resort property whilst retaining the vineyard.
>
> - **Lease**:
>   lease the resort property and vineyard and seller continues to manage both;
>   lease the resort for a lower price and the seller receives financial assistance in maintaining the vineyard.
>
> - **Joint venture**:
>   sell 49% of the resort property and vineyard and retain 51%, the seller to continue to manage the resort and vineyard.

One reason that mutually beneficial options are overlooked is the time and commitment they take to generate. The above example has only looked at some of the possibilities and then only in outline. Given the time it takes to create ideas and mutually beneficial options it is tempting to take what appears to be the short cut of splitting the difference.

Another obstacle to creating mutual options is the assumption of the fixed pie. There is an assumption that the negotiation can only ever be about a single issue and therefore the negotiators do not bother to invent options. Negotiators cannot see the negotiation as being anything other than linear, with winning and losing at opposite ends. In this climate, it is difficult to see the other options that could solve the problem.

Another obstacle is the firmly held belief of many negotiators that how the other side will get what they want is their problem. However, if the other side's interests are not satisfied you will not reach an agreement. Their problem therefore really is your problem as well.

In order to invent options you will need to allocate part of your preparation time to this activity. When negotiating in a team this can make team members uncomfortable. They may be tempted to see option-creating as a process that 'clouds the issue' rather than a process that can in the long run save time and money. You will need to spend time uncritically gathering ideas that could help you solve the problem. Do not attempt to evaluate any of the ideas as you think of them as it is important that you keep the process of inventing and evaluation separate. Inevitably if you are critical of new ideas you will stifle their creation. You may collect some outlandish ideas but, if necessary, these can be weeded out at the evaluation stage.

NEGOTIATION

Once you have assimilated the options then you can evaluate them. At the evaluation stage you will be looking to determine how practical, workable and enforceable each solution is and measuring the extent to which it is capable of meeting the interests of both side's of the negotiation. Try to select criteria for evaluating the options. Do not forget the other sides interests at this stage. Try to select options that really are mutually acceptable.

4.5.2.5 Insist on using objective criteria

The main difference between a negotiation and adjudication is the lack of an independent third party to determine the outcome. Principled negotiators attempt to bring this objective element into a negotiation by the use of objective criteria. This means that the settlement is based on an objective standard not the will or opinion of one or other of the parties (i.e., on principle not pressure).

(a) Develop objective criteria by use of precedent and independent standards, e.g., an expert where appropriate.

(b) Frame issues as a joint search for objective criteria.

(c) Use reason not positional statements in determining the standard to apply.

(d) Be open to reason but closed to pressure.

4.5.2.6 Developing a BATNA

'BATNA' stands for Best Alternative to a Negotiated Settlement and is a principled negotiator's equivalent to the 'bottom line' used by competitive or cooperative negotiators.

The purpose of a 'bottom line' in a competitive or cooperative strategy is to ensure you resist pressure exerted in the negotiation; do not succumb to temptation in the negotiation and give away more than is good for the client. However, determining when you walk away from a negotiation on the basis of a single 'bottom line' is very rigid and can be very restrictive. It assumes that a negotiation is just about trading concessions and moving along a continuum to a single point beyond which you will not go. It does not take into account information you may receive or alternatives which might be proposed in the negotiation itself, options which might be considered which, although they technically do not meet the 'bottom line', may in fact satisfy more of the client's real interests.

Planning the BATNA is an important part of preparation. Rather than looking at what your client ought to get out of the negotiation, you consider what he or she will do if no agreement is reached. By looking carefully at the client's real underlying interests, you can see the options available and which satsify those needs best. You can then identify those alternatives which are better than a negotiated agreement against which to compare proposals made in the negotiation.

You also need to consider what the BATNA is for the other side to see what proposals they may or may not accept.

The strength of your negotiating position depends on the attractiveness of your and your opponent's BATNAs. The better your BATNA the stronger your position. It is therefore important to consider and develop your BATNA by making a list of possibilities if no agreement is reached, converting as many of those into genuine practical options as possible and identifying which is the best option. The stronger your BATNA the more useful it is to disclose it to the other side.

4.5.2.7 What if they won't play

Where one side does not adopt a principled strategy but continues to make positional statements and act in an adversarial way, there is a real temptation for the principled negotiator to respond with similar behaviour, with the result that the negotiation ends up in a cycle of positional statements by both sides. The main technique suggested to avoid this is to break any such cycle by refusing to react in an adversarial way, by not using similar behaviour. They label this technique 'negotiation jujitsu' because it adopts the same basic strategy of stepping aside and using their strength to your ends.

If the other side:

(a) Sets out their position strongly:

- do not be drawn into argument
- do not reject or accept it
- treat it as a genuine attempt to solve the problem
- look behind what is said to see what principles it reflects, what interests it might satisfy. Ask them to explain how it solves the problem.

(b) Attacks your suggestions:

- do not get defensive
- invite criticism and suggestions.

(c) Attacks you:

- allow them to let off steam
- do not react
- reframe it into an attack on the problem.

On the basis that replying to a statement with a statement is more likely to escalate the confrontational stance, to produce resistance, they recommend the use of:

- questions which produce answers instead of statements which produce resistance, and
- silence which may also produce answers as people feel uncomfortable with it and may, to fill the void, continue by giving explanations.

4.5.3 PROBLEM-SOLVING STRATEGY

A problem-solving strategy shares much with the principled approach. It emphasises the importance of: identifying the underlying needs and objectives of both the parties; creating solutions which meet the parties' needs; examining closely the shared, compatible and potentially conflicting goals of the clients; and expanding the resources available by looking carefully at all the aspects of distribution: what can be distributed, when, by whom, how, how much, etc.

> In summary, by using substantive strategies such as exploring shared interests, by exploiting value differences in needs, by looking to third parties, by sharing, by aggregating or disaggregating, by neutralizing, by seeking substitute goods, by exploring long- and short-term values, and by using other specific devices, a greater number of solutions may be found. (Menkel-Meadow, Carrie, 'Toward Another View of Legal Negotiation: The Structure of Problem Solving' (1984) 31 *UCLA Law Review* 754–842 at p. 813)

The strategy also encourages more reasoned interchange in the negotiation, brainstorming for options, sharing information to genuinely assist in solving the problem, and giving reasons when discussing whether or not proposals are acceptable, etc. Thus like principled negotiation, it encourages an intellectual approach to negotiation and many of the techniques recommended for principled negotiators are equally relevant to a problem-solving strategy.

The process for the two is also similar in that it encourages full exploration of the two parties' interests before attempting to divide them.

The major difference between the two is that, while a principled strategy involves applying some objective criteria external to the parties, problem-solving seeks fair or just solutions:

> For those who seek the most effective or efficient solutions from a utilitarian perspective, it is enough to settle at a point where no party can gain without hurting the other party. (Menkel-Meadow (above) at p. 813)

Thus the test relates more to the actual needs of the clients than some external standard.

4.5.4 ADVANTAGES OF THE COLLABORATIVE APPROACH

The collaborative approaches as represented by both principled and problem-solving strategies has enormous advantages over both the competitive and the cooperative in that:

- they increase the focus on parties' real needs and interests

- rather than focusing on the division of resources on the basis that they are limited, they encourage techniques to try to expand the resources

- rather than assuming that the parties' needs and interests are directly opposed so that resources are wanted equally and exclusively by both, they encourage negotiatiors to distinguish between genuinely conflicting needs and those which may be shared or compatible

- they encourage a more rational and reasoned approach to negotiation whereby the two negotiators try to use information constructively and focus on resolving the issues rather than just swapping concessions.

Where both parties use a collaborative approach, they are more likely to have genuinely considered the parties' objectives fully, to have considered a far greater range of options for settlement, to have really considered whether the options satisfy the objectives and therefore to reach a settlement which is far more satisfactory to both parties.

Clearly the greater the range of real interests and needs of the clients the easier it is to use this approach fully. However, even where the scope for 'option creating' is limited some aspects of the strategy are useful, e.g., separating the people from the problem.

4.5.5 LIMITATIONS OF THE COLLABORATIVE APPROACH

Negotiators who use a collaborative strategy are open to some degree of exploitation by a competitive negotiator if the collaborative negotiator does not really check out what is happening. An opponent may use a very cooperative style and many of the phrases taken from principled or problem-solving strategies, e.g., 'objective standard', 'fair and reasonable', 'underlying interests', 'joint benefits', etc., but in fact be using a very competitive strategy, revealing little information and making few, small concessions.

While both principled and problem-solving strategies have a test against which to judge whether the settlement is a good one or not, these tests are not in fact as certain as one might think.

- Principled negotiation relies on the use of 'objective' criteria. As Condlin points out in his article 'Bargaining in the Dark: The Normative Incoherence of Lawyer Dispute Bargaining Role' (1992) 51 *Maryland Law Review* 1–104:

STRATEGY AND STYLE

> Objective can mean neutral or non-partisan, in the sense of treating each side's interests equally.... Or it can mean fair and legitimate, in the sense of respecting recognised entitlements of the parties and reconciling conflicts between them through the use of principles, procedures and substantive norms that are accepted as authoritative.

- Problem-solving relies on solutions which are 'fair or just' where 'no party can gain without hurting the other party' (Menkel-Meadow above). But even she recognises that this does produce problems in legal negotiations. 'When might the negotiator choose to pursue less gain for his client or actually cause his client to suffer loss so as to benefit or not hurt the other side?' In discussing this, she says 'In considering the acceptability of a particular solution, both lawyer and client might engage in a dialogue about the fairness or justness of their proposals.' As Condlin (above) says (p. 41, note 118), 'Menkel-Meadow expresses a hope that justice will take care of itself in the needs ascertainment dialogue between the lawyer and client'.

Even when using these strategies, the negotiators are left to define 'objective' or determine what is 'fair or just' in the circumstances in which they are negotiating. For those negotiating at the court door, the way in which the court is likely to view the merits will most likely be the appropriate standard, i.e., a good settlement is one in which the merits matter. How much does this conflict with the 'ethos' particularly of the problem-solving strategy? Is one's BATNA at least partially determined by this?

Finally, there are practical considerations for those negotiating at the court door. Both collaborative strategies require:

- time to explore interests, needs and options

- sharing and maximising available information on which to reach a settlement

- investigating the client's underlying interests and needs to reach a settlement to achieve these

- looking at options with both parties being open-minded with a real interest in expanding the pie and exploring the options.

The circumstances of court-door negotiations (set out above at **3.3.2**) create some potential difficulties because of the severe time pressure, lack of access to information or knowledge of the client and limited opportunities to expand the pie.

4.6 Choosing a Strategy

A negotiator does not choose one particular strategy in advance and then apply it throughout. It is unusual and counterproductive to apply one strategy across the board. You should adapt your strategy during the course of the negotiation, depending on the case, the people involved, the issues being discussed, etc.

Some negotiators may have predominant patterns and predominant behaviours, and so be generally competitive or generally cooperative. However, they should be conscious of the risks involved in choosing a particular strategy. Even where you intend to adapt the strategy to the dynamics of the negotiation, starting with one particular strategy may limit later flexibility. Thus starting with a very competitive strategy and style may make it more difficult to change to a more cooperative or collaborative one later.

Depending on your personality you may find you naturally tend towards a particular strategy. Thus if you are naturally aggressive you may automatically go into competitive mode. If you are naturally pragmatic you may find you are inclined to a more collaborative or problem-solving approach. Be conscious of this and at least try to be aware of the different strategies, the impact they have on the negotiation and their advantages and limitations.

There is some research on the effect of gender and culture on negotiations (in particular by the Harvard Negotiation Project). While some of this research points to there being differences in negotiating styles and strategies which may relate to gender and cultural or ethnic background, many other factors also influence an individual person's style and strategy. This is a highly complex subject and it is difficult if not impossible to give concise but accurate summarisies of the research to date on the influences. We have therefore not attempted to cover it in this Manual.

There is much discussion and some disagreement about which strategies are more effective and which the legal profession should be adopting. You will find different authors have differing views and argue quite persuasively for the adoption of the particular strategy they are promoting. Many 'How To Do It Guides' on negotiation are written for sales or business people and in general promote a competitive strategy.

Many of the legal professional skills courses and books promote almost unaltered the principled approach of Fisher and Ury, although some of them tend to collapse the principled and problem-solving strategies into one and label it 'cooperative'. It clearly has real advantages over both the competitive and cooperative but is not without its own limitations, which means that adopting it religiously whatever the circumstances is not necessarily a good idea.

Part of improving one's negotiation skills is to understand the different strategies and be able to pick and use those aspects of the different strategies which are useful in different negotiations and at different stages in any negotiation.

4.7 The Big Questions

4.7.1 HOW TO START?

How should you start a negotiation? Who goes first and what does he or she say? The answer to these questions will depend on a variety of factors including the type of case, your and your opponent's analysis of it, the order in which you wish to cover matters, etc.

The way in which a negotiation starts sets the atmosphere which can then influence the remainder of the negotiation. A competitive stance at the start will create a very different tone than a reasoned, rational and pragmatic suggestion that a principled approach be adopted. Both negotiators will be trying to determine the approach being adopted by their opponent. You can wait and see what your opponent does, thereby letting him or her set the tone, at least initially. Alternatively, you can state the approach you wish to take with a view to influencing the atmosphere and getting the other side committed to the desired approach.

The way in which a negotiation starts will also influence the overall structure — the order in which matters are covered. You can of course just jump in and start discussing a particular issue, offer or demand. However, there is a real risk that this will result in very inefficient use of time. Consideration of the structure of the negotiation and therefore the method of opening is an important part of preparation. Basically you need to try to use the time as efficiently as possible to enable sufficient information to be exchanged and discussion of proposals to reach a settlement. This will involve consideration of the case to date, determining what is agreed and disputed, what the real issues are, what the parties' objectives, needs and interests are and how any which confict are to be resolved. You can set an agenda, e.g., agree with the opponent the order in which matters will be discussed, although you then need to be flexible about the extent to which this is followed in the negotiation. The structure envisaged by the problem-solving approach is investigation of interests and needs, followed by option-creation and allocation. This could also be applied to the principled approach.

STRATEGY AND STYLE

Somewhere in this process will come consideration of the objective criteria or what is fair or just and you should be conscious that this is an important element of any negotiation.

We considered the process of negotiation, that is the various stages through which most negotiations go, above **2.4**. In planning how to open you should take this on board. If you wish to discuss the merits of the case generally without reference to the particular individual claims of the parties, you could suggest opening by summarising the case to date, or just focusing on the agreed facts and law or on the disputed facts and issues. Alternatively, if you wanted to focus more immediately on the claims and ensure that discussion of the merits was related to the particular claims by the parties, you could start by listing what each party is seeking.

Within the considerations of how to open is also the issue of who makes the first offer, you or the opponent. Who opens may be a matter of convention given the type of negotiation it is. There are some advantages to making the first offer. It can focus the negotiation nearer your end of the settlement range (see **5.2.6.3**). The opponent's reaction can also give you information about his or her position. The disadvantages include giving information to the other side about your range and, particularly where you do not have full information, underestimating the amount the opponent may be prepared to settle at.

4.7.2 HOW TO PRESENT THE CLIENT'S OBJECTIVES

In competitive and cooperative strategies, it is important to determine your opening demand. Both these strategies assume a fixed pie, i.e., that the parties want exactly the same thing and the negotiation is about how to divide it (see **4.2.3**). The competitive negotiator will open high and the cooperative at a reasonable level for their own strategic reasons.

Research has shown that the level of settlement achieved is often related to the opening demand. Thus the higher the demand, provided it is not outlandish, the more one gets. Judging exactly where to pitch it can be difficult. An unrealistic demand has little chance of success unless the opponent is very weak. If it is not believable (i.e., has no rational basis at all and does not take into account the strengths and weaknesses of the case from both sides) it reduces the negotiator's credibility. If it is too far above what any reasonable opponent would agree to, it may require a real climb down (i.e., many and/or large concessions) which will also reduce the negotiator's credibility.

Starting too low can severely limit the room for manoeuvre. First, it may be so close to the least the negotiator is prepared to accept that it leaves no room for further concessions. Secondly, it may increase the expectations of the other side who may assume that it is a far greater distance from what the negotiator is genuinely prepared to settle than it in fact is and maintain pressure to reduce it.

Presenting the clients' objectives in a principled or problem-solving negotiation will be more complex than where a simple cooperative or competitive approach is used. The negotiator will be genuinely seeking to determine whether there are any shared or compatible interests and whether any additional options can be created to satisfy both parties. However, even where the pie has been expanded it still has to be divided. While there may be shared or compatible interests, there are also likely to be conflicting ones. This puts the negotiators back in the realms of splitting resources. Where the ball starts rolling in this process will influence the outcome.

4.7.3 HOW TO MOVE TO SETTLEMENT

Moving to settlement involves give and take by both parties, both on the conduct of the negotiation (including the information shared) and the substantive issues being negotiated. Negotiation is about moving from differing views to agreement and one should be conscious that this can be done in a variety of ways, not just by making concessions. It can be done by:

NEGOTIATION

(a) Finding shared or compatible interests: exploring what both parties are seeking, to find interests which are shared or items on which the parties place differing values, assists in finding mutually beneficial solutions. This assists in identifying where the views really do differ and determining what items can be traded off.

(b) Persuading by means of good argument: negotiating is about persuading people to alter their views, to see the facts and law in a way which moves them towards settlement. In agreeing to a settlement at the court door, each party is at least partially weighing the risk of getting a 'better deal' in court with the costs that will entail. Argument and proposals based on the merits of the case, the facts, law, procedure and evidence (direct or indirect) are directly relevant to their considerations.

(c) Skilful use of concessions (see **4.7.4**).

4.7.4 HOW TO MAKE CONCESSIONS

Many people are afraid to make concessions, failing to plan them adequately either in considering what they will concede or how they will do it. As a result they make them too quickly and unnecessarily or just refuse to make them.

It is important to distinguish between agreeing the facts and issues in the case (which assist in identifying what is in dispute and needs to be settled) and concessions (proposals for resolving the dispute). It is also important to distinguish between making admissions (i.e., of disputed fact), unnecessarily agreeing on the applicable law (i.e., accepting the opponent's interpretation) and making concessions (proposals about what your client would be prepared to accept by way of settlement).

Planning concessions should be based on the client's objectives including his or her priorities, what the opponent's likely objectives are (e.g., there may be shared or compatible interests which do not require concessions) and on the strengths and weaknesses of the case. It is important to take on board what has been said above about the 'opening demand'.

It is also important that you only make concessions for good reasons. A good test of this is to think to yourself, 'How am I going to justify this to my client?'

You can rarely retreat from a concession once made. Do not get locked into making a concession before you know what you are getting in exchange. Make conditional statements, e.g., 'If my client were prepared to ... would yours ...'

When making proposals, think carefully before making a range of offers (e.g., 'if we were to pay between £1,000 and £2,000 ...') as your opponent is likely to accept that most favourable to him or her and you will have difficulty retreating from it.

A good settlement is one which overall meets as many of the client's objectives as possible. Thus one should keep all the issues on the table until one sees the overall package. While you may discuss individual items in turn and trade off on different issues, only agree unconditionally once all of the issues have been provisionally agreed.

A noticeable pattern of behaviour in negotiations is that concessions are usually larger at the start and decrease in both size and frequency over time and as negotiators get closer to their bottom line. This pattern sets up expectations — the negotiators reading the behaviour pattern assume a level of closeness to the bottom line.

There are also tactics which can be used in the making of concessions, e.g., bunching, false demands and false patterns (see **Chapter 5**).

4.7.5 HOW TO EXCHANGE INFORMATION

Negotiation is about exchanging information as much as making and seeking concessions. No negotiation can proceed without information-exchange. Principled and problem-solving strategies focus heavily on this aspect, both in determining clients' real needs and interests and looking for increased options. However, it is important to recognise that some people use information-exchange as a tool in their negotiation strategy, e.g., to exploit in a competitive strategy. Some also use the whole negotiation process merely as a means of finding out about the opponent's case (a fishing expedition).

It is therefore important not to underrate this element of a negotiation and think carefully about the information which is being exchanged, the purpose for the exchange and check out whether or not the other side is exploiting it.

4.7.6 A BOTTOM LINE OR BATNA?

Both a bottom line and a BATNA mark the point beyond which a negotiator is not prepared to settle, the 'walk away point'. A bottom line is a relatively simplistic method of determining this point. The BATNA gives more scope for taking on board information in the negotiation and proposals which have not been considered at the planning stage. It is important to be fully aware of the need for such a trigger mechanism to ensure that you do not end up settling for something which gives your client less than he or she could get elsewhere.

As well as having identified your walk away point, it is wise also to identify a point above this which acts as a warning that you are approaching your walk away point, a 'reservation point'. This will ensure that you do not suddenly find yourself in a corner with nothing left to negotiate, that you remain conscious of the leeway you have remaining in the negotiation.

4.8 Summary

There is much discussion and debate about the different strategies and what is and is not effective. This debate is carried on not only in the context of what achieves the best for individual clients, but also what strategies are best for the civil justice system overall. The discussion has taken on an added dimension with the rise of the concept of appropriate dispute resolution (see **Chapter 12**) and the increased use of mediation. Thus, over the course of your professional life, you may find that attitudes to what is and is not effective and acceptable in negotiation strategies change.

However, the purpose of this Manual is to prepare you for pupillage and early years. While it is important that you understand the theories and rationales of the different strategies, this must not be done at the expense of learning how to prepare and present properly and effectively in negotiations.

Strategy is largely about deciding how you are going to deal with the exchange of information and the issues between the parties. Merely labelling your strategy as 'competitive' or 'problem-solving' means nothing if you have not also thought about the objectives and issues to be negotiated, whether there are any shared interests, the strengths of your case and your opponent's, the information you are going to exchange, etc.

FIVE

TACTICS AND TECHNIQUES

5.1 Introduction

'Tactics' are the different behaviours and specific actions used in the negotiation to achieve the negotiators' desired ends. There is overlap with strategy in that certain tactics are more likely to be used with certain strategies and they include how you use your concessions, the exchange of information, etc. However, when one speaks of tactics, one is referring not to the overall plan and ethos but to particular actions used at specific points in the negotiation to deal with specific situations.

Many associate the word 'tactics' with coercion and manipulation, but they are not confined to use with a competitive strategy. Not all tactics involve tricking the other side. They are skilful devices for dealing with a variety of aspects of negotiation.

Tactics are actions consciously done by negotiators to achieve their ends (as opposed to cognitive influences which unconsciously affect a person's behaviour — see **Chapter 6**). However, because we have all been negotiating since birth, we may have developed negotiation tactics which we now use almost unconsciously. We may for example have learned as a teenager that we could avoid answering a difficult question put by a parent by deflecting the conversation on to something else (see **5.2.2.2**). We may use a strategy akin to 'anchoring' (see **5.2.6.3**) in social situations so often that we fail to recognise that we are using it in work situations as well (e.g., when 'negotiating' what film to see, wanting a nice 'light' funny one, we 'spontaneously' note the number of new light comedies, focus the conversation on these and, surprise, surprise, the discussion being largely about comedies, that is what is chosen).

Understanding the different tactics which can be used in a negotiation and the purpose for using them enables you to:

- decide whether and how to use them, and

- recognise when an opponent is using them and know how to deal with them.

Chapter 4 has dealt with the general concepts of the various strategies and the basis of these particular strategies (the use of high demands, small concessions, etc. by competitive negotiators). Set out below are some of the more common specific tactics used in negotiation. Most of them stem from the mind set of positional bargaining more than the principled or problem-solving approaches.

5.2 Specific Tactics

The following is a list of tactics (**5.2.1** to **5.2.11**). It is not an exhaustive list. It gives the main tactics you are likely to come across. Like strategies, there is not necessarily agreement on terminology nor the exact details of some of the tactics. Other books may give them different labels or approach them differently. We have attempted to categorise them to assist you to understand when and why they may be used, the risks attached to them and possible responses you might have to them.

NEGOTIATION

5.2.1 CONCESSIONS/DEMANDS/OFFERS

This group of tactics covers the different ways of dealing with concessions, seeking concessions from the other side (i.e., putting demands or proposals to them), making offers/concessions and responding to concessions sought of oneself.

5.2.1.1 Precondition demands

One party can require a condition to be fulfilled or a demand satisfied before he or she will enter negotiations. In fact this is attempting to obtain an early concession without trading anything in exchange. It can be used to test the other side to see how easily he or she will concede. If used against you, you should be clear that this is the position and ensure that it is seen by both sides as included in the negotiation. Just responding to it can be seen as being prepared to capitulate easily.

5.2.1.2 Extreme opening demand

Using an extreme opening demand, i.e., at the very margins of what is credible, can influence how the parties see 'bargaining range' (see **Chapter 4**) putting it closer to the end which gives your client the most. It can also indicate that a competitive strategy is being used. It may create doubt in the opponent's mind about his or her assessment of the case. If too extreme, however, it just undermines the maker's credibility, introducing distrust and competition into the negotiation which may then break down. Where used against you, you can counter with an equally extreme demand (thus escalating the negotiation), label it as extreme, ignore it or move to non-positional bargaining, i.e., to discussion of the issues and needs, interests of the parties (see **5.7** below).

5.2.1.3 Bunching

This tactic involves putting all the important demands together early in the negotiation. It has a similar impact to a high opening demand. However it reveals more about your position than a mere high opening demand in that it indicates which issues you consider important. Responses to it can be similar to those used with an extreme opening demand while absorbing the relevant information to use later.

5.2.1.4 Concessions early

Making early concessions is the sign of a cooperative negotiator who is trying to create trust and openness and reciprocal behaviour from the other side. It is a risky tactic as it can easily be exploited. It can also result in both parties swapping concessions without having considered the real issues in the case or the clients' interests. In responding to it be aware of the underlying ethos, that it seeks reciprocation and that it can lead to soft positional bargaining which may not consider all the options.

5.2.1.5 False demands

This tactic involves inflating the number of real issues or demands, by putting forward as very important demands which in fact are of little or no importance to the client. It serves several purposes. First, it disguises the real position. Secondly, it gives the negotiator scope for making concessions at little or no cost. Thirdly, where there is consideration of how much each side has moved to reach agreement, it can create the perception of greater movement by adding in concessions on the false demands. It can backfire on the user in that it may precipitate more demands from the other side or shunt the negotiation off into irrelevant discussion. By asking for reasons to support demands, you can attempt to guard against being taken in by this tactic.

(Note in some books this technique is labelled the 'Brer Rabbit technique' because of his ploy of using pleas not to throw him into the briar patch to get his captors to do just that. Not strictly the same thing but one can see similarities.)

5.2.1.6 Escalating demands

Most negotiators 'open high', i.e., start with the most they seek in the negotiation, and move from that position. However, some, as a tactic, escalate their demands, increasing them either from what was expected from the papers and previous exchange between the clients or from their opening position. Done with a view to determining the

TACTICS AND TECHNIQUES

toughness of the opponent or the limits of what they will concede, it is a highly risky tactic as it is likely to result in confrontation, escalation on both sides and complete breakdown. Where used against you, you can counter by increasing your demands (a dangerous response) or labelling the behaviour, refusing to consider the demands or moving from positional bargaining (see **5.7** below).

5.2.1.7 Split the difference or compromise

A negotiator may suggest that a way of settling either the whole substance of the negotiation or one issue, is to 'split the difference', i.e., both sides compromise equally. This can in fact be a reasonable suggestion and produce a reasonable result for both parties. It is also a tempting solution to go for because it is a 'focal point', i.e., easy to identify and explain as a common position. However, it can be used inappropriately.

Whether splitting the difference is fair depends on where the parties started and how far each has moved during the negotiation. It is not a genuine compromise where one party has opened with an extreme or inflated demand and made far fewer concessions than the other party who may have opened at a more reasonable level.

Splitting the difference may also not be the solution which produces the best result. It may not satisfy either party's interests. Using it as a way of resolving differences may just divert the discussion onto positions and away from the parties' real needs and interests. Because the parties are speaking in cooperative terms, it can produce a sense of fair settlement where the settlement is in fact not fair because it does not reflect the parties' needs.

When responding to such a suggestion, you can certainly acknowledge the apparent appeal to fairness but should also weigh up what has already occurred in the negotiation to see whether it does really produce a compromise. You should also move away from positions and back to consideration of the interests and needs of the client to see whether another solution or formula would not be more appropriate.

5.2.1.8 Boulwarism or the single offer approach

Named after a man who negotiated on the basis of one offer based on his perception of what was fair, it is a 'take or leave it' approach. It can be used to save time and cut through the ritual dance of positional bargaining. It can also give the person using it a sense of power and authority. The person using it may genuinely consider that what is proposed is fair. However, the other side may not believe this. In addition, such a tactic fails to take on board that it deprives the other negotiator of any participation in determining the settlement and gives him or her very little control over the settlement reached. He or she is left without any input and will probably react by straight rejection, even if the proposal might appear to be reasonable. Where used against you, you can acknowledge the consideration which may have gone in to the proposal and point out that there may be considerations from your side which have not been included and therefore need discussing, or ask for the reasoning behind the offer and how it has been assessed as fair for both parties.

5.2.1.9 Slicing/salami/nibbling

This tactic involves dividing issues up into smaller issues and can be used with demands or concessions. Used with demands, it consists of seeking and getting agreement on demands one at a time, on the basis that a series of small demands will be more likely to be accepted and it disguises the overall amount of the demand. Used with concessions, it consists of dividing up what you have to concede to increase the number of concessions made (although not the overall amount conceded). By focusing the negotiation on the number of concessions made rather than the amount both parties have conceded it produces the appearance that you have conceded more than you in fact have. In both cases, insisting on not agreeing unconditionally until the whole package is on the table guards against this being used effectively against you.

5.2.1.10 Trade-offs/logrolling/the overall package

Rather than dealing with items sequentially, i.e., agreeing each one before they move to the next, negotiators can trade off items. Where parties put different values on

NEGOTIATION

different items they can logroll, i.e., trade off items of lower value for those of higher value. To do this effectively they need to consider all the issues before reaching agreement on any of them unconditionally. They need to weigh up the relative values of the different items or issues, explore each other's preferences, and then consider the whole package. By making all proposals conditional or hypothetical until an acceptable overall package has emerged, the negotiators can discuss a variety of options to explore which really does produce the best settlement. Research has shown that negotiators who only agree to the 'overall package' generally do make better settlements.

5.2.1.11 Backtracking/reopening

Where a particular item or issue has been agreed and the negotiation has moved on to other issues, a negotiator may backtrack and try to reopen the agreed one with a view to increasing gain on the issue under current discussion or the one already agreed. This is a risky tactic as it immediately creates distrust and may cause the negotiation to break down. When used against you, realise what is happening and why, label the behaviour and refuse to deal on the basis suggested.

5.2.1.12 Misleading concession pattern

As explained above, most negotiators will reduce in size and number the concessions they make as they get closer to their bottom line. This tactic involves reducing the concessions well before the 'bottom line' and is used to mislead the other side as to the 'bottom line' and therefore the potential settlement range.

5.2.2 STRUCTURE/ORDER

Negotiators can set up a structure for the negotiation or alter the order to assist them to get the most out of the negotiation or cope with difficulties. How the negotiation is started and the way in which negotiators open is one of the tactical considerations as they can have a real impact on the whole negotiation. These have been considered above.

5.2.2.1 The agenda

By setting or suggesting an agenda, you determine the order in which issues will or are likely to be discussed. Thus, where you have a strong legal claim which is perhaps weaker on proof of the amounts claimed, you might suggest starting with a discussion of the merits of the claim first (i.e., suggest both parties set out their view of the case to date). Alternatively, there may be a variety of issues on which the strengths differ or the amount the client is prepared to concede differ (these two do not always coincide). You may then wish to determine the order in which the issues are covered on the basis of strength of case, e.g., starting with the strong ones to show a strong position in the hope that, by the time the negotiation has reached the issues on which you are weaker, the other side has been worn down (i.e., on the basis of a competitive strategy). Alternatively, you may determine the order on the basis of what you will or will not concede, e.g., start with the issues on which you are prepared to make concessions to introduce a cooperative atmosphere and encourage your opponent to concede on issues.

5.2.2.2 'Moving on'

Negotiators may discuss issues sequentially, agreeing them as they go along. Even where they agree to settle only once all the issues are on the table and have been discussed, they must discuss the individual issues or items. Some items may be more difficult than others to reach even provisional agreement on and the negotiators may therefore wish to 'move on' to other items and come back to the one causing difficulty — an efficient suggestion for keeping the negotiation moving. However, a negotiator who sees a weakness in his or her case or is suddenly confronted with new information may also use this as a device to avoid discussion of it, either until later when they have decided how to deal with the issue or altogether. It is surprising how many people 'move on' from items and never return to them particularly where they appear to be, but are not necessarily, unimportant items like costs, or date of payment. Recognise that this may be the case and that you may wish to continue discussion of the item in hand. However, be prepared to be flexible as insistence on discussing this one item until agreement is reached may produce deadlock.

5.2.2.3 Just one more thing

This tactic is to introduce a new demand near the end of the negotiation, at the point the negotiators are reaching or actually agreeing the outcome '... oh by the way, just one more [often but not always small] thing'. Done to test the resolve of the other negotiator on the basis that, in sight of agreement, he or she will give on this (little?) matter, it is risky as it might undo what has already been achieved. When used against you, label the behaviour and refuse to respond to it. Clearly where the negotiation has been done on the basis that it is conditional until the whole package is agreed, this additional demand becomes part of the package. You might require the opponent to put the full package on the table and expressly confirm that there are no more 'add ons' before you decide whether you will continue.

A variation of this, is adding an item or a condition on after agreement has been reached on the basis that it had been forgotten or a mistake made. This is a highly dubious tactic. Refuse to react to it. Once agreement has been reached, provided it satisfies contractual principles, it is enforceable as a contract. Additional terms cannot be added unilaterally. If, however, the agreement has been insufficiently specific then it will not be enforceable as the terms will be too uncertain. The potential use of this tactic is another reason why it is essential when negotiating to finalise the terms fully and precisely.

5.2.3 REFRAMING YOUR APPROACH

The ability to put one's case persuasively is an important part of a lawyer's tool kit. What is persuasive will depend on the circumstances. A negotiation, particularly a legal dispute resolution between lawyers, is done within a litigation framework. The lawyers speak from an adversarial perspective using adversarial language. (One can contrast this with the framework and language of other professions, particularly those in the 'caring' professions such as social workers whose whole approach is conciliatory, e.g., 'sharing concerns'.)

The way in which proposals are framed and the language used has an impact on the negotiation process. One can learn to 'reframe' or use language to affect the process. Using more conciliatory language, while not in any way altering the substance, can produce an atmosphere more conducive to agreement. Alternatively, using adversarial language and framing can increase the sense of competition and stress to which the opponent may react (by giving in or possibly by deadlock). The following (**5.2.3.1** to **5.2.3.3**) are just some specific examples of 'reframing' or using language to effect.

5.2.3.1 Seeking proposals/making demands

In many negotiations the two negotiators 'make demands' of each other, i.e., each puts what he or she wants to get out of the negotiation in the expectation of being beaten down (i.e., having to make concessions). The two then focus on how far each has moved from the initial 'demand'. Another approach is to ask your opponent what he or she 'proposes' by way of settlement. This moves the focus from what that side is seeking to what he or she considers reasonable.

5.2.3.2 Reasons or requests first

When asking for something from someone, one can either put the request and then say why one wants it or set out the reasons why something is needed and then put the request. Putting the request first in a negotiation may mean that the other side does not really hear the reason because he or she is busy thinking how to respond. Putting the reason why something is needed first means the other side is more likely to be listening throughout to find out precisely what is wanted.

5.2.3.3 Yes but ...

Responding to a proposal or demand put by the other side which is not wholly unacceptable or wholly acceptable, requires an indication of some agreement with qualifications. Often this is done by saying 'yes but ...'. The 'but' acts as a signal that a negative is to follow and many people will only hear the part from 'but' onwards, i.e., the qualifications, the negatives, the parts on which there is disagreement. (This is a

NEGOTIATION

well-known phenomenon in teaching as well, where the comments are 'You did x, y and z well but you need to work on a, b and c' the student only hears a, b and c. By substituting 'and' for 'but', i.e., by joining the qualifications to the agreement rather than separating them from it, people hear the whole proposal.)

5.2.4 I AM ONLY THE REPRESENTATIVE

Representative negotiators can separate themselves from the person whose case is being negotiated. Clearly it is important to have a professional approach to the negotiation and not see it as personal. A professional, not directly experiencing the problem, does have a more objective view of the issues and settlements which are possible. A representative must ensure that he or she has the actual authority to negotiate for the client and be clear exactly what that authority empowers him or her to discuss and agree (see **3.4.1.2**).

However, this separation can also be used particularly by employing the following tactics.

5.2.4.1 Lack of or limited authority

Making it clear that any agreement is subject to the client's approval at the start of the negotiation is a statement about the limits of the negotiator's authority. It enables the client to have the final say on what is agreed. However, a negotiator may unnecessarily claim lack of or limited authority. The lack or limit may have been specifically sought or in fact not exist. The claim may come near the end of the negotiation when the other side thinks that final settlement has almost been achieved. As a device, lack or limit of authority can be used to get information from the other side while reserving your position, for buying time to think or for obtaining more from the other side. Ensuring you are clear about the negotiators' authority at the start of the negotiation prevents this device being used later.

5.2.4.2 My client won't agree

A representative negotiator may be highly sympathetic to what is being proposed but say that he or she cannot agree because the client will not. This may in fact be the true position. However, it may also be a device whereby the negotiator appears to be negotiating in a reasonable and sympathetic way while in fact being tough. A variation of this tactic is for the negotiator to present the client as insisting on a particular issue, being 'locked in' to a position despite the risks attached because the client will not or cannot move. The negotiator can express views about the unreasonableness of the client's approach while insisting that the demand be met. Alternatively, the client can be presented as being reasonable but subject to forces 'beyond his or her control'. When used against you, you can press for more details (what exactly is the client committed to and why) or deal with the issues on which there might be agreement to produce a package which persuades 'the client' to agree on this issue.

5.2.5 PSYCHOLOGICAL

There are a number of tactics using behaviour and/or words which are not directed at substantive or procedural issues but affect the negotiators' thinking, emotions and confidence.

5.2.5.1 Aggressive tactics

There are a huge variety of similar tactics which can be used to introduce an emotional element into the negotiation, to wear the opponent down, cause loss of confidence or self-image, e.g., aggression, confrontation, anger (feigned or real), sarcasm, ridicule, blame or fault finding, guilt, put downs, and unpredictabilty through sudden change of mood (which many people have great difficulty coping with partially because they assume they have somehow caused it). When used against you, do not react. If necessary take time to consider how to respond in a rational way to get the negotiation back to the relevant issues. Consider labelling the behaviour and refusing to negotiate unless it is altered.

TACTICS AND TECHNIQUES

5.2.5.2 Positive emotions/strokes

We all like to be liked and are, generally, well-disposed towards those who are friendly to us. We all also like to have the positive aspects of our self-image confirmed by others, e.g., that we are clever. As in all human interactions, giving people positive strokes in negotiations, being friendly, flattering them, etc. can make them more predisposed to persuasion and making concessions. While a friendly demeanour or positive statement may be genuine they may also be being used as a tactic. Being conscious of your reactions to such use of emotions/strokes (whether conscious or not) means that you are more able to identify them and limit your response to a rational discussion of the substantive issues.

Being amused, finding something humourous, generally creates a positive atmosphere. Although different people find different things amusing or humourous, there is also much humour which is shared and which can be used to lighten the atmosphere where it has becomes too tense. It can release people to feel more predisposed to one another, more able to work together. While it can be used as a positive tactic, e.g., to break deadlock, one should be conscious that it can be used negatively as well, e.g., to disguise a move away from an issue under discussion or make the opponent feel more predisposed to make concessions.

5.2.5.3 Silence

In any interaction between people in western culture there is very little room for silence. We find silence difficult and react automatically to fill it by speaking. This cultural behaviour can be used in a negotiation. Just remaining silent can put pressure on the opponent to speak. Thus where the opponent has put a proposal with the reasons for it, remaining silent may produce more information or a variation of the proposal, possibly a further concession. To avoid being the victim of such a tactic, learn to resist the automatic response to silence. Being silent yourself is fine but both negotiators cannot remain silent for long. Think carefully about what you say if you break the silence and ensure that it is guided by the substance of the negotiation and not the pressure to speak.

5.2.5.4 Tit-for-tat

This tactic is one whereby the negotiator mirrors the strategy adopted by the opponent. He or she responds to cooperative behaviour by being cooperative and competitive behaviour by being competitive. One can also use this specifically with concessions, matching the size and frequency of one's concessions to those of the other side. This reinforces the desired behaviour (i.e., the cooperative) by giving rewards for it (i.e., concessions) and punishes the undesired behaviour (i.e., the competitive) by withholding concessions. A fairly basic strategy which is completely positional, in experiments it has been shown to produce concessions even after the negotiator has stopped rewarding the behaviour.

5.2.6 SETTING PARAMETERS/FIXING THE FOCUS

There are several devices which can be used to set the negotiation into the context, settlement range or parameters favourable to one of the parties. The underlying ethos is the same for all of them. The person using the tactic gets the negotiation discussion centred around his or her view of the issues.

5.2.6.1 The drafts

This tactic is the easiest to understand and spot. The negotiator brings a draft agreement to the negotiation and suggests the discussion proceed by going through the draft. This puts him or her in a powerful position. First, the text of the draft will dictate the agenda, both what issues are discussed and the order in which they are covered. Secondly, a solution to each of the issues is already set out in the text, leaving the other party having to counter it. While working from an existing draft by one party can have advantages, e.g., save time, think carefully about the implications if it is suggested by an opponent.

NEGOTIATION

5.2.6.2 The objective standard

While principled negotiators genuinely try to use objective standards in a negotiation to enable them to negotiate on the basis of principles rather than pressure, not all negotiators suggest using objective standards for this reason. As pointed out above, objective can mean different things and there can be different standards against which to judge settlements, e.g., precedent, norms, business practice, etc. The standard used may have a real impact on what each of the parties get. A negotiator may suggest applying an apparently objective standard in the knowledge that this particular one favours his or her client. Where an 'objective' standard is suggested, do not just assume it is objective. Check it out. Consider whether it really is objective in your case. Take time to consider what other standards might be equally or more 'objective'.

5.2.6.3 Anchoring

This tactic is more subtle than the two above but has the same purpose. Basically, by making a particular statement the negotiator fixes the focus of the negotiation in a way beneficial to him or her. By discussing the issues using a hypothetical figure or set of facts, the parties 'anchor' or focus on that figure or those facts and this can influence their thinking. Thus, for example, if the parties discuss a case 'hypothetically' on the basis that the defendant is liable, the fact that this focus has been introduced and the statement probably repeated, may influence the outcome against the defendant.

5.2.7 INFORMATION EXCHANGE

Exchange of information is a fundamental part of negotiation. There is a variety of tactics which negotiators can use in relation to the exchange of information which can affect (increase or decrease) the accuracy and/or flow of the information exchanged.

5.2.7.1 Accuracy of information

Any interchange between two people will almost invariably involve some distortion in the information passed between them, for a variety of reasons (see **6.5**). Competitive negotiators are more likely consciously to attempt to distort information to their own ends, although cooperative, principled and problem-solving negotiators may less consciously also do this. The level of distortion, the deliberateness or consciousness of it and how it is done introduces ethical considerations (see **5.3**).

- Communication can be distorted because people (consciously or unconsciously) present or hear statements as factual statements when they are not. In discussing the clients' claims, assertions of what happened, etc., a negotiator may present as statements of fact, matters which are only allegations (for which there may or may not be proof). Both negotiators may then start to treat what amounts to allegations as statements of fact. A negotiator may put his or her opinion of the value of something as a statement of fact. The opinion is then accepted as fact (i.e., this is the value).

- Bluffing is consciously masking one's position by creating an impression of greater strength (usually) or weakness (less frequent) than one in fact has. It can be done by making statements which, although strictly true, create a false impression, or by merely allowing an opponent to form a particular impression. It is completely contrary to the ethos of all but competitive strategies.

- Finally there are statements which are untrue and calculated to mislead, which is always unethical.

Be attuned to the possibility of distortion of information, listen carefully to what is said and check out the basis of the statements. Do not be taken in by over-confidence in an opponent. What is the evidence to support the statement? Is it in fact not true? Label misleading behaviour and insist on accuracy.

5.2.7.2 Flow of information

There is no rule that negotiators must reveal information. In fact most negotiators, even non-competitive ones, are slightly tentative about revealing information to the other side. As Condlin in his article 'Cases on Both Sides: Patterns of Argument in Legal Dispute Resolution' (1985) 44 *Maryland Law Review* 64–136 at p. 75 says:

> ... negotiators are likely to approach one another circumspectly, revealing as little as possible until discovering what state of affairs obtains. This is only prudent. One does not expose one's neck until it is clear the head will not be chopped off.

The amount of information revealed by a negotiator will depend to a degree on the strategy adopted. Most negotiators will be more willing to reveal information favourable to their case than to the opponent's. The opponent may then make assumptions about the relative strengths of the cases. To guard against this, think carefully about what is and is not being revealed. Do not make assumptions. Ask for further information. Seek evidence to support allegations or reasons for proposals.

Some negotiators fail to provide information even when specifically requested to do so and cover up this failure by a variety of devices.

- Diverting attention: the negotiator may divert attention and fail to provide the information requested by simply changing the topic to another issue, asking a question rather that providing an answer or focusing on an approaching deadline (real or fictitious). If the information requested is important, do not be diverted.

- Apparently answering: the negotiator may respond (like a politician) with information which only partially answers the question or which, although related to the question, does not in fact answer it and is very long and confused. The negotiator relies on the questioner not pressing for clarification because he or she feels responsible for any misunderstanding either because of the way in which the question was worded or because he or she just fails to understand the answer. Press. If you do not understand, ask for clarification.

Some negotiators may just refuse to give the information. Alternatively, they may agree to provide the information only in exchange for information or a concession. Think carefully about the importance of the information requested, how crucial it is to the negotiation and whether you really can continue without it. Think also about any price requested. It may be fine and increase the flow of information. It may be a concession which you are not prepared to make.

On the other side of the coin, some negotiators are very good at getting a lot of information from the opponent. They have learned to use the fact that most people prefer talking to listening. By asking questions and speaking little themselves, they get a great deal of information from the other side. They are careful not to ask questions which put the opponent on the defensive. Guard against being exploited by this tactic and providing too much information to someone who may misuse it. Think carefully about the question put. What is the purpose of it? Consider whether the information requested really does need to be provided. Do not get carried away by the desire to do most of the talking.

5.2.8 INCREASING THE COMPETITION

Some tactics are used to increase the apparent competition for particular items. Thus a negotiator may say that there are other people who want the particular item, hence the unwillingness to go below a certain point. A negotiator may also indicate that what the opponent wants is a scarce commodity thereby increasing the competition for it and possibly its desirability for the person seeking it. The other person and the scarcity may be real or not. Check it out.

5.2.9 USING TIME

Even negotiations between solicitors while the case is trundling its way through the litigation process will be subject to the pressure imposed by court time-limits or the wishes of the clients. The pressure exerted by lack of time in negotiations at the court door is very apparent.

NEGOTIATION

There is research to show that negotiators make lower demands, increase concessions and lower their expectations under time pressure. Negotiators can use time to try to press their opponent into reducing demands and making concessions.

- The Deadline: Negotiators may create false deadlines. Where there is a real deadline, e.g., at the court door, they can repeatedly refer to the shortage of time.

- Brinkmanship: Negotiators may delay dealing with the main issues or introduce new ones very close to the deadline to test the opponent and increase his or her anxiety that settlement will not be reached unless he or she concedes. A risky tactic, it can backfire and result in no settlement.

Being conscious of the effect of time pressure on most negotiatiors, being aware of the real time pressures, checking out any additional ones suggested by the opponent and taking some control of the structure of the negotiation to ensure best use of the time can be some safeguard against succumbing to these tactics. Remember your reservation points and bottom line or BATNA and that you can walk away.

5.2.10 FORCING THE ISSUE

Some negotiators try to make it appear that the negotiation stands or falls on the opponent's actions to induce anxiety and force concessions from him or her to reach agreement. Two common tactics to force the issue are:

(a) The Final Offer: The negotiator states a 'final offer' as an ultimatum. Whether or not settlement is reached then depends on the opponent's response. This tactic attempts to transfer responsibility for reaching settlement to the opponent and force him or her to accept the offer because of anxiety that his or her failure to do so might cause the negotiation to break down. The negotiator may or may not give reasons why it is the final offer. He or she may also make an additional concession when making the statement. It is a risky tactic to use unless it is genuine, i.e., you really are prepared to discontinue the negotiation if it is not accepted. When used against you, think carefully about the offer and your bottom line or BATNA. The fact that it is stated as a 'final offer' does not make you responsible for any break down which may follow. That is determined by the overall conduct of both parties throughout the whole negotiation. If you have been unreasonable during the negotiation, maybe what is offered is reasonable, far better than your BATNA. On the other hand it may be far worse.

(b) The Walkout: A version of the above tactic, the negotiator threatens to discontinue negotiations unless his or her proposal is accepted. It has the same risks and when used against you should be handled in the same way.

5.2.11 WHERE THERE IS A TEAM

Lawyers may negotiate in teams. At the court door, where barristers have been instructed, the actual negotiation will generally be just 'between counsel' and therefore rarely in teams. However there may be circumstances where there is a team, e.g., leading and junior counsel or the solicitor takes an active part in the negotiation.

A negotiation team may play 'Good Guy/Bad Guy'. One negotiator is friendly, sympathetic and apparently cooperative and the other is overtly aggressive and competitive. The opponent begins to see the 'good guy' as an ally, assume he or she is more cooperative than is in fact the case and as a result is more disposed to make concessions. When used against you, deal with the substance of what is said by each negotiator and use some of the tactics from principled negotiation, e.g., separate the people from the problem.

TACTICS AND TECHNIQUES

5.3 Dubious Tactics

5.3.1 GENERAL

Some tactics are clearly dishonest and unethical, e.g., deliberately misleading your opponent by pretending to have evidence you do not have. They are against the Bar's Code of Conduct and, even if they do not amount to an offence, e.g., fraud, using them can result in being debarred.

Even if the behaviour comes within the ethical boundaries (which are often difficult to determine), you need to be conscious that the tactics you use will invariably affect the reputation you build. If, for example, you use aggressive tactics you will get a reputation for being confrontational which may be difficult to get rid of it.

Some tactics, particularly the more competitive ones, although not blatantly unethical, may fall over the line. There are huge grey areas and very different views as to where the line is drawn between acting ethically and unethically. Two areas covered above where this difficulty lies are:

- Aggressive behaviour which may become sufficiently insulting or rude to amount to a breach of your professional duty to act courteously.

- Managing or manipulating information which may become sufficiently 'tricky' or misleading to amount to professional misconduct. A barrister's job is to promote the client's case as an advocate. You can quite properly pitch the case at its highest when trying to reach a settlement, even though you may not necessarily succeed in proving the whole case in court. There is not always a clear line between doing the best for your client and misleading or unfair tactics. But you must not pretend that you do know a fact or have particular instructions if this is simply not true.

5.3.2 THREATS

'Threat' is defined as 'a conditional commitment by a negotiator to act in a way that appears detrimental to the other party unless the other party complies with a request', in Donald G. Gifford's book *Legal Negotiation: Theory and Applications* (p. 143). Threats demonstrate commitment by the person making them and attempt to induce concessions from the opponent. Many negotiation tactics although not phrased as threats implicitly involve them, e.g., 'the final offer' is basically a threat to end the negotiation if the offer is not accepted.

Two questions arise in considering the use of express open threats:

(a) How effective are they? To be effective, the threat must be believed. To be believed it must be credible. The size of the threat must relate to the issue involved; if it is disproportionate it is less likely to be believed. The negotiator must also be believable. Issuing a number of threats none of which is carried out or which the negotiator is clearly not in a position to carry out reduces his or her credibility. Finally, the reaction to a threat may be to counter with a threat, escalating the aggressive behaviour and leading to deadlock.

(b) Are they ethical? It is unprofessional and unethical to introduce improper threats. On the other hand it is quite legitimate to point out potential consequences. The dividing line between a legitimate statement and an unethical threat is difficult, and is dealt with in the Professional Conduct Course and the Negotiation Course.

There are a variety of ways of responding to a threat depending on the circumstances in which it is made. You can just ignore it. You can label it and refuse to deal on the basis of threats, treat it with derision, 'If making a threat is your best line of argument ...', or express surprise at such behaviour. You can discuss the contents of the threat, see what lies behind it and whether it can be carried out. You can divert the discussion to another topic. Making a counter threat is generally not a good idea as it just escalates the hostility and increases the chances of deadlock.

5.4 General Attitude/Preparation for Tactics

The best protection against being overwhelmed by your opponent's tactics is thorough preparation, i.e., knowing the issues, the facts and the law, the objectives, the options, the arguments which can be used for and against you, planning your concessions and your bottom line or BATNA. This probably cannot be emphasised too much. Knowing the strengths and weaknesses of your case well will assist you to respond rationally to any tactic and reduce the possibility of reacting to the tactic in the manner intended.

Being conscious that you do not have to settle is another safeguard. Having considered the alternatives your client has to settlement, you are able to measure this against proposals and make rational decisions about whether or not to accept them. Using the protective tactics set out at **5.2.1** leaves you less vulnerable to buckling under pressure. Remember you do not need to agree unconditionally to any one issue until you have the full package (including any costs or procedural issues) on the table.

Being professional and detached is also a safeguard. The negotiation should not become personal. Control your reactions. Do not show surprise unless this is a tactic. Maintaining control means you are less likely to give things away unintentionally. Work at maintaining this mindset. Remind any opponent who acts unprofessionally of his or her duty as a barrister.

One can respond to specific tactics by recognising them, appreciating your natural response to them and controlling your reaction. Do not feel you have to respond immediately; if necessary, take time to consider the best response. You may wish also to label the tactic, identify the behaviour and ask why it is being used or explain that you will not continue unless it is stopped. If you consider that the opponent is acting unethically make this clear.

5.5 Dealing with Deadlock/Failure to Move

5.5.1 HOW IT CAN HAPPEN

Deadlock occurs where the two sides are or appear to be unable to agree. It can arise from a variety of circumstances. Some tactics, e.g., 'the final offer' or 'walkout' can produce it. Some negotiators can produce it by just being intransigent, unreasonable or unrealistic. Alternatively, the negotiation may just be going in circles with no progress being made or come to a complete halt because both parties have run out of ideas. In any of these cases, it may be there is no solution but to break off the negotiation. However, you should at least try to break the deadlock or get the negotiation moving again. The following are suggestions for trying to get constructive discussion going again. Different circumstances will lend themselves to different methods.

5.5.2 WAYS TO DEAL

5.5.2.1 Review progress
One way out is to review what has been discussed. Go over the progress made so far. Redefine the issues. Check whether all the issues and possibilities have been fully explored. Write a list of interests and issues. Writing them down may clarify where both parties stand and show that the differences are not as great as originally thought.

5.5.2.2 Discuss reasons for breakdown
Try to discuss why the deadlock or breakdown has happened. Try to see if emotions have interfered in the negotiation. Try to empathise, see the difficulties in reaching

TACTICS AND TECHNIQUES

agreement as a joint problem. If appropriate, acknowledge your own feelings and attempt to get the opponent to air his or hers.

5.5.2.3 Disadvantages of breakdown
Focus discussion on the disadvantages of breakdown. Look at the impact of failure on both sides. Just articulating the negative results of failing to reach settlement may produce the incentive to continue negotiating with more purpose.

5.5.2.4 Advantages of agreement
Focus discussion on the advantages of settlement for both sides. Articulating the benefits of an agreement for the future and the difficulties which might be avoided by it may produce the incentive to continue negotiating with more purpose. If appropriate, raise past positive relationships either between clients or negotiators. Create a positive mood.

5.5.2.5 Look for common ground
Restate the common concerns of the clients. Revisit the shared and compatible interests and try to build on them. Seek agreement on one issue and move on from that.

5.5.2.6 Give to get
Think of any information which you can disclose which might assist in movement. Make a planned conditional concession. Give something to get something, to get the negotiation moving again.

5.5.2.7 Move to the hypothetical
Ask a hypothetical question to get both parties thinking of alternatives, 'What if ...?'

5.5.2.8 Take a break
Suggest a break. Where appropriate this could mean suggesting a further meeting at a later date. Where this is not possible, e.g., at the court door, even a short break can be sufficient to change the atmosphere.

5.6 Other Problems

5.6.1 FEELING INEXPERIENCED

You may have to negotiate with a much more senior practitioner. While he or she may have experience, do not assume this automatically makes him or her a better negotiator. From the little empirical research done, it would appear that most lawyers are not very sophisticated negotiators. Be professional, remember your preparation, watch and try to determine what (if any) strategy he or she has. Focus on your preparation and knowledge of strategy and tactics rather than the difference in years of experience at the Bar.

5.6.2 THE UNFORESEEN

You go into a negotiation with, on your papers, a strong case. Your strategy, tactics and analysis of what can be achieved in the negotiations is based on your case being strong. Your opponent makes a statement which substantially alters the strength of your client's case, undermines it almost completely. While thorough analysis of the case prior to the negotiation should alert you to possible gaps and ambiguities, there may be times when the client has just failed to reveal relevant aspects which do alter his or her position. Do not react. Stop and think. Is the statement merely an allegation? Ask your opponent for the evidence to support it. If necessary move the negotiation on to another topic. Give yourself time to absorb the information and reassess the case.

5.6.3 PERSONALITY CLASH

Sometimes, without intending confrontation, you simply do not get on with the negotiator for the other side. Personality and emotions can get in the way. Try some of

NEGOTIATION

the tactics from principled negotiations to reduce the impact, e.g., separating the people from the problem. See also **5.7**.

5.7 Techniques for Getting Past No

The various techniques for dealing with awkward negotiators set out in *Getting to Yes* have been expanded in a further book *Getting Past No: Negotiating Your Way From Confrontation to Cooperation* by William Ury (1991), again a relatively short paperback. The strategy suggested is based on breaking through the five barriers to cooperation (i.e., getting past no) which he identifies as:

(a) Your reactions: We all do react to what other people say and do.

(b) Their emotions: The other side may have negative emotions which influence what they say and do. They may be angry, nervous or defensive.

(c) Their habits: They may only know how to negotiate positionally.

(d) Their doubts about the agreement: They may have difficulty seeing how an agreement which satisfies your client actually benefits theirs.

(e) Their perception of the negotiation as a power game.

The five steps in the strategy for doing this are set out at **5.7.1** to **5.7.5**.

5.7.1 DO NOT REACT

Give yourself space to evaluate the position and distance yourself from any impulsive or emotional response. Ury suggests using a psychological trick to create a mental image which gives you this space: 'go to the balcony'. This enables you to:

(a) Recognise the tactic.

(b) Recognise how you are feeling and 'know your hot buttons', i.e., those things to which you have strong reactions, e.g., criticism or rejection.

(c) Buy time to think by:

   (i) Pausing and saying nothing. Do not be afraid of silence and do not be pushed into responding by rantings from the other side. Think what good it is doing them to let off steam! Clearly this will buy limited time.

   (ii) Rewinding the tape. When you can pause no longer, slow the process down by reviewing what has been said. This can help to clarify it.

   (iii) Taking time out. If you need more time, take a short break if possible. If you cannot do this by physically leaving the negotiation space do it by changing the topic.

   (iv) Not making important decisions on the spot. Where a matter is sprung on you and there is no need for an immediate response, do not respond. Where an immediate response is needed, give yourself what time you can to consider it. Check deadlines imposed to see if they are real.

   (v) Remain focused on your objectives. 'Don't get mad, don't get even ... get what you want!' That is why you are negotiating.

5.7.2 DEFUSE THEIR EMOTIONS

Create a favourable climate for the negotiation. Disarm the other side by being conciliatory, acknowledging and trying to understand their feelings. The psychological trick suggested by Ury is that you 'step to their side' which means:

(a) Listening actively by:

   (i) Giving the other side a hearing. Remain focused, do not interrupt, encourage them to explain.

   (ii) Paraphrasing and asking for corrections. Sum up your understanding of what they have said and check whether you have got it right.

(b) Acknowledging his or her point/feelings. This does not mean you agree with it. It merely means that you understand how he or she see things. It may also be appropriate in some circumstances to acknowledge his or her feelings or offer an apology. This can be seen as exhibiting strength if done with confidence.

(c) Agreeing whatever you can. No need to concede, just focus on the issues on which you do agree, the common ground. Look for ways of saying 'yes' rather than 'no'. Tune in to his or her wavelength, watch the non-verbal cues, the manner of speech.

(d) Acknowledging the other person. Treat him or her with respect. Acknowledge authority and competence. Try to build a working relationship. By doing this you may change his or her perception of you, become more of an ally than an adversary.

(e) Expressing your views without provoking. Use language which reconciles rather than accentuates differences, e.g., 'yes and' rather than 'yes but' (see **5.2.3.3**). Acknowledge differences and be optimistic about resolving them.

5.7.3 DO NOT REJECT: REFRAME/CHANGE THE GAME

Some people only know how to negotiate using positional behaviour, seeing the negotiation as a ritual dance in which both parties keep stating their positions with a view to making the other side change their position. Alter this perception by probing their position and asking for more information to enable you genuinely to understand what they want. Use the psychological technique of 'reframing' to turn their position into an attempt to reach a solution by:

(a) Asking problem-solving questions, i.e., ones which require more than a 'yes' or 'no' answer, which seek reasons, information, etc. Why? Why not? What if?

(b) Asking for advice. How would you explain this offer to my client?

(c) Using silence. Do not automatically fill the silence if he or she is having trouble answering a question. Give him or her time to think, possibly to feel uncomfortable, to come up with a proposal.

(d) Ignoring or reframing positional statements and attacks.

(e) Negotiating the rules of the game: where tacit tactics do not work to change the behaviour, deal with it explicitly. Label the behaviour without attacking the person.

5.7.4 DO NOT PUSH: DRAW THEM TOWARDS YOU

A person may reject a proposal because it is not his or her idea, it does not satisfy all his or her needs, because of a fear of losing face or because it has come too quickly. Pushing him or her to agree may just increase resistance. So Ury's suggestion is to 'build a golden bridge' by:

(a) Involving him or her in the proposal. Do not 'tell' him or her the solution. Ask for ideas and build on them. Ask for criticism. Offer choices. Make the proposals joint proposals.

NEGOTIATION

      (b) Satisfing unmet interests. Ensure all interests have been explored. Try to see the rationale behind them. Do not overlook basic human needs. Try to expand the pie.

      (c) Helping him or her to save face. Find reasons which justify his or her accepting the proposal.

5.7.5 EDUCATE: BRING THEM TO THEIR SENSES NOT THEIR KNEES

Some negotiators may resist all the above tactics and keep playing a positional power game. Resist the temptation to respond. Show him or her that *this* negotiation is *not* win/lose but win/win, that the only way he or she can win is for you both to win by:

      (a) Letting him or her know the consequences of the behaviour. Ask reality-testing questions, such as 'What will you do if we don't agree?' Explain in an objective way what you will do (i.e., warn, do not threaten). Demonstrate your BATNA and use it if necessary.

      (b) Giving him or her space to decide, to choose whether to settle or lose.

5.7.6 SUMMARY

While not all these techniques are necessarily appropriate to court-door negotiations by barristers, some of the ideas in the book are imaginative and give useful insights into the psychology behind them.

SIX

COGNITIVE INFLUENCES

6.1 Introduction

Negotiators approaching a negotiation tend to focus on the practical preparation aspects such as understanding the merits of the claim, identifying what the client wants from the negotiation and devising a strategy to achieve a realistic workable settlement. Whilst it is vital to give these aspects full consideration it is necessary to be aware of how cognitive influences may affect the negotiation. This chapter focuses upon some of the cognitive influences you will encounter whilst negotiating and some of the skills you will need to develop in order to overcome some of the negative effects of those cognitive influences.

6.2 Human Influence and the Role of Emotion

As a form of social interaction, negotiation inevitably involves emotion. Emotion (strong mental or instinctive feelings) can exert significant influence in a negotiation. The impact of emotion can be positive or negative, depending on a whole range of factors. Given the role of negotiation at the Bar, and the conditions in which it can take place, there is plenty of scope for emotion to have a negative effect. For barristers, many negotiations represent the last chance for their lay client to settle a dispute before the matter is litigated with all the attendant costs and stresses that a full hearing involves. The barrister is often put under considerable pressure to find a settlement that prevents a fully litigated hearing and yet, at the stage when court-door negotiations take place, both parties will have invested considerable amounts of time, energy and money in the issues at stake. These conflicting factors can cause stress, which in turn can lead emotion to outweigh reason, in a negotiation, or at least to have a significant role. It is therefore necessary to be aware of your own emotions so that you can understand how they may be affecting the negotiation. Equally, an understanding of the role of emotion can assist you to determine your opponent's emotional status and enable you to deal with his or her emotions in the most appropriate way.

6.3 Expectations and Perception

Whenever we approach any negotiation, we have expectations about what will happen and why. Expectations assist us to make decisions both before and during the negotiation. Some of those expectations can have a positive effect upon the negotiation, e.g. if our expectation is to win, it can provide us with a determination that may make winning more likely. But expectations can have a negative effect. This is particularly so where expectations are based on limited and unreliable information, as this increases the scope for our own personal biases, preconceptions and misconceived expectations to shape our view of things, the decisions we take and the way we behave.

When approaching a negotiation it is wise to consider carefully what the other side is likely to want to obtain from the negotiation. Within the framework of the legal case, we look at what factors might be motivating them to settle, what their interests and underlying needs might be, what they are prepared to sacrifice for the sake of settlement and what remains of prime importance to secure. Our perceptions and expectations of what the other side will want and how they are likely to act to achieve it, are based upon information we can glean from a number of different sources: the brief itself, the client, the instructing solicitor, the knowledge of the opponent (if any) and perhaps, previous dealings with the case at an earlier stage.

We therefore bring to every negotiation, expectations and perceptions about the other side, and how they are likely to act, based upon this information; in turn we have expectations about our own case and what we want to achieve from the negotiation. In this context it is important to remember that nearly every negotiation, at whatever stage of the litigation process it takes place, is characterised to an extent by a lack of information. This can take many forms such as documentary evidence not yet disclosed, or lack of information concerning the characteristics and negotiating abilities of your opponent and his or her view of the case, including the concessions that are desired from you and the resistance point at which going to court becomes a preferable course of action. The greater the gaps in our information, the greater the scope for our expectations and perceptions to play a role in the decisions we take during the negotiation. This is true whether the gaps of information relate to the subject matter of the dispute itself or the personalities involved in negotiation. An example of expectancy-effects is as follows. If we believe that the opponent is likely to want to secure a much higher sum than we are prepared to consider, based upon our opponent's competitive opening statement about the case, our expectations and perceptions may lead us to take an argumentative and defensive stand that lends an air of hostility and tension to the negotiation which in turn sets the pattern for competitive bargaining. Here the expectation has shaped the negotiation. In the absence of knowing what the other side considers its best result in the negotiation to be, our expectation that it is greater than we would be prepared to consider has informed our decision about how to progress the negotiation and what negotiating style to adopt.

Expectancy-effects can exert a powerful influence in many areas. A good example can be seen where cross-cultural negotiations take place. Ignorance and lack of experience of another culture can lead to expectations of certain behaviour based upon a stereotypical model. Stereotypes are often generalised, misinformed and inaccurate, yet such expectations can influence the negotiation by dictating, or at least to some extent influencing, our behaviour.

6.4 The Self-Fulfilling Prophecy

Taking matters a step further, expectations can shape behaviour in such a way that expectations become realised: the self-fulfilling prophecy. Consider the following. In practice it is likely you will have to negotiate with a more experienced practitioner. Consider what your expectations could be and their possible impact. If you and your opponent have a conflict over the way the legal principles will apply to the facts, do you expect that there is less chance that you are right due to your lack of experience? If you concede the point to your opponent, will you attribute that to actually getting the point wrong or to your expectation that being more junior it is less likely that you are right? Do you make concessions more readily because you perceive you have less bargaining strength due to lack of experience or because this is actually the case? At the end of the negotiation, having made too many concessions, will you attribute that to your lack of experience or will you recognise the possibility that, because you expected you would be forced into making more concessions, you made more concessions based upon that expectation and not the superior skill of your opponent?

It may be that your perceptions and expectations are correct, but in all negotiations it pays to consider what expectations and perceptions we have, and why, and query with ourselves the underlying basis for such expectations and perceptions. From such an analysis you can consider whether those expectations should be informing your decisions or not.

6.5 Selective Perception

Part of the process of negotiation is the assimilation of new information and one of the difficulties negotiators experience is trying to listen, analyse and evaluate the relevance of the information received. In order to deal with the information, and process it, inevitably it is simplified and categorised. Selective filtering tends to occur as part of this process.

Regrettably, all too often we do not pause to consider our expectations, and, rather than thinking about how they might adversely influence the negotiation, they are confirmed through a process of selective perception that rejects material that is contrary to our expectations, leaving only information that confirms them.

Selective filtering can explain a negotiator's over-confidence about the merit of his or her client's position. If, during the preparatory stages, a negotiator has evaluated the strengths and weaknesses of his or her client's case and concluded that, on issue X, the client has a virtually unassailable claim, the negotiator will often selectively filter the information received from the other side during the negotiation. That which is contrary to the previously held view is not digested. The negotiator only listens and hears information that confirms his or her initial views. In such a scenario, it is possible that such a selective filtering process will assist the negotiator to secure a better deal for the client than he or she would otherwise, provided the opponent is a weak opponent. However, the danger is that by rejecting information concerning the weaknesses in the claim for X, the negotiator holds out for too much and the negotiation founders when the opponent is not willing to concede on issue X.

6.6 Concessions and Psychological Influences

The process of concession-making is part of any negotiation and it is important to consider some of the psychological factors that can be present and affect this part of the negotiation process. There are a huge number of reasons why settlement may not be achieved, despite this being the preferred option, but a common reason is the loss of credibility associated with making concessions. Fear of loss of credibility can lead to problems in attempting to move to settlement and ultimately to deadlock.

In most negotiations, a number of needs and requirements have been mapped out by the negotiators in advance. In articulating those needs and requirements, negotiators state positions or propositions that they require the other side to fulfil. Agreement to move from the stated position/proposition in a direction less favourable to the negotiator making the statement can be termed a concession. Difficulties often occur in negotiation when both sides get stuck over whether or not the stated position/proposition will be met. If both sides are adamant they will not retreat from their position/proposition a deadlock will result. The pressure upon the negotiators to move is intense, given the mounting costs, the increasing time it is taking to negotiate a deal, and the probable desire to avoid further escalation of the conflict. However, paradoxically, the longer neither side is prepared to move, the more there is at stake and the more parties become trapped in their positions.

The primary concern of a negotiator in this scenario is that any movement away from the position taken will be interpreted by the opponent as weakness and a signal that they are prepared to move, or can be pushed, not just one step away from the position but several. However, concern over loss of credibility and determination not to back down can mask the realities of the situation. Often negotiators will hold firm to their positions in a situation where the resulting deadlock will put both sides to the dispute to considerable expense. In extreme cases, the item that is being negotiated can be relatively minor compared with others on the table for negotiation, yet the fear that any movement from the stated position is an invitation to exploitation leaves the negotiation in deadlock.

In trying to deal with this all-too-common scenario, the first step is to recognise what is happening and to evaluate the consequences. Ideally, try to avoid the situation from occurring in the first place by planning the concessions you wish to make with real care. A simple example of bad concession-planning is the negotiator who only has one concession to make, who makes it early on in the negotiation, leaving the other side with the impression that they can be pushed further into making other concessions. Equally, where you do have more than one concession to trade with, do not use up the bank before reaching a crucial item you wish to negotiate over.

Remember, also, that in any deadlock the other side may well be experiencing the same concerns and anxieties over the possibility of losing credibility. Be aware that you have the power to influence the negotiation by changing its dynamic. Move to a different issue; alternatively acknowledge the problem and look for alternative ways of overcoming it, by shifting the focus onto other items that require negotiation.

It is common in a negotiation to depart from a reasoned analysis of what is an appropriate level of settlement, that is determined by the merits of the parties' positions, and be distracted by your expectations and emotions and the actual dynamic of the negotiation itself. Try to reconsider and reconfirm in your own mind the basis for what you are asking for, and reconsider whether it is realistic. Have you been overly optimistic about what you can expect? Alternatively, have they over-estimated their case, and if so, how can you persuade them to reconsider their expectations of what concessions to expect from you? Additionally, it can be helpful to reconfirm the basis for both parties' expectations by explicitly attempting to discuss this with your opponent.

6.7 Reciprocal Behaviour

In a negotiation it is easy for your opponent's behaviour to influence, and to an extent dictate, your own. Often two negotiators will unwittingly mirror each other's behaviour. This is true of behaviour that is 'destructive' as well as 'constructive'. Behaviour that is 'destructive' to the negotiation and escalates conflict, what occurs is akin to 'an eye for an eye and a tooth for a tooth'. If your opponent makes positional statements, aggressive arguments, and generally behaves in a hostile manner, it is tempting to 'reward' such behaviour in kind. Unwittingly an escalation of conflict can occur that can have disastrous consequences for the negotiation. Yet negotiators who exhibit mirroring destructive behaviour will often cling to the notion that such behaviour was justified on the basis that the opponent started it, and that their response was perfectly reasonable in the circumstances. Curiously, if negotiators are privately consulted, both will consider their own actions as reasonable whilst citing the opponent's as unreasonable. Being aware of the possibility of mirroring your opponent's behaviour, and remembering that both you and your opponent are likely to feel justified in what you do, is the basis for avoiding destructive mirroring behaviour.

The alternative is for mirroring behaviour to be 'constructive' and lead to an escalation of concessions, both negotiators trying to reward each other's 'good' behaviour. Obviously this will often lead to a settlement that is achieved quickly and painlessly. Whilst reciprocal concession-making due to mirroring good behaviour is acceptable, in as much as it leads to settlement rather than deadlock, this does not always mean that the settlement reached is appropriate for either or both of the clients. Caution is required so that the concessions made really are in the client's best interests.

A key feature of the mirroring behaviour described above is that it is unintentional and occurs as an unconscious reaction to the way your opponent is behaving. It is precisely because it can occur without a negotiator being aware of it that a negotiator needs to be able to identify it if it is happening. One of the key elements of negotiation skills is the ability to understand the process as it occurs, to be able to know what is happening, and why, as this brings control and informed decision-making.

Unconscious mirroring behaviour must be distinguished from the tit-for-tat tactic described at **5.2.5.4**. The tit-for-tat tactic is a conscious and deliberate attempt by the negotiator to mirror the opponent's behaviour with the intention of bringing about specific results.

6.8 Not Coping

Negotiating is a highly complex activity that requires considerable concentration, self-discipline and hard work if it is to be done properly. Arguably it has the fewest rules and guidelines in the litigation process as a whole. Even if you are very well prepared, you may have to digest considerable amounts of new information in an already complex case, some of which requires you to alter radically your evaluation of the merits, reflect that in your proposals, whilst dealing with your opponent's strategy, tactics and points, and considering your revised plan of action; all in a very short space of time. In this situation, at times, it can be tempting, and sometimes impossible, not to 'shut down' and resort to a pre-planned strategy ignoring what has occurred during the negotiation, relying upon the original arguments, and not revise your plan of action to accommodate the new information and the proposals put forward by your opponent. Alternatively, you may be tempted simply to throw in the towel and accept the proposals being offered without giving them proper consideration. It may not be just you that is affected. If both you and your opponent are overwhelmed by the negotiation, and the issues involved, it may result in the negotiation going around in circles with little or no progress being made.

Again recognising what is occurring is a starting point in dealing with this situation. Sound preparation can minimise the extent to which it is likely to occur, but even that sometimes is simply not enough. Do not be afraid to ask your opponent for time to deal with new information arising during a negotiation. If both you and your opponent are in difficulties, try to take a step back from the negotiation and implement a plan for dealing with the complexities in the case that are causing difficulties, such as redefining or categorising what is on the table for negotiation and what the issues are that relate to them.

6.9 Communication Skills

6.9.1 INTRODUCTION

Learning to counter the negative effects of human influences takes time, practice and a willingness to accept that human influences play a significant role in the negotiation. If a negotiation does not go as planned, it is important to spend time reviewing what occurred, and considering what went wrong, and what you could have done differently. Regrettably, in practice it may seem as if there is too little time for this sort of reflection but the alternative is the repetition of mistakes that can themselves cost time and money.

It is also important to spend time working on the interpersonal skills necessary to deal appropriately with the human influence. Negotiation is social interaction which involves the exchange of information on a number of different levels, including the spoken word, the sub text of what is said and a person's behaviour. Certain communication skills play a vital role in this process, and yet many lawyers do not give time and consideration to these skills. It is only when sound analytical skills are combined with sound communication skills that the lawyer can expect to be a good negotiator.

6.9.2 OBSERVATIONAL SKILLS

One of the primary skills necessary to negotiate well is the ability to observe what is happening and why. You need to be able to evaluate not only your opponent's actions, but those of your own, if you are to have any measure of control over what goes on. Very often negotiators focus on their opponent and are unaware of their own behaviour

NEGOTIATION

and the reasons informing it. All too often negotiators who are not self-observant fail to appreciate the interpretations that can be placed upon their behaviour and, throughout their career, adopt patterns of behaviour that can have a negative effect upon the negotiation. It is also quite common for lawyers who negotiate to adopt one particular style of negotiation that they use for all negotiations whatever the context, whoever the opponent, and give no thought to alternative ways of negotiating, that might be more suitable in certain contexts.

Negotiating with sophistication requires you to have an awareness of your behaviour and how it shapes the negotiation. This will assist you to learn what works, and when, and what does not work, and why. This information can only be gained through careful observation during the negotiation and critical reflection after the negotiation. One way of achieving such detachment is to mentally remove yourself from the negotiation and try and observe the negotiation critically as a non-partisan spectator.

6.9.3 LISTENING SKILLS

It is a stereotypical view that a barrister is paid to talk. In fact often this is not the case. A major part of a barrister's job is to listen, and listening skills play a vital role in any negotiation. Negotiation is a process of information-exchange that occurs on at least three different levels: the explicit spoken word, the 'subtext' or hidden message in what someone does not mention, and the non-verbal information they transmit. Very often, listening occurs at the first level only and even at this level negotiators do not 'hear' what is being said. Listening is a vastly underrated skill given the intense levels of concentration required particularly during a negotiation. Recognition of the obstacles to effective listening can help you train yourself to concentrate on picking up important information in the negotiation.

During a negotiation, one of the main obstacles to effective listening is your own internal dialogue as you process the information received, and consider what your next move should be. You will need to practise disciplining your own thoughts so that they do not preclude you from listening to important verbal and non-verbal messages you may be receiving from your opponent.

Part of the difficulty in learning to listen effectively is that it can appear to be contrary to the culture of the Bar. It is tempting to think that, if you are not doing the talking in a negotiation, you are somehow missing an opportunity and will appear weak. Yet saying nothing and doing nothing are two completely different things, and by listening carefully you can obtain information that can be of great assistance in the negotiation. It takes confidence and patience to become a good listener but remember that all the time you are not saying anything and simply listening you are receiving information, whilst your opponent is giving it away. Silence is itself a valuable tool and you should learn to resist filling the void in conversation/dialogue if you find that you are tempted to do this.

On a more simple (but no less distracting) level, external factors also militate against effective listening, and this is particularly true in a crowded corridor trying to negotiate a settlement, with the clock ticking, and the pressure of an impending hearing if settlement is not achieved. In these circumstances, it is easy not to hear the subtle messages and fragments of important information that your opponent may be giving you.

6.9.4 VERBAL SKILLS

Clearly, an important skill in negotiation is the ability to speak clearly and plainly and make yourself understood. Although many of the formalities of court-door advocacy do not need to be observed when negotiating, many of the primary rules of persuasive speech still apply. Your overall aim should be to speak with clarity and conviction and to articulate difficult points with precision.

Studies have shown that there is a relationship between speech styles and persuasiveness so that, aside from the content of what someone says, their manner of speech can make it more or less likely they will persuade the listener. You should be aware of the possible negative impact of certain characteristics of speech and try to avoid them.

Frequent use of hesitation statements such as 'um', 'er', 'ah', can weaken the impact of what you want to say and convey a lack of confidence. They are also irritating to the listener. Similarly, if too many words are used when making a point, then the message loses impact. Consider the following statement:

> I feel compelled to point out to you the obvious mistake in what you appear to be saying, as my client could not possibly have failed to observe the warning signs on any version of events, let alone the ones you seem to be presenting, despite the obvious distractions at the time.

Consider by contrast how much more powerful is the following statement:

> My client did see the warning sign despite the distractions present at the time.

Using speech that is clear and simple makes it easier for the listener to understand what you are saying. Negotiators who speak hesitantly, or use too many words, or are repetitious, risk diluting the impact of what they are trying to say. They also risk the listener becoming bored, frustrated and irritated. Such speech also requires the listener to expend more energy deciphering what it is that is being communicated. Unless these consequences are for some reason desired for tactical reasons, it pays to speak plainly.

SEVEN

PERSUASION

7.1 Introduction

To understand the role of persuasion in legal negotiation, it is necessary to revisit the definitions of negotiation which were variously described in **Chapter 2** as 'confer (with another) with a view to securing compromise', 'a basic means of getting what you want from others'. It is 'back-and-forth communication designed to reach an agreement when you and the other side have some interests that are shared and others that are opposed', and 'a process in which two or more participants attempt to reach a joint decision on matters of common concern in situations where they are in actual or potential disagreement or conflict'.

Common to all the definitions is mutual need for an agreement. Whether the parties are in actual or potential conflict, whether there are shared interests or not, whether the parties have equal bargaining strength or not, both sides need something from one another and they have come to the negotiation table in order to get it via a negotiated settlement. A very great part of the skill of negotiation therefore lies in persuading the other side to give you what you want.

This chapter looks at various methods and techniques of persuasion with particular emphasis on the use of argument. There is overlap with the chapters on psychology, strategy and tactics (**Chapters 4** to **6**) and you may wish to cross-refer to these from time to time.

Many of the ideas and concepts mentioned in this chapter are based on the work of Paul Bergman and Robert Condlin, references for which can be found in **Chapter 15**.

7.2 The Use of Argument

'Argument' can be defined as an exchange of views, a reason advanced, a reasoning process. It is one of the ways that a negotiator attempts to persuade the other side to move towards their settlement position. In legal negotiations, the use of argument is a primary skill that all negotiators should master. Yet, frequently, little time and energy is spent by the negotiator distinguishing between different types of argument and their possible impact. In fact many negotiators would deny that they placed any reliance at all upon the use of argument.

Of course there are cases in which a negotiator does not have to persuade an opponent; for example, both sides may discover they have entirely compatible interests and desire the same outcome. In such a scenario, simple discussion and request will enable both negotiators to get what they want for their clients. Not surprisingly such cases are rare and most negotiations require the reconciliation of differing views of appropriate settlement standards. Using argument is one way of achieving this.

Lawyers who negotiate use argument in one form or another even if they are not consciously aware of it. Yet lack of understanding of the role of argument can lead to mistakes and disappointing results. Negotiators who can distinguish different types of argument, and know how and when to use it, have significant advantages over the uninitiated. This is true whether the negotiation is dispute-resolving (i.e., that which seeks to settle conflicts over historical events) or deal-making (i.e., that which seeks to regulate future conduct), whether it concerns one issue or several, whether it is distributive or integrative.

7.2.1 LEGAL AND FACTUAL ARGUMENT

Argument in legal negotiation can take many forms: moral, social, normative, ethical, personal, factual and legal. When considering how to persuade an opponent, it pays to be able to make distinctions in your own mind between different types of argument as, depending on the context, some types of argument are likely to be more persuasive than others.

In legal negotiation, lawyers commonly adopt settlement positions based upon their view of the facts and legal principles applicable to the case. For example, a claimant's lawyer in a personal injury case might suggest a figure acceptable to his or her client, based upon a full finding of liability, on the basis that the facts do not support a finding of contributory negligence. Conversely, his or her opponent might suggest a lower figure which takes contributory negligence into consideration on the basis that the facts do support such a finding. As settlement positions are closely related to the legal principles and the relevant facts, legal and factual argument can be a useful part of a negotiator's persuasion arsenal.

Legal argument can be defined as argument about the interpretation of legal rules and principles from whatever source they may be derived, be it statute or common law; whether concerned with substance or procedure (including the rules on evidence). So, for example, a dispute may have arisen concerning whether or not your client received the appropriate notification of certain events. To be valid notification, a certain statute says your client must have received written notice at his or her 'principal place of abode'. You may be arguing over the meaning of the words 'principal place of abode' and what they are intended to cover.

Factual argument focuses on disputes over what has happened, is happening or is likely to happen and how this affects the legal principles relevant to the subject-matter of the dispute. So, for example, in a dispute-resolving negotiation concerning a sale of goods contract, factual argument might be concerned with whether or not the goods were delivered on the date specified in the contract (that term not being in dispute).

In legal negotiation the most common form of argument is probably factual, as most disputes requiring negotiation are concerned with the application of settled law to controversial facts. For example, in a contract for the sale of goods it is clear that the law requires the goods to be of satisfactory quality, but there could be considerable factual debate over whether or not the goods delivered where defective and met this standard.

It is not at all uncommon for legal negotiation to require both factual and legal argument where, for example, the applicable legal principle contains ambiguities, and where the facts relating to the rule are also controversial. Returning to the first example above, legal argument may be concerned with interpreting the meaning of 'principal place of abode' and whether the defendant's country home fell into this category. Factual argument might be based on a dispute over how many days out of the last year the defendant actually spent at the country home.

7.2.2 WHAT CAN LEGAL AND FACTUAL ARGUMENT ACHIEVE?

Having defined and distinguished legal and factual argument, it is necessary to consider what such argument can achieve.

When parties negotiate, they will decide whether or not to accept what is offered, depending on whether they can better that offer elsewhere. If you are proposing to buy

PERSUASION

a car you will judge the price offered by one garage against the alternatives that you have researched, and presumably accept the vehicle which represents the best buy, often the car of greatest quality, costing the least money.

7.2.3 DISPUTE RESOLVING NEGOTIATION

In dispute-resolution negotiations, the alternative to accepting settlement via negotiation is to go to court. Lawyers therefore judge what is an appropriate overall settlement primarily according to their view of the merits of their client's case. In other words, lawyers will settle if they think that what is offered is worth equal to or more than what they could realistically get if the matter went to court, bearing in mind the risks and expenses involved in litigation. So, for example, if, in a personal injury case as claimant lawyer, you consider that it is highly likely there will be a finding of contributory negligence of at least 15%, you will no doubt be prepared to accept a figure of settlement that takes such a probable finding into account.

Although the merits are of primary importance in determining settlement levels, it should also be recognised that in some cases there may be other factors that dictate what are acceptable settlement terms. An example would be where a client has pressing financial reasons for wanting an early settlement to litigation. This might motivate acceptance of terms of settlement that did not reflect the full strengths of the client's legal case. However, it remains true that, in most cases, the merits dictate settlement positions adopted and what terms are acceptable and therefore the merits of the case are highly significant.

Obviously making a comparison between settlement terms offered, and what you consider to be the most likely court outcome given the strengths and weaknesses, for your client's case, is by no means an exact science. It can be extremely difficult at times to know whether it is better to accept what is on the table in the negotiation, rather than to go to court. Such decisions are primarily based upon a very careful consideration of the merits of the client's case. When evaluating the merits of the case and the competing claims involved, negotiators are faced with two considerable difficulties. First, the uncertainties inherent in the litigation process, and secondly, informational uncertainty.

Uncertainties in the litigation process can take many different forms. Generally speaking, litigation is a risky business, given the focus on finding a winner and a loser. Courts can rarely impose compromise, particularly at the trial stage. Thus, for example, the way the witnesses will give their evidence and their credibility will influence the outcome and therefore be of greatest concern. The second factor causing difficulties in evaluating the merits of the competing claims is informational uncertainty. The view of the merits is not static or fixed but changes constantly, given the numerous informational changes that occur over the course of litigation. Every time a new piece of information is added, its impact on the merits of the negotiation must be evaluated. Consider, for example, the impact on the view of the merits of the case from information received on discovery, exchange of experts reports and witness statements.

Both process and informational uncertainty mean that a negotiator cannot be certain that his or her view of the merits is entirely accurate and will not need revising in the negotiation. The problem is particularly acute if new information and evidence is put forward by the opponent whilst negotiations are in process. Such uncertainty gives considerable scope for legal and factual arguments concerning the merits of the competing claims, to have a persuasive effect. Consider the following illustration that shows how process and informational uncertainty gives scope for factual argument to be used to persuade an opponent to move from a stated settlement position.

Scenario: Your client is a company defending a personal injury negligence suit brought by one of its employees. The employee is suing for damages as a result of injuries sustained when she slipped on a wet floor. Liability is in dispute with your client alleging that the company is not responsible, as the claimant was running at the time that she slipped (in an area where running was clearly prohibited) and, therefore, is the author of her own misfortune.

NEGOTIATION

Example 1. As the lawyer acting for the defendant, you intend to call a witness at trial who will give evidence that he saw the claimant running just before she fell. In the negotiation you might argue that this witness was:

- standing nearby where the claimant fell and had an unobstructed view of the entire incident;

- the safety officer for the floor where the accident happened and therefore likely to be paying particular attention to careless and dangerous behaviour.

These two factual arguments strengthen the direct evidence you have that suggests that the claimant was running before she fell. They also utilise litigation process uncertainty about the credibility of the witnesses.

Example 2. You have new evidence recently obtained that shows that the claimant had already received two verbal warnings for being late back from tea break. You may argue that:

- the claimant was returning from the tea break when the accident occurred;

- the tea break had officially ended 10 minutes prior to the claimant returning to her workstation;

- therefore the claimant was worried about being late back to her workstation and was running when she fell.

In this example you are using factual argument based upon circumstantial evidence. As your knowledge of the existence of such evidence is revealed for the first time in the negotiation you are exploiting informational uncertainty.

By using various types of factual argument that relate to the evidence, and both process and informational uncertainty, you can cast doubt upon the settlement position of the opponent where that is based upon the merits of the case.

You should remember that using argument rarely culminates in your opponent's express acceptance of your points. Rather the purpose of using argument is to cast doubt on the basis of the opponent's settlement position, so that the position is moved in a direction or in a manner favourable to you.

Just as legal and factual arguments can be used to move an opponent from a predetermined settlement level, so they can be used by negotiators to justify settlement positions adopted. In very many negotiations, opponents want to know why you will not move from a particular stance or position adopted, or on what basis you seek to justify the requests you have made. If you can make a compelling legal or factual argument you may find you get what you want, or at least more of what you want. Your argument provides justification for the opponent. This is important, especially as most settlements require the approval of the client. By justifying your stance, or request with a persuasive factual or legal argument, you give your opponent a reason to take back to his or her client, that may help him or her to accept the terms negotiated.

In this sense legal and factual arguments have a dual purpose. They seek to change an opponent's view of appropriate positions, whilst justifying your own.

7.2.4 DEAL-MAKING NEGOTIATIONS

In deal-making negotiations, legal and factual argument can also play a persuasive role. The factors that shape the settlement positions of the parties will be more diverse and heavily dependent upon the context of the particular negotiation. The following example shows how factual and legal argument can be used in the deal-making context.

Two parties are negotiating the potential lease of a property where the parties are in dispute over two issues. The landlord wants a rent of £12,000 per annum, and a covenant against subletting, and the prospective tenant is unhappy about both of these issues.

The prospective tenant might propose an alternative settlement position as follows: £9,000 per annum, and a covenant against subletting without the landlord's consent, such consent not to be unreasonably withheld. Any or all of the following arguments could be used to undermine the landlord's settlement position and move it closer to the settlement position of the tenant.

In the matter of the rent: £12,000 is well in excess of the rental sums for equivalent properties in the vicinity; £9,000 is based upon what the tenant is paying in his current accommodation, which is similar.

In the matter of the subletting clause: the landlord is protected because he can refuse to allow subletting provided the refusal is not unreasonable and recent Court of Appeal authority indicates marked reluctance to find landlords' lack of consent unreasonable.

In this example the tenant's lawyer has relied upon factual arguments relating to similar property prices in the area and what he is currently paying. Of course, how persuasive this argument will be will, to an extent, depend upon the evidence that he has to substantiate it. Similarly, with the legal argument with regard to the subletting clause, where the opponent might need to see a transcript of the relevant authorities in question.

7.2.5 THE USE OF ARGUMENT — A CAUTIONARY NOTE

If factual and legal argument is going to persuade, it must be relevant, comprehensive and intelligible, and appropriate to the context. Regrettably all too often this is not the case. Argument that is irrelevant, incomplete and unintelligible, and inappropriate to the context, can have a negative effect upon negotiation. It can do much to confuse and alienate your opponent, make the negotiation inefficient and in extreme cases lead to deadlock. In short, argument, if handled badly, can be dangerous for a number of different reasons.

7.2.5.1 The role of case preparation
(Cross reference should be made to **Chapters 3** and **9** for a fuller understanding of the steps that must be taken at the preparation stage.)

In dispute-resolving negotiation, the only way to ensure that legal and factual argument will be relevant, comprehensive and intelligible, is to have analysed the case papers properly. You will need a thorough understanding of all the strengths and weaknesses of your client's position regarding the issues in the case. From this analysis you can identify the different possible arguments you have, ranging from the strong to the weak.

The basic method of analysing case papers is no different from that required for any other activity at the Bar, be it writing an opinion, preparing for a client conference, or preparing for trial. The main aim is identification and evaluation of the issues in the case.

The starting point is identifying the cause of claim and its elements. So, for example, in a contract action, the main elements would be existence of a contract, breach and damage. The next step is to identify which elements are agreed and which are in dispute. So, for example, there may be no dispute over the existence of the contract or its terms but considerable dispute over whether its non-controversial terms have been breached. From there you can analyse the facts relevant to the disputed matters and go on to make an evaluation of the relevant evidence. This will lead to an understanding of the strengths and weaknesses of the client's position. Only once you have undertaken this type of analysis can you begin to look at the possible arguments you have at your disposal and make judgments about their quality and the wisdom of using them in a negotiation.

In legal deal-making negotiations, preparatory steps are more diverse and depend upon the context. This is because, as has been seen, settlement positions are shaped by factors more diverse than in dispute-resolving negotiation where it is mainly the merits which matter.

The main preparatory steps will relate to researching the bases for your possible settlement positions and evaluating the factual and legal arguments that support them. From here you can compare your supportive arguments for their relative strengths. So, for example, the tenant in the example set out at **7.2.4** may have chosen a settlement position of £9,000 as the quality of evidence supporting this request makes it his strongest point.

7.2.5.2 Presentation skills

Even where proper research into the basis of the particular arguments used has been made, things can go wrong, due to presentation problems. In **Chapter 6**, the issue of verbal skills is addressed. Some of the more chronic features of poor presentation involve repeated use of hesitation statements and verbosity. These problems and others can have a disastrous effect on an otherwise persuasive argument. If you are going to use argument to persuade, it must be comprehensive, logical in structure, and backed with confidence and conviction. Put quite simply, it is not just what you say but how you say it that matters. Often a negotiator who has sound arguments, but poor presentation skills, is left repeating the point. It may well be that the only thing that changes is the volume of what is said. Rather than having a persuasive effect, the opposite is more likely, as the opponent will focus on the demeanour of the negotiator rather than the content of what he or she is saying.

7.2.5.3 Argument and bargaining strategies

Much research has been done on the different bargaining strategies that negotiators use and reference should be made to **Chapter 4** for a fuller understanding of the different models. A sound understanding of the use of argument requires you to give some thought to how the arguments you use might affect your bargaining strategy or *visa versa*.

In pure form, a competitive bargainer has an adversarial approach towards negotiating. He or she wants to win and is likely to see the negotiation as zero-sum, with one party gaining at the expense of the other. He or she is likely to open with high demands, take strong, specific positions, make few concessions, be slow to make concessions, be reluctant to reveal or share information, be preoccupied with the position of his or her client and generally uninterested in that of his or her opponent.

For the competitive or adversarial negotiator, arguments, whatever their type, be they moral, ethical, factual or legal are used competitively to justify and reinforce his or her approach in terms of strategy, i.e., to justify the high and exaggerated demands, to back the refusal/reluctance to make concessions and to marginalise and undermine the arguments and position of the opponent. In its more extreme form, competitive argument has more to do with coercion than persuasion, manipulation than understanding. It seeks to exploit the fears and insecurities of the opponent.

By contrast, a cooperative negotiator is characterised by concern with fairness and being reasonable to both parties to the dispute. He or she is likely to open with moderate statements and make offers that are not an exaggerated view of what his or her client is entitled to; he or she seeks co-operation and mutual solution. For the co-operative negotiator, argument is used primarily to foster understanding of the way the case is viewed and tolerance of requests made. It is characterised by rationality and a desire to be 'fair'. It does seek to justify the client's case on the merits but only in so far as this can help both negotiators reach a 'fair' agreement somewhere between the stated positions of the parties.

Collaborative negotiators are concerned to satisfy underlying needs and interests of the parties. Collaborative negotiators, be they principled or problem-solving, will primarily be looking to negotiate with a view to mutual gain and a 'win-win' solution. They will be using argument chiefly to persuade the other side to accept their preferred solution for satisfying their client's interests and needs. Argument will be characterised by a reasoned approach that seeks to have the other side understand the interests and needs of the parties. Although the merits of the case are not ignored, many of the arguments will be directed to the client's interests and the settlement standard that the negotiator seeks to persuade the opponent to adopt.

When you are considering the use of argument and its role in the negotiation process, you may find it helpful to have these basic distinctions in mind. Obviously most negotiators do not use argument in a purely competitive way or a purely co-operative way, as negotiators will rarely use a purely competitive, co-operative or principled bargaining strategy. Most negotiators use a mixture of bargaining strategies in any one negotiation. The same is no less true for the use of argument.

Problems occur, and mistakes are made, in negotiations when negotiators are unaware of how they are using argument and its impact upon the negotiation. It may be that you have a sound point to make, but if you make it repeatedly with increasing volume, and without suggesting why you are making the point or what you want as a consequence of it, you may be viewed as aggressive, confrontational and unconstructive. Similarly, if you have a good point to make but conceal its importance, due to a keen desire to build a friendly atmosphere in an agreement, it may be overlooked.

7.2.5.4 Arguing for the sake of it

One of the cardinal rules regarding the use of argument is never argue for the sake of it. Argument is a tool and should always be used with a specific purpose in mind. To be an effective negotiator you need to identify the purpose of your arguments and to judge accurately whether your arguments are fulfilling their purpose. Many negotiations founder when argument is used incorrectly. It should be used as a reasoning process and must be distinguished from being argumentative. Regrettably all too often this is forgotten and negotiators replace reasoned argument with quarrelling and bickering about matters in dispute. This often happens when lawyers negotiate, perhaps because they work within the adversarial system where the emphasis is upon winners and losers.

7.3 Other Persuasion Techniques

This chapter has so far concentrated upon argument as a medium of persuasion. Argument is only one technique of persuasion and must not be seen in isolation but in the context of many other related techniques. These techniques, when used in combination, may well explain why some people are much better negotiators than others.

Many of the related techniques of persuasion lie in what can be considered as the general hazy 'grey area' of communication skills. It can be tempting to skate over material concerning communication skills, either because you think it contains nothing you do not know from your own experiences, or because it is so lacking in precision that it is unhelpful. Those who already have sound communication skills stand to gain the most from learning more about and attempting to improve their communication skills (rather like a gifted runner who, if he or she continues to practise, can achieve astonishing feats). If communication skills seems a grey area which lacks substance, that is probably a reflection of the level of complexity which is inevitably involved in the field of human interaction, which makes it difficult to write about with simplicity and precision. Whatever your view of learning about communication skills, to ignore the importance of this area of study and practice in relation to negotiation skills is unwise.

NEGOTIATION

Chapter 6 deals with observational skills, listening skills and verbal skills in general terms, and full reference to those sections should be made. This section looks again at some of those skills of communication albeit from a slightly different perspective.

7.3.1 LISTENING SKILLS

In the context of persuasion, listening skills play a vital role. You must be able to monitor and absorb what your opponent is saying and react appropriately to it. This involves digesting what is said as well as what is not said. Particular care must be taken when interpreting the 'subtext' of what someone says. It is easy to make mistakes when listening to someone in a negotiation. The process lends itself to a rapid exchange of information. It can help if you check your understanding with your opponent, particularly about what has been expressly stated. Equally, if you have found a more obscure message in what has been said, try to test your views before making any major decisions about it.

You also need to be aware of the power that lies in listening. Often a persuasive negotiator will be marked out by his or her ability to make the opponent feel that what is being said is being heard. Contrary to the notion that saying nothing gains nothing, if used correctly, listening can do the opposite. Aside for the obvious benefit of being able to receive information, listening can convey a number of different and positive messages to the opponent. It can show interest and commitment. It can inspire trust, respect, even honesty. It is also very reassuring. All of which can help you get what you want from a negotiation.

Caution must be employed when listening to an opponent. Be careful that you do not appear bored or uninterested. Try to show that you are paying attention and hearing what your opponent has to say (unless for some reason you feel there is an advantage to be gained by feigning a lack of interest). Equally be subtle, as it is particularly offensive to feel that somebody is deliberately trying to use 'active listening' on you. Many would-be sensitive listeners do not realise the destructive effect an unsubtle approach can have to active listening.

7.3.2 NON-VERBAL COMMUNICATION

Non-verbal communication concerns the way we transmit information through our behaviour. It does have a significant role to play in negotiation. An ability to understand what information facial expressions, hand gestures, or other movements of the body may be revealing can assist a negotiator to respond in a more effective way if the message is correctly read. Equally, being able to manipulate your own non-verbal behaviour can be very useful in a negotiation.

Learning how to interpret someone's behaviour is complex and difficult and riddled with possible dangers. When interpreting someone's body language, there is the very obvious danger of misinterpretation, particularly when you do not know the individual concerned. The solution is not to ignore a person's behaviour altogether, but to consider with care what it could possibly mean. If someone does not make eye contact with you, there could be a number of different and quite wide-ranging explanations for this. It may be they feel intimidated by the point you are making or alternatively that they are disinterested. Equally it could be that they are simply considering your point with care and cannot look, listen and think at the same time. Having thought about what their behaviour could indicate, you can create opportunities, check what you think they are indicating by their behaviour. For example, you might ask them what they think of the point made, or whether they have anything they want to add or any comments to make.

Many negotiators concentrate fiercely upon how their opponent is behaving and what their body language could possibly be revealing, without thinking of their own. Often when we view a video of ourselves, we are shocked that we do not look, act or behave as we imagine ourselves. Be aware of possible negative effects of your own behaviour. A good starting point is to consider what you dislike in someone else's behaviour and consider very carefully whether it could apply to you and in what circumstances. Many features that are commonly disliked are those that tend to indicate the listener is disinterested. Consider what it feels like to be at the receiving end of someone who constantly looks over your shoulder, will not make eye contact, is fidgeting, looking at his or her watch, does not smile, and who slouches. Be aware of how such behaviour can have a negative effect upon the negotiation. Part of persuasion is showing that you are interested, listening and attempting to understand the other side's point of view. If your behaviour can be read as a lack of interest you may have a problem if you are not aware that this is the message you are conveying.

You must now be aware of your role as a lawyer and the dangers inherent in trying to simulate certain behaviour. As a lawyer you must act ethically and try to speak plainly. Experimenting with certain behaviour techniques to evaluate their effectiveness as a negotiation tactic should not ever be at the expense of proper representation of your client.

In addition, simulating behaviour for particular effect can end up with you looking ludicrous and your opponent thinking that you are simply a little odd. Alternatively, you may be conveying unintended messages. You are not a psychologist, be conscious of the impact of behaviour on negotiation but do not get carried away and focus too much on it.

7.3.3 QUESTIONING

Questioning an opponent can form a powerful part of persuasion in negotiation, yet many negotiators neglect the use of the question. It is relegated to 'conference and advocacy skills' where for different reasons the skill of questioning is often centre stage. However, information and knowledge (for example of the other side's case and their views on settlement) are very valuable things to have. Skilled use of questioning techniques can assist you to gain information on a whole variety of matters, from the strength of the opponent's case based upon specific questioning about the facts and evidence, to a greater understanding of the other side's underlying non-legal motivation for settlement.

Questions can also be useful in trying to establish an atmosphere you consider appropriate. Some questions are clearly hostile in their content and the way they are posed (for example, 'On what possible basis do you stake that claim?'). Others clearly convey commitment to working towards terms that acknowledge the other side's position (for example, 'Is there anything else that you think we ought to know about how your client has been affected by this accident?').

Given that questioning can affect the balance of knowledge and information between the parties and have ramifications for the relationship between the negotiators, all negotiators should understand the distinctions between different types of questions and what they can achieve.

7.4 Conclusion

To persuade: to cause somebody to believe or do something, by reasoning with him or her, lies at the heart of negotiation. Yet the component parts of the skill of persuasion are difficult to identify and describe. This chapter has attempted to define and describe some of the most important aspects of interpersonal communication that must be acknowledged and practised if a negotiator is to be persuasive. Most of the concepts touched upon are the subject of extensive research and literature and this chapter seeks only to draw your attention to the importance of these aspects rather than attempting to set out any sort of directory or guide. Full reference should be made to other sources for a more complete appreciation and understanding of matters dealt with in this chapter.

EIGHT

ETHICS OF NEGOTIATION

8.1 Introduction

It is important to remember that the Code of Conduct is not limited in its application to the conduct of cases inside the actual courtroom. The principles of the Code apply equally to pretrial preparation and the conduct of negotiations with a view to compromise. Frustration may tempt you on occasions to forget this: DON'T LET IT. A reputation for underhandedness or sharp practice will be retained long after the event. The old maxim 'you can fool some of the people all of the time' has little application at the Bar. The grapevine is far too effective!

As counsel, you have a duty to conduct negotiations in a fair, honest, courteous and trustworthy manner. You should never compromise your professional integrity. This does not mean that you should adopt an apologetic approach to negotiating. The importance of fair play should not detract from your duty to promote the interests of the lay client fearlessly.

The following is a guide to the ethics of negotiation. For the sake of clarity, it is divided into four categories, setting out the main principles which are relevant to your dealings with an opponent, lay client, professional client and the court. Not all of these matters are dealt with specifically in the Code. However, where the Code itself is silent upon any particular ethical problem, you should always apply the spirit of the Code.

The Code of Conduct can only give general guidance on ethical rules when negotiating, it cannot deal specifically with every situation that may arise. Do not let this mislead you into thinking that it is acceptable to 'bend' the rules to obtain an improper advantage for a client. It is essential that a barrister acts scrupulously in all negotiations.

8.2 The Opponent

8.2.1 'WITHOUT PREJUDICE'

Negotiations with a view to a settlement are often conducted 'without prejudice'. It is vital that lawyers and clients understand the real meaning of this phrase, as it can be misunderstood. The phrase was discussed in *Guiness Peat Properties* v *Fitzroy Robinson Partnership* [1987] 2 All ER 716, where it was held to mean 'without prejudice to the position of the writer if the terms he proposes are not accepted'. If a 'without prejudice' offer is accepted it is a formal agreement to settle the claim, is immediately binding, and can be revealed. If the offer is not accepted it is ignored, and nothing said in a letter making the offer can be used as evidence (*Rush* v *Tompkins Ltd* v *GLC* [1988] 1 All ER 549).

The words 'without prejudice' should not be misused. They should be used where a letter is intended to assist in settling a claim, and not simply in an attempt to make a document inadmissible as evidence. The use of the words is not conclusive, and they

NEGOTIATION

will be ignored if they have not been appropriately used (*South Shropshire District Council* v *Amos* [1987] 1 All ER 340). It is also possible for a course of letters to be 'without prejudice' even if the words do not appear on a particular letter.

However, where the words 'without prejudice' are appropriate, they should be used to protect the contents of the letter. Anything that is divulged which is not 'without prejudice' may be used at trial (see *Re Briamore Manufacturing Ltd* [1986] 3 All ER 132), although there may be exceptions if there is a mistake (*Guinness Peat Properties Ltd* v *Fitzroy Robinson Partnership* [1987] 2 All ER 716), or if there is some earlier reason why the document is not admissible, such as legal privilege (*Goddard* v *Nationwide Building Society* [1986] 3 All ER 264).

As a refinement of the 'without prejudice' offer, there is an offer to settle (Part 36 of the Civil Procedure Rules 1998). This is an offer which is essentially 'without prejudice', but the writer expressly reserves the right to refer to the letter when costs are considered — the argument being that if a reasonable offer is made and not accepted the party refusing the offer should bear the costs of pursuing the action after the offer was refused. An offer to settle should not be used when a Part 36 payment is appropriate, but should be used where it will otherwise protect the client's position (*Cutts* v *Head* [1984] Ch 290).

'Without prejudice' letters may be sent at any stage in the case. They would normally be drafted and sent by a solicitor, but a barrister might advise on the contents of such a letter.

Negotiations between counsel with a view to a compromise are impliedly made 'without prejudice'. Such discussions are in effect privileged and must not be repeated in court or in open correspondence. The exception to this rule is where an admission of fact, which should properly have been openly disclosed, is made in the course of negotiations. For example, 'My client now admits he gave your client a gift of £500 although the balance of his claim for £2,000 was a loan.' The umbrella of 'without prejudice' does not protect such an admission. You may therefore use the admission if it is in your lay client's best interests to do so, though you should inform your opponent of your intention to do this. On the other hand, 'My client is prepared to waive £500 of his claim provided your client pays him the balance of £1,500 within 28 days' is not an admission. It is a concession made 'without prejudice' in the context of an offer of compromise.

8.2.2 'BETWEEN COUNSEL'

Counsel may discuss a matter 'between counsel'. This is not the same as a discussion 'on instructions'. Such conversations usually relate to matters of a more personal or confidential nature, for example, the fact that a client is far too upset at the moment to discuss a proposal of settlement on a rational basis.

Such conversations are *not* to be repeated. The only exception to this is an admission of fact as in the example set out above. Here again, before using the admission, you should inform your opponent of your intention to do so.

You should try to avoid discussing a case without instructions to do so unless there is clearly some useful purpose in so doing.

8.2.3 IN BRIEF

(a) Never deliberately deceive or mislead your opponent in order to achieve a more favourable offer of compromise, for example, by pretending that you have a witness to support your client's account of the events when you do not. It is, however, acceptable to use 'bluff', allowing an opponent to form an impression without positively misleading him.

ETHICS OF NEGOTIATION

(b) Do not knowingly conceal something which ought properly to have been disclosed, for example a document, in the hope of securing a more favourable settlement.

(c) Do not make an offer or commit your client to an agreement without instructions or authority to do so. Make it clear to your opponent when your proposal is subject to your lay client's agreement. For example, 'If my client were prepared to do XYZ, would your client do ABC?'

(d) Do not go back on your word, or subsequently pretend you did not say something, in order to cover your own mistake or indiscretion. Such behaviour is unacceptable. If you have made an error, admit it.

(e) Avoid bickering with your opponent; it does not do your client any good. Nor is it wise to lose your objectivity by taking on the persona of your client in the course of negotiations. For example, 'Your client is totally dishonest, he has already stolen £2,000 from us'. This merely serves to antagonise.

8.3 The Lay Client

8.3.1 THE IMPORTANCE OF INSTRUCTIONS

The central importance of acting on the instructions of a lay client has been emphasised in **Chapter 3** (see **3.4**). You should only negotiate when your client instructs you to do so, and you can only negotiate within the authority given to you by your client.

8.3.2 IN BRIEF

(a) Ensure you have your client's firm instructions or authority to either propose or accept an offer of compromise.

(b) Keep your client informed of any offer of compromise. Advise him or her of the risks involved in making, accepting or rejecting an offer of compromise, for example, the incidence of costs. Ensure your client understands the nature and effect of any agreement and/or any undertaking he or she is proposing to give to the court.

(c) Do not browbeat your client into making, accepting or rejecting an offer of compromise. The final decision is a matter for the client.

(d) Do not advise your client to either make or accept an offer of compromise in order to suit your own purposes, for example, in order to get away from court early.

(e) Do not knowingly allow yourself to be used as a tool to obtain settlement in respect of a groundless or fraudulent claim. If your client's case is without any foundation, you should not act for him or her.

(f) Ensure your client's interests are adequately protected by the machinery of the compromise. For example, a judgment debt is likely to affect your client's prospects of obtaining future credit, whereas an agreement to pay the debt contained in a Tomlin order will not.

(g) In the event of a failure to reach a satisfactory compromise, warn your client not to repeat in court what has been said during the negotiation.

(h) Your duty not to divulge information entrusted to you in confidence by your client without his or her consent continues after the case, even if it has been dealt with by way of a negotiated compromise.

NEGOTIATION

8.4 The Professional Client

8.4.1 THE DIVISION OF FUNCTIONS

Both the solicitor and counsel may become involved in seeking to negotiate a settlement in a case. The division of roles should be kept clear. Counsel might be asked to advise the solicitor on possible terms of settlement, in which case the solicitor will proceed with any negotiation. Alternatively, counsel might be instructed to try to settle a case, in which case he or she must keep the solicitor informed.

8.4.2 IN BRIEF

(a) Keep your professional client informed of developments. If such client is present, listen to his or her views on the merit of any proposal that has been made.

(b) Be courteous and even-tempered in your dealings with your professional client. Do not argue in front of the lay client. If there is a difference of opinion between you, discuss it out of the lay client's hearing.

(c) Do not, however, keep your professional client happy at the expense of your lay client's interests. For example, do not advise your client to reject a fair offer of compromise merely because your solicitor insists that his firm, rather than the one proposed, handles the conduct of the sale of the property in dispute.

8.5 The Court

8.5.1 RELATIVE ROLES

The fact that you are seeking to negotiate a settlement may deceive you into thinking of the case as being subject only to your decisions. Never forget the ultimate role of the court and the need for its approval where you are seeking a consent order. The judge may suggest some amendments to your draft order.

8.5.2 IN BRIEF

(a) If negotiations are taking place at court, keep the court informed of the possibility of a compromise. It may be sufficient to relay this information to the court via the court clerk or usher. At times, it may be necessary to explain this to the judge or tribunal. Provide the court with a realistic estimate of the further time you need to discuss any proposals. Inform the court immediately upon reaching agreement.

(b) If you have time, draw up draft minutes of the agreed terms or order.

(c) When you go into court, either hand up the draft, or, in the absence of a written draft, inform the court of the terms which have been agreed between the parties 'subject to Your Honour/Your Lordship's approval'. It may be necessary even where you have a draft order, to take the judge through its terms. Invite the judge to make the order in the terms proposed.

(d) If agreement is reached between the parties away from the court, for example, in correspondence, remind your professional client to inform the court as soon as possible.

8.6 Problems

The following problems will be dealt with in the Professional Conduct Course. They are printed here in order to demonstrate the type of problem which may arise in practice concerning the dividing line between misleading one's opponent and bluff.

ETHICS OF NEGOTIATION

1 You are instructed to represent the defendant in proceedings for damages for breach of contract. On your arrival at court, your instructing solicitor informs you that one of your witnesses has just telephoned his office to say she is ill and cannot attend court to give evidence. Her testimony is vital to the defendant's case. You have no option but to seek an adjournment. At that moment, your opponent approaches you and asks if he can have a word with you. He indicates that he has witness difficulties and invites you to agree an adjournment of the hearing for two weeks. In so doing:

(a) Do you inform your opponent and the court of your witness difficulties?

(b) If not, do you make an application for the claimant to pay the defendant's costs thrown away by the adjournment?

2 You represent the mother of two children who is responding to an application by their father for defined contact. Your client instructs you that she is agreeable to the children seeing their father every Saturday between 9 a.m. and 6 p.m. In the course of discussions outside court:

(a) Do you put forward a proposal in these terms or in lesser terms (e.g., every second Saturday)?

(b) If in lesser terms, do you inform your opponent that this is the most to which your client is prepared to agree?

(c) If your opponent approaches you and proposes access every Saturday between the hours of 10 a.m. and 5 p.m., do you mention that your client is prepared to agree to more?

(d) Would your answers be any different if the issue involved was money rather than the future contact between two children and the parent with whom they do not reside?

3 You are instructed to represent the claimant in a personal injury case. You meet your opponent, by accident, while walking up Chancery Lane. She informs you that she has recently seen the defendant in conference and that he is prepared to negotiate provided your client will concede some element of contributory negligence. You have no instructions to negotiate. To what extent do you:

(a) Discuss the case with your opponent?

(b) Encourage your opponent to explain her client's position, e.g., tell you the figure he is prepared to offer or the percentage of contributory negligence which will be acceptable to him?

(c) Indicate your client's position?

NINE

PREPARATION AND STRATEGIC PLANNING

This chapter draws on all the concepts introduced in the earlier chapters to provide a comprehensive and practical guide to how to prepare for and plan to carry out a negotiation.

Even the seasoned practitioner who appears just to read the brief and then see how things go will have done a substantial amount of preparation and strategic planning in his or her head. For the student learning the skill full preparation and strategic planning is vital. It is only with a full analysis of the individual case that you can get the most out of conducting a negotiation, and then have a proper basis for judging whether you did cover everything, whether you did get the best possible outcome, and whether or not your strategy and tactics worked.

Planning for a negotiation is at least as important as it is for advocacy. A negotiation moves ahead very quickly and has much less structure than a court case, so it is almost inevitable that you will have to deal with unforeseen circumstances on the spur of the moment. You will have to deal with new information and new views of the case much more quickly than you will normally have to in court. Inspiration can certainly help, but too much reliance on inspiration is a rather arrogant approach to dealing with a client's problems.

Preparation involves essential case preparation tasks, such as identifying objectives and analysing the law and fact. Having completed your preparation, strategic planning is then required as regards strategy, concessions and tactics.

Proper planning is a crucial part of a professional approach that seeks to achieve the best possible result for the client, that seeks to leave no stone unturned, and that seeks to avoid you ever feeling that you could or should have done better.

Having stressed the importance of preparation and strategic planning, you must be careful that this does not lead you into taking too rigid a view of the case. You will almost certainly have to take new facts, figures and views on board as you go along, and your overall planning needs to be flexible enough to take this into account.

9.1 What should Preparation and Strategic Planning Cover?

Essentially you need to carry out a full practical analysis of the case as it stands, of the options available, and of the possible outcomes. This should as a minimum cover the following areas, most of which are covered in more detail later in this section. The CAP approach outlined in the *Case Preparation Manual* can be of great assistance.

Preparation

(a) A detailed analysis of what the client really wants.

(b) A full analysis of the facts of the case, including what can or cannot be proved and how the facts show strengths or weaknesses in the case for negotiation purposes.

(c) An analysis of relevant areas of law. Any negotiation between lawyers must take proper account of the relative legal positions of their clients, and legal strengths and weaknesses are important negotiating tools.

(d) As full an analysis as possible of what you envisage the case for the other side might be.

Strategic planning

(a) What is the most the client might possibly achieve, and what is the least that the client might accept.

(b) A basic analysis of how the negotiation might be conducted most effectively, looking, for example, at what strategy and tactics are most likely to prove effective in the particular case.

(c) A basic consideration of how the particular negotiation might be most effectively structured.

(d) An identification of possible concessions that might be sought from the other side, or offered by you if necessary.

Preparation might also generally include considering whether you can find an imaginative solution to the case, or find some options that are mutually beneficial to the parties.

Preparation should not consist of simply reading your brief and trying to identify the middle ground, or looking for a proposal that simply splits the difference between the two sides. Even if your approach is to be cooperative and problem solving your professional duty is still to achieve the best possible outcome you can for your client.

9.2 Analysis

9.2.1 PUTTING THE NEGOTIATION INTO CONTEXT

The first thing to ascertain from the brief is the stage in the case at which you are being asked to negotiate, and where the negotiation will take place. The different possibilities can have profound consequences for the form and content of the negotiation, and must therefore be taken into account in planning.

Sometimes you will need to advise, in an opinion or in a conference, whether the case is an appropriate one for negotiation and whether the case has reached the right stage for the negotiation to take place. This will depend on many factors, such as whether sufficient information is available and the costs implications of continuing with the claim. Sometimes you will simply be sent a brief instructing you to negotiate as the solicitor and client have decided that this is what they wish to happen.

It is quite common for solicitors to negotiate before any claim has been commenced in an attempt to avoid going to court. In such negotiations there will not be statements of case to define the issues (though correspondence might have started to do this), and it also means that quite different information is likely to be available to each side, as there will have been no exchange of formal witness statements and no disclosure of evidence. This has advantages because you do not have to consider procedural requirements, you can always threaten going to court as a tactic, and you will generally know that your opponent has not seen the evidence provided to you by your client. It also has disadvantages because it is most likely at this stage that the lawyers will have

PREPARATION AND STRATEGIC PLANNING

been told quite conflicting stories by their clients, and because your opponent is most likely to be able to surprise you with the evidence available to him or her.

If a negotiation takes place after an action has been commenced it is vital to place the negotiation into the context of the action. What has or has not been alleged? What procedural stages have taken place and what are yet to come? Could you make use of any appropriate procedural options, for example to get further evidence? Could you use a threat of using a particular procedural approach as a tactic? The advantages at this stage are that the issues will be clearer from the particulars of claim and defence and that more evidence from the other side may be available to you (e.g., if disclosure has taken place). The drawbacks at this stage are that your opponent will also know more about your case and that you will have to give more consideration to procedural matters.

A negotiation at the door of the court just before a hearing also has particular characteristics. If you are about to go into court to try the action there may be particular pressure to try to settle, as that is the last stage at which the parties will have control of the outcome rather than leaving it to the judge. The parties may also focus their minds at the last moment on trying to avoid the stress and costs of a full trial. At the door of the court there will be particular considerations such as trying to avoid keeping the judge waiting for too long, and recording any agreement reached in a consent order.

Whatever stage a case has reached, it is important to consider what procedural possibilities there are for getting information from, or putting pressure on, your opponent. It may well be useful to mention in the negotiation that you will recommend that your client takes specific procedural steps if necessary.

Whatever stage a case has reached it is also important to focus on how much time will be available for the negotiation. Preparation for a negotiation that can take place in the comfort of chambers and which can take as long as is necessary will not be identical to preparation for a negotiation that is likely to take place standing up in a public corridor and which will have at most 20 minutes before the case is called into court. Limited time may affect the best structure for the negotiation, and how much time you will wish to spend on developing particular points.

9.2.2 ANALYSING THE BRIEF

The first stage of preparation must be to carry out a general analysis, considering both what is there and what is not there. This analysis needs to be based partly on the stage the case has reached and what should or should not be available at that stage.

The initial analysis will, to some extent, cover most of the areas of preparation, but at this stage in a fairly superficial way. Initial analysis should concentrate on clarifying the context within which you are asked to negotiate, and identifying what further information or clarification is required before you can work on the brief fully. You might for example need:

- To clarify aspects of your instructions before you can plan how to approach the case in detail.

- To ask the solicitor to supply further documents that should be available at the stage the case has reached (remembering that you will not normally be able to get documents held by the other side prior to disclosure).

- To ask the solicitor to obtain further evidence that is likely to be crucial to a negotiation at this stage rather than just generally relevant to the case.

- To ask the solicitor to get some further information from the client.

NEGOTIATION

You will of course only be trying to seek things that are important so as not to build up costs unnecessarily. You might also consider whether it is appropriate to negotiate immediately, or whether there might be any purpose to be served in waiting until a slightly later stage in the case.

9.2.3 ACTING WITHIN INSTRUCTIONS

This is a vital matter of professional conduct. The barrister must act only within the instructions of the client. The point of negotiating is not to reach a general agreement that the barrister feels is fair, but to get as close as possible to the agreement that the client wants.

It is therefore very important to start by being very clear what your instructions are. It may be useful to write the instructions down so that you can bear them in mind while negotiating and so that you can check that any agreement you finally reach is within your client's instructions. Sometimes instructions will be very general, and the barrister is simply asked to get as close as possible to the client's objectives, with the agreement reached being subject to client approval. However, there will normally be at least some specific instructions in the case. For example, the client may specify the least that he or she is prepared to accept, or may make it clear that in no circumstance does he or she wish to go to court.

Points to look for in clarifying your instructions are:

- Specific parameters (that is the client will not accept a deal if he or she does not get a particular item or term).

- General parameters (the client specifies a maximum and or minimum limit for a particular issue but is otherwise flexible).

- Are you instructed to settle the whole case or just specific issues? This may, be relevant if you are negotiating at an interim stage.

9.2.4 IDENTIFYING AND PRIORITISING THE OBJECTIVES OF THE CLIENT

Objectives can overlap with instructions, but they are not the same thing. A client will often give some specific instructions about a case, but will indicate wider general objectives relating to what he or she hopes to achieve in overall terms. It is crucial to be clear about a client's objectives in a case at every stage of preparation and performance because the whole point of what you are doing is to get as close to the client's objectives as possible. If you do not achieve something reasonably close to what your client wants the client may not approve the agreement. Time and costs will be wasted if the client is not prepared to accept a provisional agreement reached between counsel.

In a narrow sense, the client's objectives are what he or she hopes to achieve as the outcome of the case. To give the best possible service to your client you should consider objectives widely to include in a practical sense all your client's needs and interests in the case.

You need to identify *all* your client's objectives. This might well include:

- Legal objectives. The client may wish to achieve a particular legal relationship or legal rights.

- Financial objectives. The client may wish to get payments for particular things. If several issues in the case relate to money also consider overall financial objectives so that all the figures put together leave your client in a reasonable position.

- Practical objectives. A client will often want to achieve a particular position.

- Personal objectives. The client may wish to achieve something quite personal, for example to settle a case quickly to avoid stress to a spouse. Such objectives may

PREPARATION AND STRATEGIC PLANNING

not be very logical and may not be shared by the barrister, but they must be respected.

- Hidden objectives. A client will often not state everything that he or she hopes to achieve with the case.

Each objective should be defined as specifically as possible. It is of little use to say that a client's objective in a particular case is to get damages. The lawyer defining the objectives in the case should spell out the figure for the maximum damages that the client might hope to achieve, as that is the objective.

Even in a simple case a client will often have several objectives. Once they have all been identified it will be necessary to prioritise them. The criterion for prioritisation is their importance to the client, and this may sometimes have particular implications for a whole case. You may need to give more attention in preparation and more time in the negotiating process to the issue that is most important to the client. Prioritisation may have some very individual features — it may be more important to a particular client to get an apology than to recover substantial damages.

Having identified and prioritised the objectives of the client they should be clearly and actively pursued throughout the negotiation.

9.2.5 IDENTIFYING THE LIKELY OBJECTIVES OF YOUR OPPONENT

A negotiation has two sides. To be successful you need not only to prepare your case fully but also to anticipate your opponent's case as far as you can. This includes not only thinking about what your opponent is likely to want, but also thinking about what information is likely to be available to your opponent and how the case is likely to be argued in legal and factual terms from your opponent's point of view. Even if your preparation and planning or your own case is brilliant it can easily be thrown off course if your opponent is able to surprise you. You can never totally avoid being surprised, but the better you become at seeing a case from the other side's viewpoint, the least likely this is to happen.

If you have sufficient imagination, try to decide how you would approach the case if you were briefed for the other side. What would you want? How would you go about getting it? It is quite likely that your client has given you a very one sided view of things, and while you have to accept what your client tells you is the truth in presenting the case, beware of assuming that your client has told you the whole truth in an objective way.

You should try to anticipate what the objectives of the other side are likely to be, as this can help you to decide what arguments are most likely to appeal to them. Also consider the extent to which the parties may have common interests, as well as the extent to which their interests differ. In looking at the law and facts from their point of view you will need to try to identify what they will see as their main strengths and weaknesses. Sometimes this will simply be the mirror image of your strengths and weaknesses, but this will not necessarily be the case.

Where relevant take into account anything you do know about your opponent personally. The Bar is not a large profession, and especially when you have been in practice for a few years or you work in a specialist area it is quite likely that you will know your opponent. Even if you do not know your opponent personally another member of Chambers may well do so, and some barristers do build up a reputation for the way they approach negotiations. Personal characteristics should not of course have any impact on the outcome of the case for the client, but knowing something of an opponent's likely approach to a case can properly be taken into account in planning strategy and tactics.

9.2.6 PUTTING THE CASE INTO CONTEXT

This is in essence the first stage of the CAP approach as outlined in the ***Case Preparation Manual***. From the starting point of reading the brief thoroughly and identifying objectives you should move on to putting the whole case in context.

NEGOTIATION

9.2.6.1 The general context of the case
You need to be clear about:

The stage the proceedings have reached
Has a claim been launched? If it has not there may be limited information and the issues in the case may not yet be clearly defined. No court procedures will be available unless and until a claim is launched. If a claim has been launched the issues should be defined by the particulars of claim and defence, some procedural stages may have taken place, and you may be able to make use of further court proceedings, e.g., for interim relief. Once a claim has been launched you need to decide what will happen to the claim in any negotiated settlement.

The circumstances in which you are asked to negotiate
Are you being asked to negotiate in Chambers with no set limit on time and with resources for research etc. available? Are you being asked to negotiate outside court in a limited time and with few resources available? If you are outside court you may have to work very quickly and with full awareness of the time factor, which requires a very high level of preparation to provide efficiency without superficiality.

What you are being asked to negotiate
Negotiations carried out by a lawyer are likely to centre on legal issues, but the client's overall objectives may be wide-ranging. Do make sure that your list of objectives is comprehensive, and detailed.

The practical context of the case
Many negotiations have a practical context, such as a continuing business relationship or allowing neighbours to go on living together in reasonable harmony. The negotiation should be fully rooted in the practical realities of such a situation.

9.2.6.2 The factual context of the case
The first stage of preparing to deal with the facts of a case is to become fully familiar with them. When you come to negotiate you will almost inevitably find that your opponent has been given a rather different version of the facts, and may indeed have factual information that is a total surprise to you, and or that totally contradicts what you have been told by your client (which is especially likely to be the case if the negotiation takes place before any case has been commenced). You need to be fully familiar with your version of the case to be able to put new or changed material into context quickly.

You also need to be fully familiar with the facts so that you are not constantly having to flick from one paper to another during the negotiation. Spending time checking information will give you less time to think about how the case is going and what approach you should be taking at that particular minute. Your opponent may well use the time you are checking information to take firmer control of progress in the case, or may use your temporary confusion to push you into a concession you should not be making.

However, becoming familiar with facts really is only a first stage. If you deal with facts in the negotiation only by putting your client's version of events to your opponent you will not be providing a proper professional level of service, and you will be more likely to reach deadlock or a vague compromise rather than work effectively. You need to work with the facts in a variety of ways as part of your preparation, so that you can go on to plan how to use those facts to your best advantage in the negotiation.

The types of task you often need to undertake with regard to the facts are:

Identify which factual information in your brief is likely to be available to the other side as well as to you and which is not
As an example, information in statements of case, letters between solicitors and documents which have clearly been disclosed will be available to both sides, whereas any information in a client's proof of evidence, or in documents which the client has simply given to his or her own solicitor may only be known to you. Where the same

PREPARATION AND STRATEGIC PLANNING

information is likely to be available to both sides you need to go on to decide to what extent it is likely to be disputed.

Where it is likely that the other side will not have information available to you, you will need to decide how to deal with that information most effectively. Do you want to disclose the information because it is useful to you? If so, when and how could you use it most effectively? Would it be proper and preferable not to disclose the information? Do you want to use the information tactically in any way, for example by seeking a concession in return for disclosing it?

Identify which facts the other side is likely to agree and which they may dispute
There will usually be little point in spending much time on facts that are agreed, unless these facts are of particular importance to you. Where facts are likely to be disputed you will need further work on how to deal with them.

Identify gaps in the information available to you
This is of course a basic fact management task, but it has particular implications for a negotiation. Where you are attempting to negotiate a case well before it is ready to come to court there will almost certainly be a lot of gaps in the information available to you. Your identification of the issues in the case and the client's objectives should help you to decide how important a gap in your information is. If the gap is important you will have to think through how the gap in information could be filled, by whom, with what time delay and at what cost, so that you can weigh up what to do.

An important way to fill gaps in your information is to ask your opponent. There are tactical as well as practical considerations here. Asking your opponent is relatively easy and cheap, and asking for detailed information on important issues can show how well prepared you are. On the other hand, your opponent is not bound to answer your questions, and you could appear weak if you ask questions about very basic matters.

Prepare to deal with any relevant figures fully
Most cases have money as one of the issues, even if the case does not primarily turn on money. It is very important to be fully prepared to deal with this aspect of the case as it is all too easy to get confused about figures in the heat of a negotiation. The starting point is clearly to do the basic arithmetic and add up accurately all your client's financial claims, but that is only the starting point.

In many cases your opponent will see the figures in a different light, and may, for example, wish to argue that loss of profit should be calculated on a different basis, or for a different period. If you are not ready for this you may easily be led into making concessions you do not wish to make, or you may at least get confused and waste time or lose any initiative you had. If it is clearly foreseeable that your opponent is likely to see the figures in a different way for the whole or part of the case you should be ready to deal with that alternative. Even if you do not foresee this, you should try to prepare your arithmetic in a flexible way so that you can quickly adapt it if necessary. Try to do the arithmetic in clear blocks in which you can reasonably easily alter one or two figures and make a new calculation rather than scribbling on the back of an envelope and coming up with a single figure that you cannot unpack in any way if it is challenged.

9.2.6.3 The legal context of the case

As a lawyer preparing to carry out a negotiation you will need to identify a legal framework for the case. This involves identifying all the areas of law relevant to the case. This should be relatively easy as a case approaches trial as the issues will have been defined, but it can be difficult if no claim has been commenced, unless the issues have been adequately defined in correspondence.

The point is not simply to spot the main legal areas involved but to consider all the possibilities that might be of use to you in securing the client's objectives, or which might be raised by your opponent. You might for example be able to secure a tactical advantage for your client by using an inventive legal argument that your opponent may not have foreseen and may not be prepared to counter. Equally you need to be aware

NEGOTIATION

that this could be used as a technique against you. It is also important to consider different types of law, as it may be relevant to argue law in any of the following ways:

(a) Substantive law. Clearly this is particularly important. If it is alleged that your client has broken a contract you may need to argue all sorts of points of contractual law such as what the terms of the contract were, what constitutes a breach, whether the contract was varied and so on.

(b) Remedies. This may be an important area of law in relation to achieving the client's objectives. For example, if damages is an issue it may well be relevant to argue about remoteness, foreseeability, mitigation etc.

(c) Procedure and practice. It may be relevant to argue about the use of a particular type of court procedure that has been used or might be used in the case. For example if one is negotiating a settlement of an interim application for an injunction it may be relevant to make points about whether the application has been properly made and about the test for getting interim injunctions.

An approach that may be used where it is appropriate (and one that is favoured by some student negotiators, though not always where it is appropriate!) is to take the view that you are not in court when you are negotiating, so the answer does not necessarily depend on strict law, and it might be better to try to find a practical solution rather than argue detailed points of law. Such an approach is justified if there are few legal issues in a case, where the client's objectives are primarily practical ones, or as a matter of tactics if your client's legal position is very weak. Such an approach is rarely justified if there are substantial legal issues in the case, and would almost certainly be wrong if your client's legal position is strong. In any event you should not risk failing to analyse the legal position properly — you always need to be prepared for the fact that your opponent may have strong legal arguments which you must be ready to meet.

9.2.7 ANALYSING THE ISSUES AND THE EVIDENCE

This is the second stage of the CAP approach as outlined in the *Case Preparation Manual*. The negotiation should focus on issues and on strengths and weaknesses with regard to those issues, and not on simple statements of fact and law. Appropriate structure and tactics will often relate closely to what is actually in issue, and the relative importance of different issues.

As with objectives, what matters is not to identify obvious issues in a simplistic way but to identify all issues, to identify them as precisely as possible, and to put the issues in order of importance for the case.

Potentially anything that needs to be resolved between the parties is an issue for a negotiation, though legal and factual issues will normally form the main meat of the case. Do bear in mind that the stage the case has reached or the client's instructions may place some limitations on the issues to be negotiated. If, for example, a negotiation takes place at an interim stage, the negotiation may be limited to the substance of the interim application and may or may not include the main case.

There are three main ingredients that need to be integrated in analysing the issues in the case:

- Identify the factual issues. You need to be clear about areas of factual disagreement, and how important each area of disagreement is for the case.

- Identify the legal issues. This should arise from applying the facts of the case to the legal framework you have identified.

- Analyse how the available evidence relates to the factual and legal issues in the case.

PREPARATION AND STRATEGIC PLANNING

When you put these ingredients together you should get a clear view of what the case really turns on, and of its strengths and weaknesses.

9.2.7.1 Analysing factual issues

For each factual issue that is in dispute you need to consider as a whole what you do know, what you do not know, what you can prove, what you cannot prove, and what your opponent may know. From this you can work out where your case is factually strong and where it is factually weak.

Make sure that you have a complete list of factual issues, that you have analysed all aspects of each issue in this way, and that you have formed a view of which factual issues are most and least important in pursuing your client's objectives. From this sort of analysis you can go on to prepare to present your case and to present your arguments as discussed below.

9.2.7.2 Analysing legal issues

Once you have a basic legal framework for the case, the most important thing is to establish the legal analysis of the case that most favours your client, in terms of substantive law, of the remedies sought, and of the procedural position. Where the law clearly favours your client you should be ready to press the advantage, and you should be very slow to concede on a point of legal strength on which you would be likely to succeed if you went to court. Where there may be some dispute as to what the law is or how the law applies to the case you have a legal issue that you need to investigate and prepare.

In addition to the areas of law which are clearly in issue on the face of the brief, other areas of law may be relevant and/or tactically useful in arguing the case. The brief will often not spell out that remoteness of damage or particular procedural details are in issue — it is part of the barrister's job to look for and develop such points where appropriate.

In preparing to deal with legal issues it can be tempting to do too much legal research, simply because you do not know how your opponent will argue the case. You need to take care with this, as if you have too many notes on legal points you will simply not be able to use them effectively in the negotiation. You need to develop your skill in identifying the legal issues in a case to the level where you can define fairly precisely what law is most likely to be argued in the case, so that you can research and prepare your arguments in a very focussed way.

There are various circumstances in which you may wish to bring a case authority into the negotiation — because it is very close on the facts, because it is particularly up-to-date, or because in tactical terms it may help to bolster an ingenious argument. Consider how to summarise your legal research for this purpose and whether to photocopy the head note or relevant part of the judgment to take with you and to offer to your opponent.

9.2.7.3 Dealing with evidence

Analyse the evidence relevant to each factual and legal issue. What evidence do you have? What evidence might you be able to get? What evidence is the other side likely to have? Although you do not have to formally prove anything in a negotiation, an allegation of fact is no more than an allegation, so where a fact is in dispute argument might well turn to who has, or is likely to be able to get, the best evidence. There are a lot of tactical possibilities here; you might use the evidence you have to try to force concessions, or you might challenge the other side to produce evidence on an important factual issue in dispute.

9.3 Planning the Presentation of the Case

This is the third stage of the CAP analysis (see the *Case Preparation Manual*), and it is as crucial for negotiation as it is for advocacy. You need to be very clear in advance about what your client's key objectives are and how you are most likely to achieve them. This includes:

NEGOTIATION

- how you will use legal and factual strengths to develop arguments to support your case (see **9.3.1**);

- what approach and structure are most likely to assist you in achieving your client's objectives (see **9.3.2** and **9.5**);

- precisely what you should or should not concede (so that you do not make mistakes on the spur of the moment) (see **9.4**);

- what approach is most likely to convince your opponent of the merits of your case (in terms of strategy and tactics) (see **9.5**);

- making sure that you have a comprehensive list of all the areas to be covered;

- being clear about how the negotiation should be concluded and made enforceable (see **Chapter 10**).

9.3.1 DEVELOPING ARGUMENTS

Having done the analysis you need to identify how you can use the strengths of your case and the weaknesses of your opponent's case to assist you in the negotiation. You also need to identify how your opponent might use the strengths of his or her case and the weaknesses of your case against you and how you can counter or minimise this. In short, you need to formulate and evaluate the arguments which you and your opponent may use in the negotiation and identify how best to use argument to assist you to reach a good settlement for your client.

Some people are nervous about 'arguing' their case in a negotiation for fear that it is 'confrontational', will only antagonise their opponent and work against reaching a settlement. Some of the literature on negotiation also treats argument as inherently 'positional' and to be avoided. However, this is to misunderstand the nature and purpose of argument in negotiation.

It is part of your professional job as a lawyer to test the case and ensure that you get the best possible settlement for your client. In the context of a court door negotiation, you will generally be testing the case against the likely judgment of the court which will be based on the merits of the case as argued in court. Persuasive argument is one of the essential tools of an advocate. It is also essential in negotiation.

You need to differentiate between the 'settlement standard' (i.e., what you assess is achievable for your client on the basis of the facts and law) and the 'arguments' used in the negotiation (the rational basis for the claims by either side for their desired outcomes). The arguments used can be based on the merits of the case, i.e., the facts and law (substantive, procedural or evidential) or on practical considerations (e.g., what your client can practically do or not do) and justify why you are seeking what you are seeking from your opponent or resisting what your opponent is seeking.

You need to identify the arguments which can be used by and against you in the negotiation on the various matters which are likely to be discussed. You need also to evaluate the arguments, consider the relative strengths of the various arguments, how strong or weak are they? For example, is the law quite firmly on your side but the evidence to support your version of events weak?

There are a variety of things you can do in advance to present factual issues as effectively as possible. One is to develop practical arguments (especially for areas where the evidence is not as strong as it might be!), for example you might argue that an accident must have happened in a particular way simply because that makes most sense.

Another possibility, though it will not apply to all cases, is to prepare how you will physically present factual argument to your opponent. You might for example prepare a schedule of figures in a format that suits you and hand a copy to your opponent, which may pull your opponent into arguing about the figures on the basis you have chosen, and which may even confuse him or her into making concessions. If you have evidence in your brief that you think the other side will not have and it is clearly favourable to you you might choose to photocopy it so that you can actually hand over the copy, which may have the effect of making your evidence seem more real, and which may lead to a concession. On the other hand, you may choose to provide your opponent with a swift glance at the evidence if you would prefer that he or she did not have a chance to analyse the evidence in full, or to take it away.

You need to decide how to present the legal issues to your opponent. This will normally be done quite differently and less formally than in court. As you are negotiating with another lawyer you can often present legal issues simply by using the appropriate terminology, for example 'your client is clearly in breach of an implied term' or 'I can't see that there is any problem with forseeability here'. Sometimes you will need more. If you are arguing on the basis of a statutory provision or a regulation you might consider taking a copy for your opponent as well as for yourself (this can be a good tactic if you have a particular legal strength — it can be more difficult for your opponent to refuse to argue a legal point if you have thoughtfully provided a piece of paper and it is placed in the opponent's hand!).

Finally you need to decide how your evaluation of the strengths and weaknesses will affect the order in which you deal with the issues. You might for example plan to start with an area where your case is factually or legally strong and to leave an area where you are factually or legally weak until your opponent has started making concessions.

9.3.2 PLANNING AN OVERALL APPROACH

Once you have developed arguments you should be in a position to plan an overall approach to the case. In most negotiations it is reasonably easy to spot where the client wants to be in terms of objectives and the real skill is in planning how to get there. Some lawyers always negotiate in the same way and build a reputation for it. This normally happens because they find from experience that a particular approach suits their personality and can generally be effective for them. For example, a negotiator might always start by setting out what he or she expects to achieve and then spend the negotiation justifying that position, making very few concessions.

With experience each individual will find what approach tends to work best for him or her, but it would be wrong to assume that any particular approach will always work best, or that the same sort of approach is appropriate for different types of case. When you are learning to negotiate it is worth taking an experimental approach to get a feel for what works for you in what types of case.

It is not possible to provide a simple recipe for planning an overall approach to a case, but there are some basic options. Are there a lot of issues of equal importance, or just a few issues that will dominate the negotiation? Is the case primarily about fact and evidence or primarily about law? On balance, does your client have most of the strengths in the case or most of the weaknesses? Are your strengths primarily legal or factual?

Your overall approach must also be based on the best outcome you could possibly get for your client on each issue (which your negotiation should clearly aim for), and the lowest outcome that your client would accept on each issue (which you should avoid getting near and never sink below). Your overall approach should also reflect the BATNA (the best alternative to a negotiated agreement) because you need to be clear about the precise point where your client would be better off not settling and when you should walk away. Never lose sight of what you think the outcome would be if you went to court. This must always be a yardstick — you should never settle for less than you think the client would get in court unless the costs or risks of going to court would be high.

Finally, you also need to evaluate your case in terms of what it is really worth. Once you have dealt with all the above areas you should be in a position to put your client's objectives into a realistic context. One of your client's objectives might be based on such a strong legal and factual foundation that there should on no account be any

NEGOTIATION

concession there. Another objective might be so fundamentally undermined by law and/or evidence that it will be very difficult to achieve. Do not get too pessimistic. Your opponent may not be as well prepared and you may be able to persuade him or her to concede more than you anticipate. Your opponent might have information that puts your case in a better light than you think. If your client has asked for something you should do your best to get it. However, your expectations, and eventually your outcome, should be related to a sound and detailed evaluation rather than a series of unconnected preparatory notes.

9.4 Planning Concessions

9.4.1 THE IMPORTANCE OF CONCESSIONS

Negotiation is about moving towards agreement. Each side must know what moves (concessions) they will offer to make and what moves (concessions) they will seek from their opponent.

Seeking and making concessions is one of the main ingredients of reaching settlement and will be one of the principal activities in a negotiation. It is therefore very important for you to plan what concessions you will seek from your opponent and what concessions you are prepared to offer.

At this point it is worth revising **4.7.4** in **Chapter 4** to remind yourself of the factors involved in planning how to make concessions and **5.2.1** in **Chapter 5** on how concession making/seeking can be used tactically.

9.4.2 CONCESSIONS DISTINGUISHED FROM CLARIFICATION; STATEMENTS OF LAW; ADMISSIONS OF FACT

In planning your concessions, it is important to distinguish between making and seeking concessions and:

- Clarifying what the issues are in the case and what facts are agreed and disputed. This is not conceding anything but merely assisting to clarify what is in dispute and what needs to be settled.

- Agreeing or seeking agreement on interpretation of disputed areas of law or evidence. Agreeing with your opponent's view on areas of law in dispute can unnecessarily weaken your case. Seeking his or her agreement with your interpretation can make him or her more entrenched. While it may be a tactic to try to get your opponent to agree on this, it is not essential to reaching settlement on the items on which your client is seeking to settle (unless your client is seeking a statement from the opponent that he or she accepts a particular interpretation of the law).

- Making/seeking admissions of disputed fact. Making admissions can unnecessarily weaken your case. Seeking admissions from the other side can decrease your opponent's willingness to bargain because he or she may well recognise that this weakens his or her position and case. As with agreement on the disputed legal issues, while it is useful to get admissions from your opponent, it is not essential to reaching settlement (unless your client is seeking a statement from the opponent that he or she accepts a particular view of the facts).

9.4.3 WHAT DO YOU WANT TO ACHIEVE — POSSIBLE OUTCOMES

Planning for the outcome is extremely important. You will only be able to negotiate very effectively if you are very clear about where you are trying to get to. As your professional duty is to achieve the most you can for your client, you should have clearly in mind a detailed list of the most that you could possibly achieve, even if you feel that you will not realistically get everything. Such a list will be of substantial use in helping you to develop as a negotiator — for each negotiation you carry out you should be able to identify each issue on which you did not get as much as your client wanted, so you can go on to try to identify how you could have got more.

PREPARATION AND STRATEGIC PLANNING

It is useful to consider the following prior to a negotiation:

(a) The best outcome you could possibly get for your client on each issue.

(b) The lowest outcome that your client would accept on each issue (that is, your walk-away point).

(c) If more than one possible outcome might be acceptable for the client, what are the main options and which would be best if you could achieve it?

(d) What is your BATNA (best alternative to a negotiated agreement)? (You need to be clear about the precise point where your client would be better off not settling because he or she would have a better alternative, such as going to another supplier.)

(e) What do you think the outcome would be if you went to court? (This may well be a yardstick. Generally you should never settle for less than you think the client would get in court unless the costs or risks of going to court would be high.)

(f) Look for variables that give most scope for negotiation. For example, your client may want a set price for a contract, but might be open as regards the timeframe for fulfilling the contract, or offering further contracts on terms favourable to the purchaser.

(g) Look for ways of 'expanding the cake'. There may be some possibilities that offer mutual advantages to the parties, or an advantage to your opponent at no great cost to your client. This sort of possibility may not be clear on the face of the brief, but may be very helpful in reaching an agreement (but be careful not to make imaginative offers that might cause problems for your client). For example, it might be reasonably cheap and easy for your client to offer free advertising to the other side.

(h) Consider possible objective standards for determining the outcome of the case. It may be that you could call on an objective assessment or an industry standard to decide the outcome on a particular issue.

9.4.4 CONCESSIONS BASED ON ANALYSIS AND EVALUATION

In **Chapter 3** we emphasised the need for proper preparation and planning of concessions and you may wish to revisit **3.6.3** on this.

You can only plan the concessions you will seek and make once you have thoroughly analysed the case, are clear what items are likely to be the subject of the negotiation and evaluated the arguments which can be used for and against you on each of those items.

In planning concessions (those which you will seek or make) you need to list the items which you wish to be the subject of the negotiation and which, from the papers, you think the opponent may wish to include in the negotiation. On each of the items:

- Consider what your client wishes to achieve. In addition, consider the priorities your client puts on the individual items. In particular, be very clear on each item that you *must* get for your client (e.g., the least acceptable amount of money, or the terms of employment which are crucial to him or her).

- Consider what your opponent might be seeking. Are there any shared interests, i.e., any items on which there is no dispute between the parties (e.g., they may wish to continue trading).

- Apply your analysis of the facts, law and evidence and identify the arguments which:

NEGOTIATION

— you can use to persuade your opponent to move towards your client's objectives, and

— your opponent may use to persuade you to move towards what he or she is seeking.

Do not assume that the arguments on all items will be the same. Although there may be a claim (e.g., for breach of contract), which underlies all the items being negotiated, different items may have different underlying legal arguments (e.g., a claim based on a dispute as to the terms and repudiation). The facts alleged on the different items will probably differ as may the evidence. Having considered each item you may find that, in fact, the same or very similar arguments can be used on several or all of the items. However, without having considered each item separately, you may have missed some good arguments which can be used for or against your client and which would have influenced your evaluation of the case and what concessions to seek or make.

- Consider what information you need or would like to have to fill any gaps or clarify any ambiguities before making or seeking a concession (e.g., is your view of what the opponent may be seeking accurate, precisely what facts are being alleged, what evidence does the other side have to support their allegations).

On the basis of your client's priorities and your evaluation of the merits of the case, you are now ready to plan what you will seek and offer, taking into account any potentially shared interests (see above) or compatible interests (i.e., where the parties are perhaps in less conflict than others, for example, where one party's real need is to have a certain sum of money but over a period of time and the other party's real need is to have time to pay).

9.4.5 PLANNING THE CONCESSIONS YOU MAKE AND SEEK

Having completed the analysis above, carefully consider each item of the case and what your client is *claiming* (e.g., in Particulars of Claim, affidavit, statement, etc.). Is this a (potentially) shared objective with the opponent and, if so, how do you introduce this into the negotiation. If not shared (or it is uncertain if it is shared and you may need to argue) consider the following:

- What is the *most* you can get for your client (given the arguments which can be used for and against).

- What *must* you get for your client (i.e., the point beyond which you cannot go, e.g., the least amount he or she will accept or terms of employment which are crucial).

- How can you use what the opponent appears to be seeking to achieve your client's objectives (e.g., where both parties wish to continue trading, can you propose that profits from future trade could offset a damages claim from the opponent).

- What offer can you make to your opponent which has the smallest impact on what your client is seeking and how are you going to present this (i.e., what argument/reasoning will you have to support the offer you are making to persuade your opponent to accept it or at least move towards you). What arguments might your opponent use against you?

- What staged concessions can you make (i.e., small fall back steps between your opening offer and the least you can accept) so as to increase the offer gradually (i.e., not move directly from your opening offer to your 'bottom line') to ensure that the settlement you reach reflects as far as possible what your client is seeking. What reasoning/argument can you use to try to persuade your opponent to accept what you are suggesting. What arguments might your opponent use against you?

PREPARATION AND STRATEGIC PLANNING

Provided you are clear what you are seeking on each item and what concessions you are prepared to make and how you can stage those for maximum effect, you can then use this planning in the negotiation either in discussing a particular item and what each party is prepared to do on it or in discussing proposals involving concessions on different items by the two parties.

9.5 Strategy, Structure and Tactics

As well as planning for where you are going, you need to plan how you will try to get there.

It is not possible to provide a simple recipe for planning an overall approach to a case, but the following factors will often be involved (**9.5.1** to **9.5.4**).

9.5.1 PLAN YOUR PROPOSED USE OF STRATEGY AND TACTICS

Strategy and tactics are dealt with in detail elsewhere (**Chapters 4** and **5**). For each case decide which strategy or approach is most appropriate. You should also plan in advance as many possible tactics as you can. Though it is quite possible to have inspiration in the middle of a negotiation you will all too frequently think of the best way to present a point only when it is too late. The best remedy for this is to try to think of as many tactics as possible in advance.

9.5.2 CONSIDER THE POSSIBLE ROLE OF OFFERS AND CONCESSIONS

One of the main ingredients in reaching a settlement will be the seeking and making of concessions. If dealing with offers and concessions will be one of the main things you are doing during a negotiation, it is clearly an important part of preparation to consider what concessions you will be seeking and what you might be prepared to make. Concessions are considered in detail elsewhere (see **Chapter 5** and **3.6.3.6**).

A concession can be defined as 'any modifiction of a negotiator's bargaining proposal, making it less advantageous to his or her client'. It is important to distinguish a concession from making an admission of fact or accepting a legal argument. As your primary task is to fulfil your client's objectives, you need to focus on the concessions you want from the other side. Try to identify what would need to be conceded to meet your client's objectives in full.

You will also need to identify in advance the concessions that you might make, so that you do not end up conceding more than you need to in the heat of the moment. Are there any concessions that you might make at no cost at all to your client? What size of concession would you make (given that you do not want to offer more than you have to)?

9.5.3 PLAN YOUR OPENING

The part of the negotiation that you are most likely to be able to predict in advance and to control is the opening (though this cannot be guaranteed if your opponent has very different ideas). It is very wasteful to throw this away by not planning a good opening for the case. You might choose to use the opening to make your client's objectives clear and/or to make your strengths and strategy clear. Alternatively, you might wish to open by asking your opponent to set out what he or she wants.

9.5.4 MAKE PROVISIONAL PLANS FOR OVERALL STRUCTURE

One of the main difficulties one can face in negotiation is maintaining an effective structure. This is dealt with in more detail in the next chapter. It is not easy to implement a full planned structure for a negotiation because the two sides will often have different views on what structure is most likely to be effective, and unpredictable turns and problems in the negotiation are virtually inevitable. However, this does not mean that it is pointless to plan structure in advance, it simply means that your plans need to be flexible. If you do not make some provisional plans for structure you may find it difficult to put across your strengths in the most powerful way, you will probably find it more difficult to make effective use of time, and it is more likely that you will get bogged down in something and find it difficult to move on.

A provisional plan for structure might consider the following questions. Should you try to deal with issues in order of importance to your client, in order of the strength of your case, or in some other order? (For tactical reasons you might alternatively prefer to start with unimportant issues and save your main points for later.) Do you want to try to persuade your opponent to make major concessions as quickly as possible, or do you want to build up slowly? In what order might you make the concessions that you are prepared to make?

9.6 Your Written Plan

An experienced practitioner will almost certainly not use a full written plan, but most practitioners will still plan the same elements for a negotiation, and will have strengths and weaknesses, possible concessions, etc. quite clear in their head even if they do not write them down. Many practitioners will continue to do some preparation in writing, even if it is limited to chronologies and notes on relevant law.

It is strongly recommended that while you are learning the skill of negotiation you do prepare a written plan for each case. This will help you to check that you have thought through everything that you should in advance, and should help you to evaluate your performance afterwards. A good written plan should have the following characteristics:

- Be no more than a few sides long.

- Be clearly based on the client's objectives and how to achieve them.

- Be clearly focused on what is important in the case.

- Be practical and easy to use (in note form with sub-headings and underlinings).

- Be capable of being useful during the negotiation (for example having checklists of things to be covered).

There is little practical purpose in a written plan that has long full paragraphs like an opinion or an essay, that simply states things that are obvious or very superficial, or that is difficult to use to find relevant points.

It is not possible to prescribe a set format or content for a written plan that will be suitable for any case. The plan must depend partly on the case in question. For example it may be useful to have a chronology of events if the facts are complex, but pointless if the facts are straightforward. You may need quite a long section on law if there are several legal issues, but quite a short section if there are few legal issues.

The elements which might be useful in a written plan are:

A specific and prioritised list of the client's objectives
You need to keep all the client's objectives in mind while you are negotiating to be sure that all are covered and that you get as close as you can to achieving what the client wants. The checklist needs to be reasonably detailed and prioritised to be of real use.

A prioritised list of your opponent's likely objectives
Try to predict what your opponent will want, again looking at detail and prioritisation. This should prove particularly useful in persuading your opponent to accept a particular course and in negotiating over concessions.

PREPARATION AND STRATEGIC PLANNING

A summary of issues and arguments
You may choose to include basic chronologies and summaries of relevant law, but what is most useful is an in-depth analysis of issues that will help you to form arguments to put to your opponent.

Such an analysis should include, in relation to each issue to be negotiated:

- Legal strengths in substantive and procedural law.
- Legal weaknesses and how they might be addressed.
- Facts that are in dispute, and how to deal with such a dispute.
- Factual gaps and ambiguities that you may need to question your opponent about.
- Evidential strengths and weaknesses in areas of factual dispute.
- All relevant arithmetic.

A plan for possible concessions
This must be based on a sound grasp of your 'bargaining range' (i.e., the most that you think you can achieve for the client and the client's bottom line), and of what you think the other side may want. You must think through in advance the areas in which concessions might be made and how they could be staged or you will almost certainly make unnecessary or too generous concessions on the spur of the moment.

Notes on proposed strategy and tactics
List the possible changes in strategy and the tactics that you have identified as being of potential use in the case. On the spur of the moment it is quite easy to forget a clever approach that had occurred to you in advance. Strategy and tactics could usefully focus on how to make the most on your strong points and how to mask your weaker points, while still acting ethically.

Notes on proposed structure
There is limited point in planning structure in detail, but notes on structure can provide a useful reminder if you are getting bogged down or going off course in a negotiation. If you have limited time for a negotiation, for example because you know that you will be called into court in half an hour, it is especially important to plan in advance how to use time to best effect and concentrate on the key issues.

9.7 Sample Written Plans

Read the *Megadell* case before you read these two sample plans (see **Chapter 14**).

It would also be useful to try to prepare a plan for that case yourself before you read the suggested plans. The first plan, for the defendant, is very detailed and shows the level of analysis and understanding of the law needed to be fully prepared in a negotiation. It is larger and more detailed than you could realistically prepare in a couple of hours. The second plan, for the claimant, is much shorter and demonstrates 'jogger notes' to assist you to remember more detailed points. Both plans are just suggestions and neither is the only way to prepare a plan.

NEGOTIATION

9.7.1 NEGOTIATION PLAN FOR THE DEFENDANT

MEGADELL FOODS LTD v ANGUS WARLEY (t/a CHOC FOLIE)
(Plan for ANGUS WARLEY)

THE ITEMS TO BE NEGOTIATED

GETTING JUDGMENT SET ASIDE

Proceedings	issued	20.12.99
	served	???
Judgment	entered	16.2.00 (regular?)
	served	25.2.00 (regular?)
Applied to set aside		6.3.00
Hearing		13.3.00

FOR D: primary consideration whether defence on merits (yes — see below); why D allow entered (car crash 17.12.99; in hospital until 24.2.00 applied to set aside 6.3.00).

FOR C: see final demand 18.11.99 > 14 days or sue (BUT: serious? nothing further from C; when was summons served?)

SO: likely judgment set aside but D pay costs of today (ours are £175 — what are C's?).

CLAIMANT'S CLAIM

1. **Instalment One** (500 Kilo delivered 11.9.99; price £1,260)

FOR D (NO LEGAL ARGUMENTS, MAY HAVE TACTICAL ONES)

- If judgment set aside (likely) C have to wait for money.
- Query profit margin (32.5% profit margin — cost per Kilo to D £2.52 see P of C para. 7 for loss of profit by C).

FOR C (STRONG CASE; ALL LEGAL ARGUMENTS ON C'S SIDE)

- D accepted and used.
- D says 'satisfactory' (para. 7 ws) (para. 5 statement 'extremely impressed').
- Term pay 30 days of invoice (para. 3iii of P of C and para. 3 of ws in which D accepts contract and terms).
- D states invoice delivered with goods (para. 5 statement).
- Monies due under contract (whatever dispute on implied/express terms or repudiation — see below).

SO: DIFFICULT FOR D TO RESIST PAYING THIS.

2. **Interest on Instalment One** (per contract 11.75%) (from 11.10.99; daily rate 44p) (68 days to issue = £29.92).

PRO D (SOME WEAK ARGUMENTS POSSIBLE TO COUNTER)

- If judgment set aside (likely) C have to wait for money (but interest continue to run).
- Query high rate of interest 11.75% — well above bank rate to cover potential loss by C of not being paid (i.e., if have to borrow money). NO LEGAL BASIS FOR THIS AS AGREED RATE.

PRO C

- Contract term (P of C para. 3iii) D agree terms (para. 3 ws) include rate of interest (D statement agree invoice delivered with goods on 11.9.99).

SO: DIFFICULT FOR D TO RESIST PAYING THIS.

PREPARATION AND STRATEGIC PLANNING

3. Instalment Two (500 Kilo delivered 9.10.99; price £1,260)

PRO D (NON-ACCEPTANCE OF AT LEAST 1/2 AS OF POOR QUALITY)

- C liable until D accept (para. 3 ws) D not accept until chance to inspect s. 35(2), SOGA 1989; D right to reject s. 14(2) if not satisfactory quality; D right to reject part s. 35A, SOGA 1989.

- Poor quality; 1/2 whitish residue on surface; not usable; try to contact Mr H by phone — messages left mobile and office — (para. 4 ws) (WHY NOT USE? THE LOOK AND/OR TASTE — see para. 7 statement that 'mouldy' — argue for show so both look and taste are important).

- Representation by Mr H re quality and immediate action by company (para. 3 ws; para. 3 statement) and D reliance on statements (para. 4 statement).

- Unpacked same day and attempts to contact Mr H 10-15; Mr H 'first port of call'; messages left (para. 5 statement — BUT WHAT SAID? WHO LEFT WITH? RECORD KEPT? OTHER SIDE HAVE RECORD?).

- Appears to have used good part of chocolate (query exactly how much bad — says 'approximately half' in para. 4 ws and 'about half' in para. 5 statement (assume must pay for this — if half = £630).

- Still has the 'mouldy' chocolate; No duty to return to C, s. 36, SOGA; C no attempt to inspect to date (para. 7 statement — no request); WHAT C SAY ON THIS? WOULD CHOC HAVE DETERIORATED SINCE? (5 MONTHS) WHAT PRECISELY WRONG WITH IT?

PRO C (little from papers but may argue)

- D did accept — no notice or contact until 27.10.99 (para. 7 statement). Delay too great for period of inspection (it's perishable goods).

- D no evidence that chocolate faulty — not offer on 27.10.99 to allow to inspect; not state what was wrong (see para. 7 statement — no details of conversation and D puts phone down).

- Inspection of chocolate now not suffice (deteriorated).

- Cannot use chocolate now as too old?

TRY TO FIND OUT: C'S KNOWLEDGE OF CALLS MADE PRIOR TO 27.10.99; MR H'S RECORD AT CO (QUERY SLOPPY); CO RECORD KEEPING SYSTEM (NOT SUFFICIENT); WHAT SAID IN CONVERSATION ON 27.10.99 - BUT NOT REVEAL OUT LACK OF KNOWLEDGE.

CONCESSIONS

Pay for some of chocolate £504 (40% not quite half) > £567 (45%) > £630 (50%) (provided C not claim interest and pay our losses on Choc weekend and shops (see below).

NEGOTIATION

4. **Interest on Instalment Two** (per contract 11.75%; 44p per day from 8.11.99; to issue 20.12.99 = 40 days = £17.60)

- See above for arguments on this with qualification that interest only due on that portion which reflect satisfactory goods (30% = 15p per day; 50% = 22p per day).

- Query argue D's illness intervene in interest running (out of action from Oct (marginally) or *Dec 17* (completely) until *Feb 24* (2 months)).

CONCESSIONS

Resist paying interest (goodwill gesture by C) but if necessary offer as per payment on chocolate with reductions in time starting with 2 months (1/2 amount = 22p per day).

4. **Lost Benefit of Remainder of Contract** (5,000 Kilo @ 82p per Kilo = £4,100)

PRO D (NOT STRONG ARGUMENTS ON WHO REPUDIATED BUT STRONGER ARGUMENT ON LOSS BY C)

- Repudiation by C by faulty 2nd instalment; breach of condition of satisfactory quality s. 14(2), SOGA; only 2nd intalment in 12 instalment contract; reaction by C (Mr RB para. 5 ws and para. 7 statement) (law: s. 31, SOGA; ratio fault to contract and probability of future breach (Maple Flock); also further in to contract > less likely = repudiation (*Cornwall* v *Henson*).

- C just not deliver further instalments. C's decision NOT D's decision so D not liable for C's decisions (weak).

- C prove loss: s. 50(3) *prima facie* measure; no loss if resold to another; no loss if sell now to us (BUT can argue specialist goods etc. — see below) BUT C must still PROVE his loss.

PRO C (STRONGER ARGUMENTS ON REPUDIATION — COMBINATION OF T/C AND FAILURE TO PAY; NOT SO STRONG ON LOSS)

- P of C para. 6 fail/refuse to pay sums due = repudiation (see above para. 7 statement); use Maple Flock etc. — reverse of D's argument above — ratio — only 1 instalment; other perfectly good; NOT suffice for repudiation.

- P of C para. 6 D terminate contract: in phone call 27.10.99; para. 5 ws 'told Mr B that if not re-supplied not wish to be suplied further'; para. 7 statement — exploded, told not get a penny/not pay for anything else delivered.

- Section 50 measure: no available market (specialist goods); lost sale (*Centrax* case). Ditto argument if sell to us.

CHECK: IF STILL HAS CHOCOLATE; WHAT STATE; HOW MUCH; WHAT EFFORTS TO SELL; WHAT IS MARKET (BELGIUM CHOCS BIG IN UK); HOW ARGUE LOST VOLUME (IF DOES); HOW CALCULATE PROFIT — i.e., WHAT DOES HE PAY THE £1.70 COSTS FOR; WHAT PROOF OF PROFIT; ON WHAT TERMS SELL TO US?

PREPARATION AND STRATEGIC PLANNING

CONCESSIONS

- Offer to purchase chocolate remaining; 500 Kilo per month at contract price PROVIDED assurance by MD that no problems/prompt action AND chocolate still good — test: D's opinion? independent expert? (10 months left at £2.52 per kilo), Argue: C then no loss.

- If no chocolate remaining: offer buy more from C (as above and future business wipe out loss by C — WEAK).

- If any purchase of chocolate by D accepted by C: resist paying any further money, if essential offer small % of loss claimed (notional sum 'goodwill' — start £200 — work up to £1,000) ALTERNATIVELY? offer increased price e.g., £20 per month (i.e., 4p per kilo) to 6p per kilo (£30 per month = £300 for whole contract) (query this get client into higher prices faster).

- If no purchase of chocolate (i.e., not wish to trade further) — start £200 (C produce problem) — work up to £2,000 — i.e., 1/2 on basis that split blame).

6. **Interest on Lost Benefit** (s. 69, CCA — %)

PRO D

- Only get on money judgment for damages.

- Unlikely to get all claimed (see above for arguments).

- Run from loss — from what day? (10–15 delivery — when was profit lost?)

- Calculate from 15th each month: Nov = 117 days; Dec = 87 days; Jan = 61 days; Feb = 25 days).

- Complicated to calculate for very little money.

- At most C should only get part as also liable.

PRO C

- Will get on money judgment for damages; so a right to it.

- Small amount but worth pursuing.

CONCESSIONS

- Resist paying (C goodwill gesture?).

NEGOTIATION

DEFENDANT'S CLAIM

1. **Loss of Profit on Chocoganza Weekend** (£2,000 loss of profit because only paid 2/3 contract price as goods not as ornate as ordered)

FOR D (OVERLAP WITH INSTALMENT TWO ON NON-ACCEPTANCE AND NOTIFICATION OF BREACH WHICH ARE STRONG. LESS STRONG: CONTENT OF 27.10.99 T/C AND SHOWING THAT CONTEMPLATION TEST SATISFIED TO CLAIM LOSS OF PROFIT)

- Loss flows from breach by C (delivery of faulty goods on 9.10.99).

- Can claim loss of profit where in contemplation when contract made: C did have notice on making contract (para. 3 statement) and on breach (phone call; fax etc.).

- Took all reasonable steps to mitigate loss (reasonable attempts to get supply from C, phone call 27.10.99 only three days before event and D offer clearly not suffice particularly in light of fax (investigate on Nov delivery — i.e., AFTER event) then purchase from usual suppliers.

- As claim is for loss of profit and not related to price of substitute goods: not double recovery if get this and reduced price for 2nd instalment.

FOR C

- Consequential loss: s. 53(2), SOGA this loss of profit claim not in contemplation of parties; what said to Mr H not suffice — not liable.

- Notice on fax and phone call end of Oct not suffice. (Content of phone call?)

- D not give C opportunity to rectify (t/c 27.10.99).

NOTE: DOES C HAVE RECORDS OF DISCUSSIONS BEFORE CONTRACT AND PHONE CALL AFTER DELIVERY? PROBE WITHOUT GIVING AWAY WHAT LITTLE WE HAVE

CONCESSIONS

- Reduce claim in small steps e.g., £200.

- Aim for 1/2 of amount (on basis that equal responsibility for loss).

- Overall weak arguments so final amount dependent on overall agreement and what C accepts on his claims.

2. **Loss of Profit on Shops** (£1,500 in October compared to Oct 98)

FOR D (STRONG: OVERLAP WITH INSTALMENT TWO ON NON-ACCEPTANCE AND NOTIFICATION OF BREACH; CONTEMPLATION TEST SATISFIED TO CLAIM LOSS OF PROFIT. LESS STRONG: CONTENT OF 27.10.99 PHONE CALL)

- See above INSTALMENT TWO ARGUMENTS RE NON-ACCEPTANCE AND NOTIFICATION AND REPRESENTATIONS BY MR H.

- Loss flows naturally from breach by C; s. 53(2), SOGA (delivery of faulty goods on 9.10.99 and failure to replace once notified that faulty).

- Can prove loss of profit by comparing accounts for the two months.

- Did all necessary to mitigate loss (see above — but delay in obtaining goods and the quality was not as good).

PREPARATION AND STRATEGIC PLANNING

FOR C

- No opportunity to inspect/see if breach.
- No opportunity to rectify IF was breach (argue based on phone call of 27.10.99 — see para. 7 statement).

CONCESSIONS

See above (but stronger on remoteness issue so seek more from C) reduce loss in small steps (amount dependent on overall settlement and what C agrees on his claim).

3. Loss of Future Customers?

(See para. 5 aff — 'long-term' loss.)

A weak argument; little to support in papers — use as a possible concession.

COSTS

D's to date £250 and £175 for today = £425.

C's to date ? and ? for today.

For C to prove good service of summons (presumably via court); C's action precipitous given C knew of complaint re 2nd delivery.

Usual order: for D pay to have set aside but in hospital so query ordered.

Resist any request to pay C's costs/probably can't argue that C pay D's costs.

OVERALL ASSESSMENT

In best interests of both to continue trading.

On balance C's claims are stronger (particularly 1st and at least 1/2 of 2nd instalment); weaker arguments on loss of profit; D's claims are not strong > D probably pay C money and NOT vice versa; SO argue large payments from past disagreement may jeopardise future trading.

STRUCTURE OF NEGOTIATION

Link C's claim for 1st and 2nd instalment (and interest) with our claim for loss on Chocoganza weekend and shops.

Link C's claim for loss of profits to future trading.

Argue costs at end — in line with not jeopardising future relationships.

NEGOTIATION

RELEVANT LAW

SETTING ASIDE JUDGMENT — CPR, r. 13.2

- Apply by notice of application and witness statement.

- If wrongly entered: varied as of right.

- Otherwise: only if D has real prospect of successfully defending the claim/some other reason.

    - court also take into account D's explanation for allowing judgment to be entered/delay in applying to have set aside.

- May set aside on terms: D pay sum into court.

- Costs incurred usually awarded against D.

CONTRACT FOR SUPPLY OF GOODS

Sale of Goods Act 1979 and Sale of Goods and Supply of Services Act 1994 (contracts MADE after 3.1.95). NOTE: no exclusion clause pleaded. Non-consumer contract.

Instalment contract (test: where instalments delivered and paid for separately > severable (instalment) contract not entire contract). For delivery and acceptance each instalment regarded as a separate contract which can be sued on (*Jackson* v *Rotax Cycle Co.* [1910] 2 KB 937, CA).

1. Failure to pay Breach? Seller sue for Price

- Section 27 B duty to accept/pay.

- B 'accept'. Section 35 if intimate to S; B does act inconsistent with S ownership; B retain without intimate to S rejected; not deemed until B reasonable opportunity to examine goods.

- B right to reject.

    - failure to comply with implied terms (breach of condition)

    - implied condition include s. 14(2) of satisfactory quality includes: s. 14(2A) meet standard reasonable person regard as such taking account of description, price, relevant circumstances; s. 14(2B) state and condition (including fitness for purpose, appearance and finish, freedom from minor defects, safety, durability)

    - s. 15A if breach so slight to be unreasonable to reject > breach of warranty (not condition but burden on S to show)

    - can be lost by deemed acceptance (see above s. 35) > breach of condition > breach of warranty

- — if reject, B no duty to return (s. 36) but must make available for collection at place of examination

  - — lawful reject > property revest in S; B sue for non-delivery BUT no lien.

- S sue for price:

  - — s. 49(1) if property passed to B and B wrongfully rejected or refused to pay

  - — s. 49(2) even if property not passed to B: where date fixed for payment irrespective of delivery and wrongful failure to pay

  - — property pass (specific v unascertained goods, s. 61 — here unascertained become ascertained when separated and irrevocably attached to contract; s. 18, Rule 5: property pass when unconditionally appropriated to contract (by S with consent of B or by B with assent of S).

2. Set Off?

- Section 53(1)(a) B may set off counterclaim for breach of warrants or where B elects/compelled to treat breach of condition as breach of warranty against S claim for price.

- Breach of warranty: normal *Hadley* v *Baxendale* measures (1. directly and naturally resulting and 2. unusual in contemplation of parties). (Section 53(2).)

- Section 51 (damage for non-delivery) goods rejected where there is a market: *prima facie* measure difference between contract and market price.

- Loss of profit recoverable where at time of contract S knew/ought to have known the use to which goods were to be put and that B intended to produce a profit and breach likely to reduce/extinguish that profit.

- Damages may also be available for loss of repeat orders from customers (*GKN Centrax Gears Ltd* v *Matbro Ltd* [1976] 2 Lloyd's Rep 555).

3. Repudiation?

SALE OF GOODS

Section 31(2): instalment contract for sale of goods, where S make defective delivery/B fail to pay for 1/more instalments > terms of contract and circumstances of case > whether breach = repudiation of whole contract or severable breach of one instalment.

- Failure to perform must go to root of contract (*Mersey Steel and Iron Co.* v *Naylor Benson & Co.* (1884) 9 CA 434.

- Main tests are

  - — the quantitative ratio of the faulty instalment to the whole contract

  - — the degree of probability that breach will be repeated (*Maple Flock Co. Ltd* v *Universal Furniture Products (Wembley) Ltd* [1934] 1 KB 148, CA).

- The further the parties have proceeded with performance of the contract the less likely it is that one party entitled to claim contract repudiated by one breach (*Cornwall* v *Henson* [1900] 2 Ch 298).

GENERAL CONTRACT

By renunciation: where one party evinces unconditional intention not to perform or be bound by contract or essential term (*Freeth* v *Burr* (1874) LR 9 CP 208).

Anticipatory breach: where party renounces before time to perform > innocent party may elect to accept repudiation and sue OR wait for time for performance.

4. Seller's Claim for Damages

Section 50 B refuse to accept/pay > S sue for damages for non-acceptance

- Section 50(2) measure is estimated loss directly and naturally resulting in the ordinary course of events from B's breach.

- Section 50(3) available market > difference between contract and market price at time ought to have been accepted (*prima facie* rule which may be displaced if unjust/inappropriate (*WL Thompson Ltd v Robinson (Gunmakers) Ltd* [1955] Ch 177). (What is 'available' reasonable for S to sell in?)

- Section 50(3) no available market (e.g., unique, manufactured to B specification) > usually contract price and price at which sold (*Gebruder Metelmann GmbH & Co. KG v NBR (London) Ltd* [1984] 1 Lloyd's Rep 614).

- 'Lost volume' S — recover loss of profit (e.g., B throw back onto S's hands good of same type as in stock, difficulty shifting because supply exceed demand) > prevented opportunity to sell to same B the S's remaining stock. Profit on 2nd sale recoverable, presumed to be same as profit on sale to B (*WL Thompson* above).

PREPARATION AND STRATEGIC PLANNING

9.7.2   **NEGOTIATION PLAN FOR THE CLAIMANT**

MEGADELL FOODS LTD v ANGUS WARLEY

NEGOTIATION PLAN FOR THE CLAIMANT

Client's objectives (taking into account opponent's claims)

- Get paid for the chocolate actually supplied:

  —For first installment £1,260 plus contractual interest.

  —For second installment as much as possible of £1,260 plus contractual interest.

- Get as much as possible of the lost profit of £4,100 (plus court awarded interest) on the remainder of the contract.

- Resist counterclaim from the defendant for loss of profit (£2,000 for Chocoganza weekend and £1,500 for loss of profit on shops).

- Get costs of £400 and £150 paid by the defendant (as his delays led to the need for court action) and resist any claim for payment of his costs.

- Get a long-term commercial relationship with the defendant, provided agreement on above matters is satisfactory (but only if the terms for this relationship are clear, and are no less favourable than the claimant's standard terms, and not at the expense of losing too much profit on the current contract).

Chronology

July 99	Choc Folie introduced to Megadell
16 July 99	Written agreement
Aug 99	Bulk delivery to Megadell
11 Sept 99	First delivery
9 Oct 99	Second delivery
9–15 Oct 99	Messages left at Megadell
20 Oct 99	Chocolate running low
25 Oct 99	Fax
27 Oct 99	Telephone call terminate
28 Oct 99	Get replacement chocolate
30 Oct–31 Oct 99	Chocoganza weekend
4 Nov 99	Could deliver new chocolate
18 Nov 99	Letter before action
17 Dec 99	Defendant in car crash
20 Dec 99	Issue
Jan 00	Bulk delivery to Megadell
16 Feb 00	Judgment
24 Feb 00	Defendant out of hospital
25 Feb 00	Judgment served on defendant
2 Mar 00	Defendant makes witness statement
6 Mar 00	Apply to set aside

NEGOTIATION

Analysis of strengths and weaknesses

Factual and evidential strengths

- Defendant seems to be bad at running his business. Warned of legal action in November but seems to have done nothing. Bad at expressing his problems on the telephone. Silly threat to throw the chocolate away. Probably will not make a good witness on his own behalf.

- The claimant has generally acted reasonably. There is no record of phone calls to the company, and they have carried out their normal procedures for delivery and seeking payment. Rupert Bryson could probably be a good witness on this.

- The defendant has paid nothing, while accepting that at least one and a half deliveries were OK.

- The defendant's actions support the allegation that he repudiated the contract.

Factual and evidential weaknesses

- It is admitted that there was no proper customer care in the defendant's area from September (when Mr Haalen left) to the end of November.

- Problems with getting full evidence to support claimant's case. What was said about quality? Query if we could find Mr Haalen to act as a witness to what was agreed, whether there were messages on his mobile etc., and query if he would be a good witness.

Factual and evidential gaps

- What backup systems did the claimant company have for customer care in the claimant's area? Could offer to find this out from client.

- What has happened to the chocolate delivered to the claimant. Has it all been used? Was any thrown away? If not, is it available for inspection now? Ask opponent about this.

- What has happened to the chocolate not delivered to the claimant? It seems the rest of the first consignment was sold on elsewhere, but we still have the second consignment in store.

- Possible factual problem with the figures. Sometimes the papers mention gross figures for cost of consignments and sometimes the papers simply talk of loss of profits. Important not to get confused in discussion.

Legal strengths (could include more detail on relevant law)

- We have judgment in default, and we can argue that we will stand by that if necessary.

- We have a clear contract for sale of goods.

- The defendant is clearly in breach of contract for failing to pay for goods delivered.

- Burden on defendant to prove breach by claimant on delivery — query what evidence he has if disposed of chocolate/given delay.

- Facts support claimant's version, i.e., that defendant repudiated contract by his statements/behaviour.

- Defendant's loss of profit probbly not foreseeable by the claimant.

Legal weaknesses (could include more detail on relevant law)

- Will not necessarily be able to defend the default judgment if the defendant has been ill.

- The claimant may be in breach of an implied term in the second delivery that the goods are of satisfactory quality. Breach may have entitled the defendant to reject the goods.

- The defendant may have rejected rather than accepted the second delivery.

- Severable contract: breach of the second instalment may suffice to warrant the defendant treating the contract as ended by the claimant.

- Do we have a right to try to remedy any breach of the implied term that the goods would be satisfactory through re-delivery?

Issues to be negotiated

1. *First installment (£1,260 and interest)*

Law: Clear breach of contract.
Fact: Chocolate delivered and used.

No concessions on this.

Interest calculation 68 days × 0.44p = £29.92.

2. *Second installment (£1,260 and interest)*

Law: The defendant is also in breach of contract in failing to pay for this delivery. Argue defendant accepted the goods. Judgment in default given.

Facts: May be some problems over acceptance and inspection of alleged defect.

Part of the second delivery might be defective.

Concessions to offer if necessary. We would like an expert to examine it if possible. At least get payment for half.

Interest calculation 40 days × 0.44p = £17.60.

3. *Our loss of profit (£4,100 and interest)*

Law: The defendant did improperly purport to repudiate the contract, and should therefore pay damages for the claimant's loss of profit. Maintain the position that there is no justification for repudiation just because part of one delivery might have been defective.

Do not rush to concede as our case is maintainable. Do not just cancel out with his loss of profits as the figure is smaller and his case less strong. However, if we did manage to sell the chocolate on, to the defendant or elsewhere, some concession might be made (but be slow to concede all as have lost some business).

NEGOTIATION

4. Opponent's claims for loss of profits (£2,000 and £1,500)

Law and fact: Argue as strongly as possible that these losses are not within the contemplation of the parties and/or not foreseeable, though there are some doubts on this.

May concede some payment as a goodwill gesture.

5. Our costs (£550)

Mr Warley has not acted as a reasonably efficient businessman and should therefore pay the claimant's costs, especially if concessions are made on the majority of payments claimed.

Difficult to see that any concession should be made on claiming our costs or paying theirs unless terms are otherwise very good.

Minimum acceptable: costs of judgment in default/set aside application as defendant's fault.

6. Future commercial relationship

Needs sorting out to ensure clear terms and not less favourable than standard terms. Could leave detail to parties, to be recorded in a new written contract.

Possible structure/strategy/tactics

Start strong by making it clear that claimant will stand by the default judgment, and does wish to recover its full loss of profit on the contract. Maintain this approach while dealing with the main issues, as the claimant seems to be in the stronger legal and factual position. But indicate will be cooperative about future relationship later.

Establish that should be paid for first, and at least part of second, installment early on.

Try to discuss our loss of profit before the defendant gets on to his.

Agree to have a future commercial relationship on standard terms, but only if all else is agreed satisfactorily. If necessary tie this in with getting a good agreement on costs.

Most that can reasonably be achieved:

- All of first instalment plus interest.

- All of second instalment plus interest.

- Bulk of loss of profit of £4,100 plus interest.

- No payment for loss of profit to the defendant.

- All claimant's costs paid by the defendant.

- Future commercial relationship on claimant's standard terms.

Least acceptable:

- Payment for first instalment with interest.
- Half of second instalment with no interest.
- Some further payment for loss of profit that is not totally cancelled out by any payment for defendant's claims.
- Claimant pays costs of application to set aside.

NEGOTIATION

9.8 Checklist for Preparation

(This checklist seeks to summarise the points made in this chapter. This checklist will not apply equally to all negotiations as some aspects will be more important in some cases than they are in others. This checklist summarises all the things to work on and think about — you would not necessarily include all these things in a written plan.)

- Client instructions General instructions:

    Specific instructions.

- Client objectives Comprehensive and detailed analysis:

    Prioritised list of objectives.

- Issues in the case Identify what is in dispute and agreed:

    Place the issues in order of importance for your client.

- Facts of the case What additional factual information would you like from your solicitor/client?

    What additional factual information would you like to get from your opponent? What facts can you prove now? What are you likely to be able to prove in the future? What are you unlikely to be able to prove? What are your factual strengths? What are your factual weaknesses? What factual information that you have would you be prepared to reveal? What do you wish to keep secret?

- Relevant law What are the legal strengths of your case?

    What are the legal weaknesses, and how might they be addressed?

- Your opponent's case What are your opponent's objectives likely to be?

    What are the main strengths your opponent is likely to have?

    What are the main weaknesses your opponent is likely to have?

- Concessions What concessions will you ask the other side to make? Which concessions are most important?

    How will you set about getting those concessions?

    What concessions might you make if you have to? Which concessions are easiest for your client to make?

- Possible outcomes What is the most you can hope to gain for the client on each issue?

    What is the least the client would accept on each issue?

    What would you anticipate getting if the case went to court?

    What is the BATNA?

PREPARATION AND STRATEGIC PLANNING

- Strategy and tactics   What overall strategy do you feel is most likely to be successful for you in this case?

    What particular tactics might be effective in this case?

- Possible structure for the negotiation. How do you plan to start? What overall structure is most likely to be effective?

- Documents. Is it worth preparing a page of figures or facts to offer to your opponent as a basis for discussion?

    Is it worth preparing a rough draft of terms for the agreement to be reached?

TEN

CONDUCTING A NEGOTIATION — MAKING THE MOST EFFECTIVE USE OF THE PROCESS

Like the previous chapter, this chapter seeks to draw on the concepts introduced earlier in this Manual to provide a reasonably practical guide to assist you in carrying out a negotiation effectively.

It is not possible to provide a single clear outline for how to conduct any negotiation. Every negotiation is different and presents different problems depending on the type of case involved and the approach you and your opponent take. Therefore this chapter will concentrate on the general elements of the process of negotiating rather than looking in detail at any single model. Two things are of general importance. You should always be aware of the context in which a negotiation takes place — a negotiation in limited time outside the door of the court will be different from one in chambers. Whatever the context you should make efficient use of time — do not spend ages on common documents and things you did in preparation but get to grips with the issues.

The chapter relates primarily to a negotiation taking place between two barristers negotiating face to face. Most of the principles would apply to other types of negotiation too.

10.1 Working to Achieve the Client's Objectives and Acting Within Instructions

The whole purpose of a lawyer conducting a negotiation is to come as close as possible to achieving all the client's objectives, and to achieving them in full. Everything you do in the negotiation should be focused to this end. This does not necessarily mean that you have to be aggressive or competitive. It may be that you judge that you can achieve more for your client by taking a cooperative approach, but it does mean that whatever approach you take you should be equally focused on the detailed, prioritised objectives of your client.

Your professional duty to your client is to promote and protect fearlessly your lay client's best interests, and to do so without regard to your own interests or any consequences to yourself or any other person. You do not owe a duty to your opponent, beyond the general professional duty not to act dishonestly, or to act in any other way discreditable to a barrister.

The importance of identifying your instructions as part of preparation was dealt with in the previous chapter. To the extent that you do not have specific instructions, the outcome of a negotiation will be subject to the approval of the client. You should make this clear to your opponent at the start of the negotiation, and remind your opponent of it as and when you reach agreement to avoid any misunderstanding.

10.2 General Factors Regarding the Negotiation Process

10.2.1 ACTING ETHICALLY

The importance of observing the principles of professional conduct while negotiating was dealt with in detail in **Chapter 8**. Areas of ethical difficulty can easily arise in the course of a negotiation when barristers are fighting hard for their clients' interests, and a real appreciation of how to approach ethical problems may be required for individuals to act properly at all times.

While it is important to put your client's case in the best possible light you should never positively mislead your opponent as to the facts of the case, your own instructions, or the relevant law.

On the other hand, there is no general duty of disclosure during a negotiation, and you should consider whether it is in your client's interests to reveal information that does not have to be revealed. For example, you are not obliged to answer questions from your opponent about the facts of the case or your instructions, and you could refuse to answer, or simply move on to another topic, if this is in your client's interests.

10.2.2 EFFECTIVE PRESENTATION

Effective presentation is very important, and can indeed be decisive. A well-prepared case can still fail to achieve the client's objectives if it is not presented effectively, and very effective presentation can sometimes work wonders for a weak case. In a negotiation there is no judge to intervene, so that a strong presentation of a mediocre case can achieve more than a weaker presentation of the same case (subject to the skills of the opponent).

The most important factors in effective presentation are as follows. Some of the factors are those required for good advocacy, but they can be more difficult to achieve in the faster and less controlled atmosphere of a negotiation.

- Clarity and conciseness. It is generally better to make your points as clearly and concisely as possible. This is most likely to impress your opponent, limit argument and lead to progress. Sometimes making a point at length can be effective because an opponent becomes worn down or confused, but this should be a matter of tactics rather than of lack of skill.

- Coherent presentation. Your presentation is more likely to be effective if your approach is coherent, especially as regards what you are seeking and the types of argument you are using. Jumping about and using surprise points can confuse your opponent into making concessions, but again should be used as a planned tactic rather than through lack of skill.

- Use of argument and persuasion. These matters are dealt with in detail elsewhere (see **Chapter 7**). There is little point in simply putting your brief to your opponent. Your role as a professional is to 'add value' by conveying the reasons why your client's point of view should prevail, and persuading your opponent to accept your client's view. There any many different ways of being persuasive: you may rely on the detail of your argument, you may rely on the logical and practical coherence of your argument, you may persuade by initiating suggestions and pursuing them strongly, or you may persuade by your facilitative approach.

- Use of law and fact. You need to select the appropriate amount and detail of law and fact to use for this case. You may need to adapt what you have planned to fit the particular opponent you have. You may need to use evidence as part of the argument and persuasion on each point.

CONDUCTING A NEGOTIATION — MAKING THE MOST EFFECTIVE USE OF THE PROCESS

- Appropriate use of language. If one barrister is negotiating with another it is appropriate to use legal terminology that one might not use with a client. As you do not need to explain legal concepts you should be able to make points quite easily. The way you express things can underline your approach to the case, or can be used as a tactic, for example saying, 'I don't think my client would accept that' rather than saying, 'I won't accept that'.

- Pace. Pace is important, especially if you have limited time. Practitioners negotiating at the door of the court will often get straight into a main issue in the case, and may negotiate almost in a form of legal shorthand because both are familiar with the case, and both anticipate well the points that the other is likely to make. The student learning to negotiate may well progress more slowly than the practitioner, and speed is not necessarily a virtue if it means that an important issue is not properly explored, but generally speaking if your case is well prepared you should be able to deal with it at a reasonable pace and use time effectively.

- Flexibility. Flexibility is vital. You will rarely find that a negotiation goes exactly as you wish it to. You will almost inevitably have to adapt to the approach and style of your opponent, to new issues, new facts, new evidence, a different approach to the law, and/or alternative version of the figures in the case. Flexibility does not mean that detailed planning is of little use. It means that your planning must be capable of adaptation and growth as the circumstances require.

10.2.3 RESPONDING EFFECTIVELY

Although effective presentation can have a strong effect on the outcome of a case, presentation alone can rarely win anything, unless an opponent is very weak and poorly prepared. It is the response gained which indicates whether the presentation was really effective in achieving its ends. The most important elements of responding effectively are as follows:

- Picking up points quickly and accurately. You can sometimes get something by being obtuse as a matter of tactics, but generally speaking you will work most effectively if you pick up the point your opponent is making and respond to it efficiently.

- Maintaining a coherent picture of your case. Your responses should keep a clear focus on your client's objectives and your picture of the case, rather than showing you can be pulled off-course.

- Making an effective reply. If you are fully familiar with your case and your arguments you should normally be able to respond directly using fact/law/evidence as appropriate. Whether your approach to the case is competitive or cooperative you can find an appropriate way of pointing out the weaknesses of your opponent's position.

- Avoiding concessions. You should avoid responding with a concession unless it is an appropriate and planned concession. Responding with an unplanned and/or unforced concession will often suggest weakness.

- Listening carefully. Make sure that you are listening to what your opponent is saying. If you are too busy concentrating on what you will say next you may miss something important.

- Getting the most you can out of your opponent rather than just dealing with your own case. Ask for clarification or justification of what your opponent is saying whenever this will be useful.

NEGOTIATION

10.2.4 DEALING WITH YOUR OPPONENT

Trainees learning to negotiate, and some practitioners early in practice, can be apprehensive about the effect that an opponent can have on a negotiation. They fear that an opponent who is for example particularly aggressive and entrenched, or particularly weak and ill-prepared, can undermine their own performance.

It is inevitable in a negotiation that you will need to adapt your case to the approach that your opponent is taking and the information that he or she has, but being able to adapt effectively is part of the skill of negotiation. You will hardly ever be able to present a case to an opponent in the perfect way you plan in advance, and you need to use the experience you get from this to develop your skill. For example, some opponents will use a tactic of appearing to be very friendly and easy to deal with to get you to make concessions that you should not be making and you will learn to recognise these tactics and respond appropriately.

There is rarely a real need to fear for the outcome of the negotiation as there are techniques for dealing with the problems that different types of opponents can present. It can be less satisfying to deal with a particularly strong, weak or difficult opponent, but the test for the negotiation is whether the lawyer has done the best for his or her client in the circumstances.

The following list provides some examples of how to deal with a difficult opponent:

(a) The aggressive/entrenched opponent. Avoid getting emotional or personal if you possibly can. If you stay calm and smiling your opponent is likely to see that his or her approach is failing and back down. You can ask the opponent to justify his or her position on the law/the facts/the outcome. Alternatively, you can point out why it is that your position is reasonable, or the ways in which your opponent is not serving his or her client's best interest by taking an entrenched position. If arguments fail you can always say no. If you are really getting nowhere at all you can always walk away. If your opponent is taking a hard line because he or she really does have the best case then you may have problems, but normally your opponent has been briefed to try to reach a settlement, and will not want to push you into walking away.

(b) The weak/ill-prepared opponent. It is not your job to make up for the weaknesses of another lawyer. If you have a weak or ill-prepared opponent you should use this to get the best deal that you reasonably can for your client, bearing in mind that there is no point in exploiting your opponent's weaknesses to the point where the agreement is not one that his or her client will accept.

(c) The opponent who will not agree with your approach on issues/law/fact. This is the sort of problem you will normally have to some degree or another! What do you do in an extreme case, if for example you feel that it is important to argue law in some detail and your opponent refuses to do so? One possibility is to persevere, and make the points that you wish to make briefly and clearly even if your opponent is not keen to listen. Another is to stress that you will be making these points in court if you have to, so it is in your opponent's interests to be aware of them. Alternatively, you could try to ask your opponent why he or she is taking a particular stand — for example is your opponent refusing to discuss law because he or she feels that his or her legal case is weak?

10.3 The Stages in the Negotiating Process

10.3.1 SETTING UP THE NEGOTIATION PROCESS

A number of practical things may need attention before you start. These are considered at **10.3.1.1** to **10.3.1.4**.

CONDUCTING A NEGOTIATION — MAKING THE MOST EFFECTIVE USE OF THE PROCESS

10.3.1.1 Will the negotiation be face to face?
Negotiations may be conducted wholly or partly face to face, by exchange of letters or by telephone. If there is a choice the relative pros and cons of each method may need to be considered.

10.3.1.2 Where will the negotiation take place?
Sometimes there will be little or no choice. A negotiation at the door of the court may simply have to take place in the nearest bit of corridor. But you can often have at least partial control of the surroundings. There can be particular problems in negotiating in a corridor if it is noisy or busy, or if the clients are nearby and want to take part or keep staring at you. You might at least enquire if there is a room in the court building that you could use, or try to find a better bit of corridor!

Negotiating in a corridor can present particular problems for dealing with papers if there is no opportunity to sit down, or if there are seats but no tables. You need to be aware of the problems of not being able to refer to papers easily, and to avoid dropping everything when you are trying to make your best point!

If you have any choice about the location of the negotiation you should make the best you can of it. Is it tactically better to try to hold the negotiation in your office where you have everything to hand and you have control over who has coffee when, etc.? Is it better to meet in your opponent's office so that you do not have to bother with things like making coffee, and it is easier to threaten to walk out if necessary?

10.3.1.3 Who will be there?
There are no set rules for who should be present at a negotiation, so you should consider what is most appropriate for the case. The barristers appearing for both sides may simply be briefed to meet together. Having solicitors present will be more expensive, but may be useful if for example there is a lot of documentation to deal with. It may occasionally be useful to have an expert such as an accountant present for at least part of the negotiation.

Sometimes the clients themselves will wish to be present. This can make it easier for the barrister to take instructions, but it is generally thought to be undesirable because clients may quite unwittingly undermine the strategy or tactics being used with oral interjections or body language. It is generally better for clients to be available in (separate!) rooms nearby so that they can be asked for instructions or be briefed on what is happening privately as and when appropriate. If the client is present, the role of the client in the negotiation should be clearly agreed beforehand.

10.3.1.4 Arrangements for seating and papers?
A negotiation can be facilitated or frustrated by simple things like comfortable chairs, adequate table space for papers, etc. To the extent that you have control over matters like this you can support your strategy and tactics for the case by offering your opponent good provision or inadequate provision in these areas. Do you want to show a competitive start by taking all the space available for your papers, or do you want to make a facilitative start by arranging the chairs more comfortably round the table? If you want to make any point about existing arrangements at the start of a negotiation you should see this tactically as part of the negotiation itself.

10.3.2 OVERALL STRUCTURE

The general stages in the negotiation process have been analysed in different ways. A basic outline for the stages is set out at **2.4**. It can perhaps briefly be summarised as follows:

- Opening/orientating/positioning.
- Exploration/discussion.
- Proposals/bidding.

NEGOTIATION

- Bargaining.
- Convergence.
- Settlement/breakdown.

The stages are not all equally important in every negotiation, and will not necessarily follow each other in a clearly discernable way. Nonetheless, an awareness of the stages can be of great assistance in developing your skill. The following material (**10.3.3** to **10.3.9**) is not divided into precisely these stages, but endeavours to give practical guidance on each.

A good structure is very important for a negotiation. If you can maintain a clear structure it can:

- assist you in putting across your points in the most effective way,
- help you to work most coherently to achieve your client's objectives,
- help you to plan and use the time available to best effect,
- help you to ensure that you cover all the things you need to.

Having said this, it can be very difficult to maintain a good structure, as unexpected points can come up, and your opponent may not share your views on the best structure to use. If you do allow your structure to become weak there are many potential dangers:

- It is much more likely that you will slip into repeating points, or reach a deadlock.
- Your case is less likely to come across in a coherent and consistent way, and is therefore less likely to impress your opponent.
- It is more likely you will make poor use of time.
- It is more likely that you will forget to make some of the positive points you had planned.
- It is more likely that you will fail to achieve all you want to, and that you will fail to cover all appropriate details.

There are many options for structuring a negotiation, depending on the type of case you are dealing with, and what you find works best for you. Some of the main options are as follows:

(a) You start by agreeing with your opponent a list of the issues in the case and the order in which they should be considered. You then follow what has been agreed. This sort of structure is fairly easy to follow because it is consensual, and it may well be appropriate in a case where you wish to be as cooperative as possible.

(b) You try to take the initiative in guiding the structure for the whole negotiation. You start on what you consider to be your high ground, and then you seek to move through the issues in the order that suits you. This sort of structure can be very good if you wish to show how committed you are to achieving your client's objectives, and it can be achieved if you do plan the structure you want in advance and you concentrate on sticking to the structure you want. On the other hand this sort of structure can be very difficult to implement if your opponent wants to follow a very different structure, and you can appear weak if you seek to start very strongly but you are forced to compromise on structure at an early stage.

CONDUCTING A NEGOTIATION — MAKING THE MOST EFFECTIVE USE OF THE PROCESS

(c) You may choose to start by finding out more about your opponent's case, and then take final decisions on structure when you see how what matters to your opponent fits in with what matters to you. This can be useful in strategic terms if your case is weak, or if you have limited information and wish to find out a lot more from your opponent. However, this sort of structure can easily make you appear very weak, and can easily turn into having no structure at all if it is not carefully handled.

Whatever overall structure you choose, use of time will be important. In practice you will have to be able to carry out quite complex negotiations in less that half an hour outside court, and you should develop the ability to work at this speed even though you will often have more time than this in chambers. Negotiations tend either to start with a lot of energy but then start to slow down after 10 to 15 minutes, or to take a long time to get going and only do anything useful after 10 to 15 minutes. This is not necessarily bad, but do try to avoid losing momentum too much, or taking too long to build up any useful momentum. Always make sure you are spending most time on the most important issues.

10.3.3   OPENING THE NEGOTIATION

The start of a negotiation is of great importance. Your energy is likely to be at its highest at this stage, and you will be setting the climate for what comes later. Each negotiator is giving key messages to the other as to what he or she hopes to achieve, what approach he or she will take, and how strongly he or she intends to argue. It is possible to make a real impact at this stage and show from the start that you are fully in command of the case and will not make any unnecessary concessions. You throw away a great potential impetus if you do not give careful thought to how to start each negotiation.

On the other hand the start can be particularly difficult, especially if both negotiators have very clear but very different views about who should start and the overall structure that should be used. You may indeed find that the first thing you need to negotiate is how to start! As with all issues in a negotiation, you should plan the start that you feel is best for the case and you should do what you reasonably can to achieve what you want. You may need to be flexible, but try not to immediately back down on what you have proposed if this may make you appear very weak.

The options for how to start inter-relate with your choice for overall structure. The main choices are as follows (**10.3.3.1** to **10.3.3.3**).

10.3.3.1   A mutually agreed start
A mutually agreed start can form a sound basis for any negotiation. However, even if you are agreeing what issues should be discussed, and in what order, you still need to ensure that all the issues of interest to your client are put on the agenda, and that the order of the agenda is as favourable as possible to your client. You should never choose a mutually agreed start simply because it is easier, and you should not allow the fact that you are trying to agree issues and structure to lead you into making any unnecessary concessions about how the negotiation will be conducted. Even if you intend to act in a cooperative way, try to avoid stressing how keen your client is to reach an agreement if this may give your opponent the impression that you will be keen to make concessions just to get an agreement.

If you start by agreeing how to proceed you will often set an agenda. If you do start by setting an agenda, do it properly and not superficially. You need enough detail of issues and order to ensure that everything will be covered, and you need an adequate note of what is agreed to ensure that you follow your plan.

It is possible to have a mutually agreed start that does something other than, or in addition to, setting an agenda. You might for example agree to review the facts of the case mutually. This will only be appropriate if there are real doubts about material facts, and you should of course focus on areas of fact that are in doubt or dispute and not waste time with facts that are agreed.

NEGOTIATION

10.3.3.2 Starting with your view of the case

It will almost inevitably give you most control of the negotiation, and a good opportunity to get early advantages, if you start by stating your view of the case. If you do choose to start then make sure that you do get the greatest possible advantage out of starting by putting the strengths of your case clearly. You do not have to do this in an antagonistic way — you could for example offer your opponent a chance to outline his or her case once you have outlined yours.

If you are going to start by outlining your view of the case, decide what to cover. You may simply wish to stress what your client is expecting to achieve in the case. You may wish to go on to say something about your confidence that you will achieve your client's objectives, and the legal and factual strengths of your case that found this confidence. The more you say the more you may impress your opponent, but there is a danger that saying too much can give your opponent clues as to where he or she most needs to attack your case. Beware of setting out your case in full detail at the start if there are any major areas of uncertainty on which you need to probe your opponent.

10.3.3.3 Getting your opponent to start

It can be a useful tactic to get your opponent to start. This can help you to evaluate as quickly as possible where your opponent's main strengths and weaknesses are and what the opponent hopes to achieve, so that you can polish your planning on how to approach the case. This can also help you to get more factual information before you reveal your hand. If your opponent has outlined his or her case first you can choose whether to outline your case in reply, or whether to immediately attack the case your opponent has outlined.

Getting your opponent to start is not an easy option, as you will need to ensure that your opponent does give you the information you want if you are to get the advantage you anticipate. You may need to push your opponent to give you more detail before moving on.

10.3.4 EXPLORATION AND DISCUSSION

There are all sorts of ways of moving forwards, depending on the type of start that has been used and how successful that has been. What matters is to move forwards in a structured way towards an identifiable goal rather than just to pick on a issue at random. **10.3.4.1** and **10.3.4.2** outline what will normally be the main ingredients in moving forwards. Although the precise order of things may vary, you must make sure you have full information on a point before moving to others or concessions.

10.3.4.1 Gathering of information

In many negotiations you will want to get some further information from the other side. This is an important element of negotiating — no brief will tell you everything you need to know, especially regarding the case for the other side. You may want further factual information, you may want to know what documents or other evidence they have, or you may want to know what they want to achieve. You can seek to get the extra information by having a specific section of the negotiation where you ask questions, or you might just ask individual questions at appropriate times on different issues. Having an information-gathering section can yield very useful results by giving you a lot more relevant information about the case. On the other hand your opponent does not have to answer your questions, and you might get more from occasional questions that take your opponent off guard than from subjecting the opponent to a long interrogation.

Note that the competitive negotiator may see this stage differently from the co-operative one. You may for reasons of tactics wish to leave some factual areas vague.

10.3.4.2 Argument on specific issues

In most negotiations you will end up arguing your case on several issues. On each separate issue you are trying to achieve the most you can for your client, presenting the strengths of your case to the best possible advantage and using persuasive

CONDUCTING A NEGOTIATION — MAKING THE MOST EFFECTIVE USE OF THE PROCESS

argument. You therefore need to move forward in the best possible way for each issue rather than bounding in hopefully.

For each issue you should consider whether the strongest approach is for you to outline your case or for you to ask your opponent to outline his or her case. Alternatively you might want to start by asking some questions, or by setting out what your client wants to achieve on that issue.

10.3.5 PROPOSALS AND BARGAINING

10.3.5.1 Making offers and concessions

When should you discuss offers and concessions? You might wish to demand a concession from your opponent at an early stage as a matter of tactics. You might at least wish to ensure that your opponent is asked to make a concession or offers a concession before you do.

You may wish to offer small concessions, or concessions on matters of little interest to your client, without full debate as a matter of tactics. However, you will often only move on to this once you have the fullest possible information on an issue, and once the issue has been fully argued. It is risky to offer a concession at an earlier stage as you may give something away quite unnecessarily if you do not know how strong your opponent's case is.

In addition to timing you need to consider the size of any concession that you demand or offer. You should never make a unilateral concession or a concession that is bigger than that you need to make to secure your desired end unless you could immediately give a clear practical/tactical reason for what you have done. It may help to imagine that your client is listening to each concession you make. If you feel that your client might have gasped in horror at what you are about to say then think very hard about whether you ought to say it.

Always ensure that the wording of a concession or offer is clear and sufficiently detailed to avoid any misunderstanding. Concessions are dealt with in more detail in **Chapter 5**.

10.3.5.2 Provisional offers and concessions

If you cannot quickly move to a full agreement on an issue that comes as close as possible to meeting your client's objectives, you may find it useful to discuss possible offers and concessions in an effort to find a way forward. If your opponent does not offer any concessions you could suggest a concession that he or she might make, or if you do not want to commit yourself to making a concession but would like to raise an area where a concession might be possible, then you can start a theoretical discussion on the point, for example, 'If you were to reduce your claim by £5,000 then my client might be prepared to consider it' or 'If my client were prepared to redraft the restrictive covenant, would your client be prepared to reduce the term?'

While provisional offers and concessions can be very useful they must be made with care. If you do not make it clear that a concession you make is provisional then your opponent may assume it is binding. There is also a danger that, even if you make it clear that an offer by you is provisional, your opponent will see this as a weak spot and will seek to attack your case in an area where you have suggested you might make a concession.

If you make a provisional offer or concession, make it clear what it is provisional on, for example, your opponent making a concession too, and if necessary make it clear at what stage the offer is withdrawn.

10.3.5.3 Considering offers and concessions

Take adequate time to respond to an offer or concession made to you. If necessary start by clarifying what is on offer. Then move on to see if you would like the offer modified in any way before you can accept it. If an offer seems a bit mean test whether it might

NEGOTIATION

be increased before you accept it. If an offer seems very generous consider why — is your opponent aware of a weakness in his or her case that is not immediately clear to you?

Be wary of an offer that simply splits the difference between the two sides. If you have the better case your client should get more than half. Also beware of an offer that simply trades off claims by each side that on the face of it are of equal value. This is not a good thing to do if your claim is much more soundly based than your opponent's.

10.3.5.4 Tactics

You may choose to move forward through the use of a tactic that you have identified as being potentially useful for your case. Plan as many tactics as possible in advance, and then choose which to use depending on how the negotiation progresses. Tactics are dealt with in more detail in **Chapter 5**.

10.3.6 DEFINING PROGRESS

You may find it useful to define your progress at certain points. If you simply discuss one area and then move immediately to another you can lose a lot of potential advantages. Even if you have not managed to reach a final settlement of the area you will normally have made some progress that can usefully be used in one or more of the following ways:

- Summarise the main arguments that each side has on the issue (and perhaps note them), so that as and when you return to the issue you do not waste time covering ground already covered.

- Summarise what each side is seeking to achieve on the issue, so that you can more easily discuss a possible compromise later.

- Confirm any additional information you have obtained, even if you have gained nothing else.

- Define any concessions that might be made by one or both sides, even if the actual making of the concession may come later or depend on agreement on another issue.

10.3.7 GETTING STUCK

Virtually every negotiation will run into problems sooner or later. It is inherent in the process, even if you make every possible effort to pursue an effective structure. To ensure that your case is not undermined by running into difficulties you should be aware of the reasons why you might get stuck, and what to do to find a way forward. The paragraphs **10.3.7.1** to **10.3.7.6** below aim to provide a starting point, but you will need experience to develop real expertise.

10.3.7.1 Coping with a lack of factual information

It is almost inevitable that in the course of a negotiation you will find that some pieces of factual information are relevant to the negotiation, but neither you nor your opponent knows what the factual situation is. You will simply have to make the best progress you can on the issue, and there are various ways of dealing with the situation.

The first thing to do is decide how important the information really is. It may be that it is relevant but far from crucial, and you can proceed to make a full settlement without finding out the answer. If the information is important you need to consider how difficult and expensive it will be to find the answer. If it should be relatively easy and cheap to get the information then you may be able to agree a formula settlement (for example agreeing that if the answer is X then the claimant wins on that issue, but if the answer is Y the defendant wins). Alternatively, you may agree that you will simply finalise the settlement of that issue by telephone when the information is available.

CONDUCTING A NEGOTIATION — MAKING THE MOST EFFECTIVE USE OF THE PROCESS

Sometimes it will be expensive and/or difficult to get the relevant information, in which case you should show a proper awareness of practicalities and costs. For example you may need to consider how you could make progress without the information, or how you could get it most easily and cheaply.

If you do have incomplete factual information, you can always argue on the basis of what the answer is likely to be on the balance of probabilities, or on the basis of what is likely to be held if the case goes to court, taking into account who would then bear the burden of proof.

10.3.7.2 Going round in circles

You should never find yourself repeating at length anything that you have already said. You should put your arguments in their strongest, most persuasive form the first time round, and if that fails to work there is little to be gained from simply doing the same thing again. Occasionally you may bore or wear an opponent into submission, but this should not normally be a strategy of choice! If your opponent does not accept your argument you should simply summarise your main points briefly, perhaps make it clear that you are unlikely to see your way to compromising in this area, and move on.

Equally you should not waste time listening to your opponent repeating something that he or she has already said. You can normally deal with this by pointing out that your opponent is simply repeating points already made and moving the negotiation on.

10.3.7.3 Getting bogged down

You may find that you are spending far too long on a single issue. It is worth spending a reasonable time on the issues that are at the centre of the case, but you should ensure that you do not spend too long on something that is peripheral, especially if you are negotiating within limited time. If you are properly prepared and are presenting your case efficiently it should not be your fault that things get bogged down. It should only be your fault if you have not prepared things properly in advance or if you allow yourself to be sidetracked too much.

The best way out of getting bogged down is to try to return to a sound structure for the negotiation and efficient use of time as quickly as possible. Summarise the main points that have been made while the negotiation was getting bogged down as briefly as possible and then move on.

10.3.7.4 The opponent who will not co-operate with your approach

You will often find that your opponent does not agree with the approach you wish to take to the case. Your opponent may disagree with the order in which issues should be dealt with, the facts that appear from your instructions, or with your view of the relevance of the law to the case. Often such problems can themselves be dealt with by negotiation. You may compromise on the order in which issues should be dealt with, or you may let your opponent state his or her view of the relevant law even if you do not agree with its importance.

Sometimes problems cannot be settled in this way, and there is a danger that the negotiation will grind to a halt. If you fear this is about to happen you need to consider the effect for the clients. If achieving nothing and paying the wasted costs of the negotiation is better than anything that can be achieved then it is best to grind to a halt. If there are strong reasons for the clients to settle and they cannot afford to waste costs then you need to do the best you can to carry on. You might for example point out to your opponent that he or she is not serving his or her client's best interests by being unreasonable.

10.3.7.5 Emotions get in the way

In theory, if you are negotiating in a professional way, personal emotions should not surface. In practice, you will occasionally find that an opponent does bring you close to losing your temper, for example because he or she refuses to shift position on an issue even though you feel that your arguments are overwhelming. Sometimes an opponent may even try to make you lose your temper as a tactic, to undermine your

NEGOTIATION

presentation of your case. The more frequent problem is that you will find that something about the way your opponent presents his or her case is rather irritating.

If there is any risk that your emotions may affect your performance, remember that it is vital to stay as calm as possible, so that nothing you have planned is lost. You need to be patient, and to persevere in your attempts to achieve your client's objectives (though you may need to modify your approach slightly to get away from the thing that is irritating you). There are many ways to deal with emotion, depending on the circumstances. For example, it may help to try to discuss with your opponent why he or she is taking the approach that is irritating you, it may help to try to focus on the positive rather than the negative aspects of what is being discussed, or you may need to move to another issue.

10.3.7.6 Reaching a dead-end

It is quite possible that once you and your opponent have gone through all the arguments on a particular issue you will be able to see no way forward. If there are no possible concessions to be sought or offered you may appear to have reached a dead-end.

There are various ways out of a dead-end, some of which should be avoided or used with great care. There is rarely any point in repeating arguments you have already put forward, as this will just waste time. You should not offer a concession that is not justified simply to suggest a way forward but with no real benefit for your client. Do not be afraid of simply being quiet for a moment or two while you review where you are, though you should not need to be quiet for long if you are fully prepared.

More positively, you can move to a different issue. Another alternative is to propose theoretical concessions, just to see if your opponent might concede something if you concede something.

10.3.7.7 Reaching deadlock

This is more serious than reaching a dead-end. You reach a dead-end if both sides have exhausted their arguments on all issues and there is no obvious way forward. You reach deadlock if it is clear that the objectives of the clients and/or the approaches of the lawyers are fundamentally opposed.

It is possible to reach a deadlock from which there is no escape. If you really have argued every point fully and to the best of your ability but you simply cannot reach terms that would be acceptable to your client then you may have no alternative but to stop negotiating. You should be slow to walk away if your client has instructed you to reach a settlement, not least because the costs of the negotiation will be wasted, but sometimes you may have no alternative.

It is however relatively rare to reach a deadlock of this kind. You should try to explore all the issues before deciding that the negotiation is deadlocked, as you will often find that sooner or later one issue provides a possible way forward. You should also try to explore theoretical concessions even if no concessions are actually made, just to see if anything can be done. If the case does seem to be reaching deadlock it is worth exploring whether that is the outcome that your opponent wants, as the opponent may also be instructed to reach a settlement, and may be prepared to make some concession rather than to walk away empty handed. Unless the atmosphere is very bad-tempered you can at least review the main points that have been made on each issue to clarify the views of the parties, and see if that might lay the foundation for the future conduct of the case, and possibly for a future negotiation.

10.3.8 MOVING TOWARDS A SETTLEMENT — CONVERGENCE

There are many ways of moving towards a settlement. The important thing is to be clear about when something has been agreed, and what precisely has been agreed. All too often there can be misunderstandings about this. One lawyer may assume that a particular issue has been finally resolved whereas the other may think that the

CONDUCTING A NEGOTIATION — MAKING THE MOST EFFECTIVE USE OF THE PROCESS

agreement is only provisional, and will lapse if other issues are not resolved too. A whole negotiation can collapse as a result of misunderstandings of what has been agreed, so do make sure that you are always clear about what has been agreed and whether it is final, and make sure that you make an unambiguous note immediately.

The main elements in moving towards a settlement are set out at **10.3.8.1** to **10.3.8.3** below.

10.3.8.1 Agreements on individual issues

Most negotiations will involve several different issues. One approach is to discuss each issue separately, and to reach a final agreement on each issue before you move on to the next. This sort of approach can help you to ensure that each issue is fully argued, and can help you to avoid any confusion as it is reasonably easy to stop at the end of the discussion of each issue and write down what has been agreed. Even if you do not manage to resolve all the issues, you can at least take away to your client a final agreement on some issues. If you negotiate effectively you can also get a better deal by dealing with items individually.

The drawback of this type of approach is that it limits your flexibility in reaching an overall deal. If each issue is dealt with separately you cannot very easily try to balance a demand in one area with a concession in another. It is possible to say, 'Well, I made a bit of a concession on the last issue so I think it's your turn to make a concession now ...', but you cannot get into a complex trading of concessions.

10.3.8.2 Agreeing a formula rather than a final solution

Sometimes you cannot reach a final agreement on an issue on the spot. This is most likely to be the case if you decide that you need further factual information or instructions from your client, or if you want further information from a third party. It will often not be in your client's best interests simply to leave such an issue open, if that is likely to mean that a further meeting of lawyers will have to take place with the accompanying costs. It is normally better to agree a formula by which the final solution can be reached without any further meeting.

For example, it may be that you decide that you need to know the value of a piece of property so that you can decide how much one party should pay the other in respect of it. Rather than simply agreeing that the parties will get the property valued you can agree on the spot a formula for dealing with the resulting figure. For example, you can agree that the claimant will pay the defendant one-quarter of whatever the value is found to be.

If you do agree a formula do make sure you agree enough detail to make it workable. Decide, for example, how the valuer will be found and agreed.

10.3.8.3 Agreeing an overall deal

An alternative to reaching a final agreement on each issue as you go along is to discuss all the issues fully and only try to reach an overall agreement at the end. You may do this as a matter of choice, or simply because it proves impossible to reach any agreement on the separate issues as you go along. This sort of approach can be useful in that it enables you to get more of an overall feel of the strengths and weaknesses of your opponent's case before you commit yourself to anything, and it does give more scope for flexibility and imagination in terms of the agreement that is finally reached.

The possible problems of not reaching at least provisional agreement on some items until the end of the negotiation are that one is more easily tempted to jump from issue to issue, and it can be more difficult to reach an agreement as a lot of time is spend arguing before anything is finally agreed.

10.3.9 CONCLUDING THE PROCESS

Finalising a negotiated agreement and making it enforceable are dealt with in **Chapter 11**. This section simply deals with bringing the actual process of negotiating to an end, though inevitably the two are closely linked.

NEGOTIATION

Even during the negotiation you need to give some thought to how the particular process in which you are engaged is likely to end. This may inform the structure and pace of the negotiation, or it may influence what is agreed and how. For example, if you are negotiating outside the door of the court and you know you will be called in within 20 minutes it will generally not be appropriate to indulge in a detailed discussion of legal principle that might be useful in a negotiation in chambers that has no strict time limit.

As you come to the conclusion of the negotiating process you need to be clear about what sort of conclusion is appropriate:

(a) Be clear about the precise terms that have been agreed. Unless the agreement is very simple you should write the terms down, preferably agreeing with your opponent what should be written down. This will not only help to avoid any future dispute about what was agreed, but it will assist anyone who has to draft any document to enforce the agreement. If you do this yourself you should not just assume that you will remember, as you may well work on several other cases before you come to do the draft and you will almost certainly forget some details.

(b) Can you conclude the matter yourselves because the agreement is so simple that it can be endorsed on briefs, or because the barristers themselves will be agreeing the wording of an order?

(c) Will you need to present your conclusions to a third party in written form, so that you need a written note clear enough for someone who is not present to understand? This might happen if, for example, a solicitor is not present but will be asked by the barristers to draft a letter, contract or deed to record the agreement.

(d) Will you need to present your conclusions to a third party in oral form? You will often need to discuss the proposed settlement with your client. Sometimes you will also need to present the position to a judge, if for example you are negotiating prior to an interim application.

If you do manage to reach an agreement on all issues you need to ensure that the following have occurred before you end the negotiation:

(a) Double-check that the agreement you have reached is within your instructions, meets your client's objectives as closely as possible, and is likely to be acceptable to your client.

(b) Double-check that the agreement does cover all issues in dispute, and all subsidiary matters such as costs.

(c) Ensure that the agreement is clear. Try to ensure that the parties do not have different understandings of what a term means.

(d) Ensure that you have agreed each term in sufficient detail. All too often an agreement falls apart after the barristers have completed the negotiation process because the parties cannot agree details when it comes to drawing up a document to record the agreement.

(e) Ensure that you have covered negative things as well as positive things. For example, if you are negotiating before a claim has been commenced, do not just assume that on the basis of the agreement reached no claim will be brought — make it clear that this is a term of agreement.

(f) Do consider the overall impact of the deal if you have reached separate agreement on separate issues. If you have agreed that the claimant will pay the defendant certain figures, and the defendant will pay the claimant certain figures, look at what the net balance will be.

CONDUCTING A NEGOTIATION — MAKING THE MOST EFFECTIVE USE OF THE PROCESS

(g) Pause to consider whether the overall agreement is practical and realistic. It is quite possible in the heat of the moment to agree something that really will not work. Do try to allow yourself a little time for reflection at the end of the negotiation before you rush away. It is not good practice or easy to try to unpick an agreement that has been reached, but if something is unlikely to work it is better to discuss it now than just to leave things to fall apart.

If you manage to reach an agreement on some issues, but not on all issues, you have achieved something that needs to be properly recognised. You should do the following:

(a) Cover any appropriate procedural points as well as the substance of the case. For example, if a case has been commenced, will that claim be stayed on the basis of the terms agreed?

(b) Think forward as far as you can. Might there be any problems in carrying out or enforcing the agreement you have reached that should be addressed now?

(c) Be very clear about what is or is not settled. It is probably worth running through the issues that are still open as well as the ones that are agreed, to avoid any possible confusion.

(d) Be clear about the basis upon which some of the issues are settled. Are they settled once and for all whatever happens, or is there any possibility that they could be reopened if other issues are not settled?

(e) As far as the issues are settled, consider as far as relevant all the points to be covered in dealing with a full settlement.

Even if you have not managed to reach an agreement on any issues you should try to ensure that the negotiation is as useful as possible:

(a) At the very least you have probably got some further factual information about your opponent's case and how it is being presented. Make sure you record this for future use. You might orally wish to check some of these points with your opponent before you part.

(b) You should have got some ideas about where your opponent's case is weakest and where you are most likely to get concessions even if you have not got them yet. Again this is worth noting, and possibly worth running through with your opponent if you want to try to encourage your opponent to come back with an offer for settlement.

(c) Similarly, you should have a clearer idea of where your own case is strongest, and you might well choose to impress this upon your opponent.

10.4 Reviewing Your Conduct of a Negotiation

Every negotiation you perform should assist you in building your skill by providing you with further insights into the negotiation process. It is therefore worth spending at least a few minutes reviewing what happened. While you are learning to negotiate it is well worth discussing what happened with your opponent.

The following checklist suggests the sort of things you might usefully consider.

Meeting the client's objectives

- In what ways did you not meet your client's objectives in full?

- If you did not reach your client's objectives in full, why was this?

NEGOTIATION

- Do you envisage any problems in persuading your client to accept the agreement you have reached?

- Did you get all the concessions you sought from your opponent? If not, why not?

- Did you make any concessions that were not really necessary?

Structure

- Was the start that you chose effective? If not, what might have been more effective?

- Did you use your time efficiently? If not, why not?

- Was the general conduct of the negotiation effective and did it keep up a good pace? Could any sections have been cut out?

- Did you get stuck at any point? Could this have been avoided? Did you get out of it as effectively as possible?

Your presentation

- Was your presentation as strong, clear and persuasive as possible? What could you have done better?

Responding to your opponent

- Did you always respond to your opponent as effectively as possible? With hindsight, which of your responses could have been better?

Strategy and tactics

- Did your intended strategy work? If so, why? If not, why not?

- Did your intended tactics work? If so, why? If not, why not?

- Were your opponent's strategy and tactics effective against you? If so, why? If not, why not?

ELEVEN

RECORDING AND ENFORCING A NEGOTIATED AGREEMENT

When you reach a full, negotiated conclusion to a case the natural reaction may well be to heave a sigh of relief, and quite possibly to open the champagne. Unfortunately, although an oral agreement is binding in contractual terms, you have not fulfilled all your duties to the client until you have got a detailed, comprehensive and enforceable written record of what has been agreed. It is clear that a lawyer who does fail to ensure that an agreed term is recorded in an enforceable way may be open to a claim for negligence (*Bell v Peter Braune & Co.* [1990] 3 All ER 124).

It is probably wise to see this written agreement, rather than the oral agreement, as the final goal of the negotiating process. The point of negotiating is to reach an agreement which is clear to the parties, which is capable of being carried out and which is actually carried out. Keep this in mind throughout the negotiation.

Chapter 10 gave some brief suggestions as to how the concluding stages of a negotiation need to focus particularly on how the agreement will be recorded. This chapter looks more fully at the issues surrounding the making of a final agreement, and looks specifically at the main ways in which a negotiated agreement might be recorded and enforced.

Do note that the one thing you do not do when you have successfully concluded a negotiation is to shake hands — it is a professional convention that barristers do not shake hands, however cooperative and successful their negotiation has been!

11.1 The Vital Role of Client Acceptance

There is no point in reaching a negotiated settlement that one or both clients will not really accept. It is simply a waste of your time and a waste of client costs.

You breach the rules of professional conduct if you reach an agreement that is outside your instructions, and you breach your general professional duty if you do not reach an agreement that is as close as possible to your client's objectives. Even if you are taking a cooperative approach, the point is not to split the difference and come up with something that is vaguely fair, but to do the best that you possibly can for your client. That is what the client is paying you for, and if the client is disappointed the negotiation can be fatally undermined.

The first possible problem is that a client may refuse to accept a proposed agreement. It may be possible to save the agreement by renegotiating one or two terms, but this situation should be avoided if at all possible. To the extent that an agreement is subject to client approval you should be aiming to produce terms to which the client will just say, 'Yes'. When preparing for or carrying out a negotiation you should consider how you would persuade your client to accept a particular outcome. If you foresee real difficulty in persuading your client you need to fight hard on the point. You cannot

NEGOTIATION

impose an agreement on the client simply because you think it is reasonable. Note also that even if you are negotiating very effectively and your opponent is negotiating very weakly you should not exploit the position so far as to push your opponent into a deal that his or her client is unlikely to accept as your effort will be wasted.

The second possible problem is with enforcement. Even if a client grudgingly accepts agreed terms, if the client is fundamentally unhappy because the agreed terms are so far away from his or her objectives then carrying out the terms may well prove difficult. You do need to consider whether such a problem might arise with respect to either client.

11.2 General Elements of a Final Agreement

11.2.1 CHOOSING AN APPROPRIATE FORM

While you are negotiating you need to have in mind what form is likely to be appropriate for recording any agreement you reach. The main options are outlined below. Occasionally you will be presenting agreed terms orally to a judge, but normally you will decide that the agreement will need to be recorded in writing. You should think through what sort of detail you need for the written agreement. For example, if you are negotiating following an application for a interim injunction, it may be appropriate to decide what might be recorded as an injunction and what as an undertaking.

11.2.2 THE CONTEXT OF THE AGREEMENT

The form in which the agreement should be recorded must be appropriate for the stage the case has reached. If no legal claim has been started then the agreement will simply be between the two parties, and would therefore normally be recorded by an exchange of letters, or by a contract or deed. Once a legal claim has been started then the court will normally need to be involved in some way to record that all or part of the claim has been settled. If the claim is nearing trial then a consent order may be sought. At an interim stage an appropriate procedure may be employed, such as having the claim stayed on terms. The appropriate procedure must take into account whether the whole substance of the claim has been settled or only part of it. See the *Civil Litigation Manual* for further guidance.

11.2.3 THE ISSUES TO BE COVERED

The recorded agreement should cover all issues in the case, leaving nothing simply as an understanding. All the following may need to be included:

- the solution to any legal issues (any matters relating to the legal status of the parties, or any legal relationship between them, for example redrafting contractual terms),

- the solution to any factual/practical issues,

- any further terms that may help to make the agreement practical and effective,

- fringe matters, such as costs.

11.2.4 THE AMOUNT OF DETAIL TO INCLUDE

Each point of agreement must be spelt out in appropriate detail. Just to give some examples of the type of detail that would be appropriate:

- If you are negotiating revised terms for a contract, ensure that each term is fully drafted, and that it is clear to what extent the new contract supersedes the old one.

RECORDING AND ENFORCING A NEGOTIATED AGREEMENT

- If you are agreeing that money should be paid by one party to another do not just agree how much but when it should be paid by, how it should be paid (if this matters), whether it will carry interest if it is paid late, etc.

- If you are agreeing practical terms, for example that one party will provide free publicity for the other, agree the details of who will provide copy and pay for printing, how the publicity material will be distributed and for how long, etc.

- Make sure that an agreement about costs is comprehensive. Does the agreement include the costs of the negotiation itself? Will it include any costs of drawing up the agreement?

11.2.5 PROVISIONS FOR ENFORCEMENT

To avoid future problems you should try to think forward in a realistic and tactical way as to how the agreement will actually be carried out.

- Have you agreed time limits for each thing that is to be done?

- Have you agreed, where appropriate, what will happen if something is not done on time?

- Are the different things to be done by each side inter-related in a sensible way, or could your client carry out all of his or her side of the bargain only to find that the other side had done nothing and the only remedy was to go back to court again, incurring further expense?

- Cover necessary consequential actions. If for example you agree that some real property belongs to one side rather than the other, provide for any necessary conveyancing and/or registration to take place.

- Have you made appropriate arrangements for anything still to be agreed? For example, it may not be sensible just to leave something to be agreed between the clients themselves (since they are currently dealing with each other through lawyers). It may be better to arrange for instructing solicitors to act to agree the particular point.

11.3 Forms for an Enforceable Agreement

11.3.1 GENERALLY

There may well be a choice of methods for recording a particular agreement, and you may need to negotiate with your opponent about which should be used. The more important the case is for your client, and the more important the concessions you have won, the more important it is to have a legally strong form for recording the agreement.

You may also need to negotiate who should actually prepare the written draft of the agreement. Sometimes it may be appropriate simply to leave it to instructing solicitors to exchange letters recording what has been agreed, but do be aware of the risk that something may be lost if the solicitor has not carried out the negotiation personally! For tactical purposes it may be that you want to prepare a draft agreement yourself. Although you are only recording what has been agreed, you can thus ensure that wherever there is any shadow of doubt the wording favours your client, and drafting the agreement may jog your memory as to some detail that has been forgotten.

Do bear in mind that in some circumstances you will have final control over how the agreement is recorded and in other cases you will not. You can agree the precise wording of something endorsed on briefs. You can ask to see a draft prepared by your instructing solicitor, but the final agreement will also need to be approved by your opponent. If you are drafting an order then the final outcome will be at the discretion

NEGOTIATION

of the judge, who does not have to make an order in the terms agreed and may wish to amend your draft.

Whoever prepares a written draft, and whatever form it takes, the basic requirements of a good draft, such as conciseness and clarity, should be present.

11.3.2 ENDORSEMENT ON A BRIEF

An agreement can be recorded simply by writing the terms on the backsheet of the brief of each barrister. The agreement is dated, and signed by both sides to signify acceptance. The endorsement simply provides written evidence of the agreement made. An endorsement can also be used to record that the client is satisfied with the terms agreed, or agrees to be bound by them, if this seems appropriate in the case.

This is very quick and very cheap, and it might be appropriate in a fairly simple case with very simple terms, and where there is no need for the clients to have copies of the terms.

Endorsement on the brief alone is not appropriate where there is any great complexity in the terms agreed, where there are a number of terms agreed, or where it is for any reason useful to the clients to have a full separate written agreement.

It may be possible to enforce an endorsement by returning to court where an endorsement is used to record an agreement at an interim stage, but it may be necessary to start a new claim to enforce an agreement recorded by endorsement if the claim is over or no claim was commenced.

Examples of endorsements on briefs

1. In a case where one substantial issue is in dispute (like the ownership of beneficial interests in real property), a smaller issue might be settled by endorsement on a brief rather than by separate argument in court.

JAMES BROWN

V

AMANDA SMITH

It is hereby agreed that:

(1) The claimant shall have ownership of the dining room table and chairs

(2) The defendant shall have ownership of the painting known as 'Conflict Rationalised'

(3) The collection of silver teaspoons shall be sold and the proceeds divided equally between the claimant and the defendant.

Signed (client)   Signed (client)

Signed (barrister)   Signed (barrister)

Dated

---

2. If an interim order has been made or a case adjourned the parties may record an agreement on claims pending a further order in the case.

RECORDING AND ENFORCING A NEGOTIATED AGREEMENT

RANJIT SINGH

v

QUICK SUPPLIES LIMITED

Upon the adjournment of this matter by consent, it is agreed that pending a further hearing in this case:

— the defendant will continue to make supplies of stationery material to the claimant upon the terms of the contract dated 1st April 1997

— the claimant will pay for all such supplies within 28 days of invoice.

Signed (client)   Signed (client)

Signed (barrister)   Signed (barrister)

Dated

---

3. If a court makes a general order, such as that contact with a child should be as agreed between the parties, detailed terms can be endorsed upon the brief.

DARREN JONES

v

TRACEY JONES

In pursuance of the order herein, whereby it is ordered that contact with the child Jeremiah Jones should be as agreed between the parties, it is hereby agreed that the defendant should have contact with the said child on alternate Saturdays, commencing on the Saturday immediately following the making of this order. The precise times and places of such contact shall be agreed by the parties by telephone at least 24 hours in advance.

Signed (client)   Signed (client)

Signed (barrister)   Signed (barrister)

Dated

11.3.3 AN EXCHANGE OF LETTERS

An exchange of letters between solicitors can usefully provide a written record of agreed terms. One solicitor would write a letter setting out the terms proposed and the other would write in reply to express agreement. Again, the letters simply provide written evidence of what has been agreed.

The expense of solicitors exchanging letters will be relatively small. This form of record is appropriate where the agreement is a little too long and complex to be endorsed on a brief, and/or where it is useful for the clients to have a written copy of what has been

NEGOTIATION

agreed, but where there is no need for the additional expense and formality of a contract or deed.

An exchange of letters is not appropriate where the context and/or the complexity of the terms merits a contract or deed, or where possible problems with enforcement might be lessened by the formality of a contract or deed. Once a claim has been commenced, an exchange of letters alone would not bring the claim to an end, though it might in practical terms mean that no further steps in the claim are taken.

Example of an exchange of letters

1. Offer of settlement prior to claim by proposed defendant.

1st September 2000

Dear Sir,

<u>Without Prejudice</u>

Re: The Gardens at Manor Lodge, Great Thrushfield

I am writing with regard to the claim of your client, Mrs Anita Singh, respecting damage allegedly caused to her garden by my clients, Green Fingers Ltd. A contract for the laying of a terrace in Mrs Singh's garden at Manor Lodge was made orally on 10th May 2000, and the work was carried out by my clients in June.

I have been instructed by my clients to make the following offer to you in full and final settlement of your proposed claim for damages.

While making no admission of liability, my client is prepared to make an offer regarding the cracking of the concrete used in the building of the terrace and the damage to the beech hedge surrounding the maze in the garden. The sum of £3,600 is offered in full and final settlement of these claims. My client denies all liability with regard to the breaking of the statue of cupid at the centre of the maze.

This offer is made on the basis that your client agrees not to make public in any way the nature of her allegations against my clients, or the terms of this proposed settlement.

Yours faithfully,

(Solicitor for the proposed defendant)

---

2. Acceptance of the above offer by the proposed claimant.

10th September 2000

Dear Sir,

Re: The Gardens at Manor Lodge, Great Thrushfield

With regard to your letter of 1st September, I have discussed your proposed terms with my client, and she is reluctantly prepared to accept them. I am therefore instructed to inform you that my client will accept £3,600 in final settlement of her claims relating to the work on her garden by your client, provided that this sum is paid within 14 days of today. I assume that it is your intention that both sides should bear their own costs.

I look forward to receiving the agreed sum on behalf of my client.

Yours faithfully,

(Solicitor for the proposed claimant)

RECORDING AND ENFORCING A NEGOTIATED AGREEMENT

3. Letter setting out terms of a negotiated settlement.

1st April 2000

Dear Sir,

Megadell Foods Ltd v Angus Warley (t/a Choc Folie)

I am writing to you to record the terms of negotiated settlement of this case reached by counsel for the parties on 20th March, the detailed terms being subject to client approval.

I understand the terms agreed to be as follows:

1. That there should be a new contract for the supply of chocolate by the claimants to the defendant, to commence within 28 days of the date of this letter. It has been agreed that this contract will last for a minimum of 2 years, and will provide for a minimum delivery of 500 grammes of chocolate per month. The defendant and a representative of the claimant will meet within one month of the date of this agreement to agree full detailed terms for this contract.

2. On the basis that approximately half of the Luglian Chocolate held by the claimant has already been sold to an alternative purchaser, and the rest will be used to meet the new contract with the defendant, no payment will be made with regard to loss of profit by the claimant, save for that provided in (3) below.

3. The defendant will pay to the claimant the sum of £1,890 in respect of one and a half deliveries of chocolate plus interest of £150. This sum is to be paid within 7 days of the date of this letter.

4. The chocolate from the second delivery remaining in the possession of Angus Warley will be inspected by an independent expert within 1 month of the drawing up of this agreement. If the chocolate is found to be of satisfactory quality Angus Warley will retain it and pay for it forthwith. If it is not found to be of satisfactory quality Megadell Foods Ltd will collect the chocolate forthwith and no payment will be required.

5. There will be no payment with regard to the defendant's alleged loss of profits. However, the claimant and the defendant will discuss the possibility of a joint advertising promotion of the Luglian chocolate products manufactured by the defendant.

6. Each party will pay their own costs, save that Megadell Foods will pay the costs of drawing up this agreement.

I have discussed these terms with my client and he is prepared to accept them. I look forward to hearing from you that your client is also prepared to accept the terms.

    Yours sincerely

    (Solicitor for the claimant)

NEGOTIATION

4. Letter accepting the above terms.

10th April 2000

Dear Sir,

Megadell Foods Ltd v Angus Warley (t/a Choc Folie)

I am writing in reply to your letter dated 1st April setting out proposed terms of agreement for this case. I have confirmed with my client that he is prepared to accept these terms in full and final settlement of the case. Indeed my client is looking forward to a more positive commercial future with your client.

Yours sincerely,

(Solicitor for the defendant)

11.3.4 A CONTRACT OR DEED

A contract or deed drafted according to the ordinary principles for drafting such documents can be used to record the outcome of a negotiation. This contract or deed would then itself be a separately legally enforceable document.

This option is more expensive, but the complexity of the terms, the value of property involved or the context may mean that it is a preferable option. If for example the negotiation is between an employer and employee or between businesses involved in trade a new contract may well be appropriate. The essential difference between a contract and a deed is of course that if both sides are making concessions then a contract is made, whereas if only one side is making concessions (and therefore providing consideration) a deed will normally be required. A deed may also be more appropriate if for example the negotiation relates primarily to rights over property.

A contract or deed will not be necessary if the terms agreed are relatively simple. Once a claim has been commenced a contract or deed alone will not have the effect of ending the claim, though it may lead to no further steps in the claim being taken.

If a contract or deed is drafted to record an agreement, it is useful to include a preamble setting out that the document is intended to set out the terms for settling particular claims, so that it is clear what the agreement is supposed to cover should there be any later problem.

Example memorandum of agreement

(This example is an alternative to the exchange of letters above. A further alternative might be to have a new contract between the parties, which would probably be based on a standard form contract used by Megadell Foods Ltd rather than being a wholly separate document.)

THIS AGREEMENT is made on 1st April 2000 between Megadell Foods Limited of the one part and Angus Warley (trading as Choc Folie) of the other part.

WHEREAS the aforesaid Megadell Foods Limited and Angus Warley have been in dispute regarding alleged breaches and alleged repudiation of a contract for the supply of chocolate by the claimant to the defendant in a contract dated 19th July 1999.

NOW IT IS HEREBY AGREED by way of compromise of the said dispute as follows:

1. A new contract for the supply of chocolate by Megadell Foods Limited to Angus Warley will be entered into within 28 days of the date of this order. This contract will last for a minimum of 2 years, and will provide for a minimum delivery of 500 grammes of chocolate per month.

> 2. Angus Warley will pay to Megadell Foods Limited the sum of £1,890 in respect of one and a half deliveries of chocolate plus interest of £150. This sum is to be paid within 7 days of the date of this agreement.
>
> 3. Each party will pay their own costs, save that Megadell Foods will pay the costs of drawing up this agreement.
>
> IN FURTHERANCE OF THIS AGREEMENT:
>
> 1. Angus Warley and a representative of Megadell Foods Limited will meet within one month of the date of this agreement to agree full detailed terms for continued delivery of chocolate by Megadell Foods Limited to Angus Warley.
>
> 2. The chocolate from the second delivery remaining in the possession of Angus Warley will be inspected by an independent expert within 1 month of the drawing up of this agreement. If the chocolate is found to be of satisfactory quality Angus Warley will retain it and pay for it forthwith. If it is not found to be of satisfactory quality Megadell Foods Ltd will collect the chocolate forthwith and no payment will be required.
>
> Dated:
>
> Signed   Signed
>
> In the presence of   In the presence of

11.3.5 AN INTERIM COURT ORDER

An interim order can only be made by a judge once a claim has been commenced, and if an appropriate application to court for the interim order has been made.

One possibility is that an application for an interim order has already been made, and the negotiation between the parties takes place just prior to going into court. This might happen if for example there is an application for dismissal or an application for an interim injunction. In such a case the barristers will need to agree what they are going to ask the judge to do — whether they want to ask for the interim order to be made in the terms they agree, or whether they wish to ask the judge to dismiss the application altogether because they have agreed terms.

An alternative possibility is that the parties might need to seek an interim order to put an agreement that they have reached into operation in whole or in part.

If you are reaching an agreement at an interim stage you must be clear about whether the agreement will mean that the claim will proceed no further, whether the claim will proceed in part, or whether the settlement relates to the interim application alone.

Examples of interim orders

1. Setting aside a judgment in default on agreed terms.

(Since there has been an application to set aside a judgment in default, the following is a further alternative to the exchange of letters or the memorandum of agreement above.)

NEGOTIATION

IN THE TAUNTON COUNTY COURT   Claim No. TA501001

BETWEEN

MEGADELL FOODS LIMITED   <u>Claimant</u>

and

ANGUS WARLEY (t/a CHOC FOLIE)   <u>Defendant</u>

DRAFT MINUTES OF ORDER

Upon hearing counsel for the claimant and for the defendant

By consent it is ordered:

1. The judgment in default obtained on 24th February 2000 be set aside upon the basis of terms agreed between the parties.

2. Each party to bear their own costs.

Dated

(The precise terms could then be recorded in a separate contract or exchange of letters.)

---

2. An adjournment upon agreed terms

IN THE WINCHESTER COUNTY COURT   Claim No. 9876

BETWEEN

ALGERNON SMYTHE   <u>Claimant</u>

and

HONEST JOHN MOTORS LIMITED   <u>Defendant</u>

BY CONSENT it is ordered that the claim and Part 20 claim in this action be adjourned generally upon the terms set out below:

1. That the Defendant pays to the Claimant the sum of £5,000 within 28 days of the date of this order.

2. That the Claimant returns to the Defendant the Ford Fiesta motor car registration number M 143 SUE within 28 days of the date of this order.

AND IT IS FURTHER ORDERED that in the event of the terms being carried out by the parties the claim and Part 20 claim be and are hereby dismissed with no order as to costs.

AND IT IS FURTHER ORDERED that in the event of any of the terms not being carried out, either party shall be at liberty to restore the claim for trial.

11.3.6 FINAL COURT ORDER

You can only get a final order from the court, even by consent, if the claim has been commenced, and if that claim is sufficiently advanced for it to be procedurally possible to ask for the case to be listed for an order to be made.

RECORDING AND ENFORCING A NEGOTIATED AGREEMENT

If a case has reached such a stage then it will often be appropriate to record an agreement reached in the form of a consent order. If the case has not reached such a stage then one can only ask the judge to make an order that the case be dismissed upon agreed terms.

Remember that a judge can only order those things that he or she has the power to order in the case in question. The judge cannot order anything at all simply because an agreement has been reached by consent (*Hinde* v *Hinde* [1953] 1 All ER 171). There are however, techniques for getting round this, such as having the order made on the basis of certain undertakings, or putting things that the judge cannot order directly into a schedule, upon the basis of which the judge's order is made. Do note that undertakings to a judge can only be given in an interim or final order and are not otherwise generally available as part of a settlement of a case.

A Tomlin order with a Schedule can be useful where the terms agreed are particularly complex, where the use of a schedule to list property aids clear drafting, or where the schedule can be used to set out terms that cannot be ordered by the judge in the body of the order.

Example court order

IN THE HIGH COURT OF JUSTICE   2000 T No.7564

QUEEN'S BENCH DIVISION

BETWEEN

        TOP WOMEN (a firm)   Claimant

        and

        MANAGEMENT CONSULTANTS PLC   Defendant

DRAFT MINUTES OF ORDER

Upon hearing counsel for the claimant and for the defendant.

And upon the defendant undertaking:

1. Not to take any action to exclude the Claimant's clients from the Defendant's offices.

2. To continue to pay the Claimant's clients as specified in the agreement dated 6th March 1998.

By consent it is ordered:

1. The Defendant to pay to the Claimant damages of £40,000 within 4 weeks of the date of this order.

2. The defendant to pay the costs of this action.

Dated

Example Tomlin order

IN THE HIGH COURT OF JUSTICE   2000 C No. 666

QUEEN'S BENCH DIVISION

BETWEEN

COMPUTER PRODUCTS PLC   Claimant

and

UNITED DISCS PLC   Defendant

Upon the parties having agreed to the terms of settlement set out below.

By consent it is ordered that all further proceedings in this action be stayed upon the terms set out in the attached Schedule, save for the purpose of enforcing the terms, with liberty to apply for such purpose.

And it is further ordered that there be no order as to costs.

SCHEDULE

1. The warehouse at Lot 9, Molesworth Industrial Estate, Polehurst, Hampshire be sold within 6 months of the date of this order for the best price obtainable, and the net proceeds be divided as to 60% to the Claimant and 40% to the Defendant.

2. A valuation of the computer software remaining in the warehouse will be obtained by each party within 14 days of the date of this order, the Defendant to pay to the Claimant a sum half way between the two valuations obtained within 3 months of the date of this order. Should the sum not be paid within this time it will carry interest at the rate of 10% per annum.

3. The Defendant will destroy all copies of the 'Drawpro' program remaining in their possession forthwith.

11.4 Enforcement of Negotiated Agreements

As has been said, an oral agreement following a negotiation will itself be enforceable (save in so far as the terms are subject to client approval). For examples see *Smallman v Smallman* [1971] 3 All ER 717 and *Chanel v F.W. Woolworth* [1981] 1 All ER 745. This can be an advantage in so far as the terms are advantageous, but not in so far as it may be difficult to prove the terms agreed if there is any disagreement, or if you would like to re-open what has been agreed (see *O'Boyle v Leiper, The Times*, 26 January 1990). You therefore need to be careful before reaching final oral agreement, and to move on to getting a full written agreement as soon as possible after an oral agreement is concluded.

As has already been said, the lawyer should have in mind how any agreement might be enforced when negotiating its terms. If there are options then the lawyer should normally go for the one that will be easiest to enforce (for example because it is simplest or will require least monitoring or assistance). Note that terms can only be enforced if they are sufficiently clear (*Wilson & Whitworth Ltd v Express & Independent Newspapers Ltd* [1969] 1 WLR 197).

You should also consider enforcement when negotiating the detail of terms, such as when money will be paid and whether there will be any penalty if it is not paid on time.

The options for enforcing an agreement if necessary are as follows (**11.4.1** to **11.4.5**).

11.4.1 BUILDING ENFORCEMENT OPTIONS INTO THE AGREED TERMS

If the terms of the agreement are not adhered to, then the cheapest and easiest form of enforcement will normally be one that is within the wording of the agreement itself. If, for example, the agreement is for your client to pay the other side £50,000 and for the other side to give specified property to your client then it is best to provide in the agreement that your client will only give the money once he or she has been given the property.

You can provide for such terms either when you are negotiating orally or when you come to draw up the appropriate form of written agreement. It is best at least to mention enforcement points during the oral negotiation, and if you foresee any particular problems with enforcement you may particularly wish to offer to do the draft of the agreed terms yourself. Try to cover all reasonably foreseeable eventualities in the terms you agree.

11.4.2 RETURN TO COURT IN AN EXISTING CLAIM

The agreement reached will normally terminate any claim that had been commenced, and you should not assume that there will be any easy or cheap route for returning to court for enforcement.

If there has been an interim or a final judgment it may be possible to return to court to ask the judge for assistance in carrying out the agreement. You will normally need to reserve liberty to apply for this purpose. Note that the words 'liberty to apply' can only allow a party to return to court to clarify a detail, or to seek the directions of the court on the implementation of an order, and they cannot more generally be used to remedy any defect or as a sort of appeal (*Practice Direction* [1980] 1 All ER 1008).

11.4.3 RETURN TO COURT PURELY FOR ENFORCEMENT OF AN ORDER

In certain circumstances you will be able to go to court purely to enforce the order, using normal enforcement methods. You will also be able to return to court for enforcement if an interim injunction or an undertaking to a judge is breached.

11.4.4 APPEAL

It will generally not be possible to appeal where an order has been made by consent. If you have agreed to an order you will generally be estopped from any further action or appeal relating to the same matter. The only possibility for appeal will generally be where the substance of the order has been undermined by fraud, mistake or duress (see for example *D & C Builders* v *Rees* [1966] 2 QB 617).

11.4.5 COMMENCING A NEW CLAIM

The most expensive option, and therefore the one best avoided unless there is no alternative, is to commence a new claim. This may be necessary if a claim was never started in the first place, or if a contract or deed needs to be enforced, or if an endorsement on a brief needs to be enforced (see for example *Green* v *Rozen* [1955] 1 WLR 741). Since a new claim will have to be taken through all its stages, there will be all the attendant cost and inconvenience.

For further precedents for written agreements when settling a case, see *The Law and Practice of Compromise* by David Foskett (4th edn, 1996).

TWELVE

APPROPRIATE DISPUTE RESOLUTION

12.1 Appropriate Not Alternative

Over the last decade there has been increasing concern about the civil justice system and the need to reform it. The major but not fundamental changes made by the Woolf reforms attempt to address some of these concerns. Time will tell how successful the reforms are.

Around the world, serious consideration is being given not only to reform of the civil litigation process but also to alternative methods of settling civil disputes. A movement which started in the US looking for Alternative Dispute Resolution methods (ADR) has spread to other countries and arrived in the UK a few years ago. Increasingly there is international discussion about the best methods of resolving civil disputes which has begun to look more widely and creatively at the problem. Two things are happening. First, those interested in developing a method which really does provide an efficient, fair system which gives access to justice to all, are looking at a range of methods used in a variety of jurisdictions to get a broader view of what is possible. Secondly, some are beginning to question whether litigation should be seen as the principal method with others being described as 'Alternative'. There is a real movement to consideration of 'Appropriate' Dispute Resolution methods with litigation being seen as one of a variety of methods, and not necessarily the dominant or most appropriate one.

Use of alternative methods and consideration of what is appropriate, has come later to the UK than some other countries, e.g., Canada and US. However, many in the UK are making up for lost time and taking to heart the opportunities this provides for developing a variety of methods to resolve different types of civil disputes.

12.2 What is Wrong with Litigation?

The English civil justice system has traditionally relied heavily on the litigation process, i.e., largely through courts, to settle civil disputes. Tribunals are also an important part of the system, although often overlooked in consideration of the system. The underlying ethos, whether using court or tribunal to settle the dispute, has been an adversarial system whereby the two parties in dispute put their cases to a third party to decide. The third party (the decision-maker) relies on the two disputing parties to put all the relevant evidence and arguments, usually in the form of an oral hearing. The decision is then made on the basis that one side wins and one loses (i.e., the decision-maker 'finds' for one side only).

The nature of the process has meant that both parties do as much as they can to demonstrate the strengths of their case and hide or disguise the weaknesses. Rules have developed to ensure that there is some control over the degree to which the parties can do this. Because the disputes are legal, the system has largely been controlled by lawyers who, as a result of their training (and possibly also personality types), are

NEGOTIATION

interested in the interpretation and application of rules. This, combined with the adversarial nature of the system by which each side uses the weapons available, has produced an incredibly complex and costly system which parties require lawyers to guide them through. Some of the disadvantages of resolution through the courts are:

(a) It is highly complex, with a large number of procedural steps and devices which take time to explain and which parties do not understand.

(b) The lawyers and court rules often seem to 'take over' control of the case, leaving the parties feeling powerless and often deferring unnecessarily to the lawyer's views or the court structure.

(c) The adversarial nature of the system emphasises confrontation rather than resolution of the issues.

(d) The combination of lack of understanding of the system, the transfer of some control to the lawyers and the adversarial nature of the system increases the anxiety for the parties.

(e) It can take a long time for cases to come to trial.

(f) Trial dates are not fixed for the benefit of the parties but to fit in with the court diary and, possibly, the lawyers.

(g) Although judges do bring objectivity to the process and can determine the case on the basis of the weight of evidence for the two parties, they cannot necessarily offer expertise in the particular area in dispute.

(h) The system is based largely on hearings in public, which means that private concerns are made public. This can increase the anxiety for the parties.

(i) It is EXPENSIVE!

While the Woolf reforms aim to make litigation more open and less adversarial, they do not fundamentally alter the system and many of the above disadvantages of litigation are likely to remain.

For a whole variety of reasons, therefore, people are looking at more fundamental ways of altering the civil justice system. This means two things for potential barristers. First, the range of methods of resolving disputes may expand and the methods used within that range may alter radically over their working careers. Secondly, the skills needed to do the job may also change radically, e.g., with a reduced emphasis on oral adversarial advocacy skills.

12.3 The Alternatives

There are a number of alternatives to court or tribunal claims which already exist and which may develop with the new thinking on civil dispute resolution:

(a) Complaints procedures. Many professions and commercial concerns have specific procedures for the investigation of complaints as an alternative to legal claims. These procedures vary in their powers and effectiveness.

(b) Ombudsman procedure. Increasingly used by public services in particular, e.g., local authority, insurance, banking, housing associations, ombudsmen are available to deal with a wide range of disputes which individuals have with the providers of the services. This system enables people to enlist the assistance of the ombudsman service to investigate a complaint in a particular area. The person who does the investigation is conversant with the area and will have specific powers to deal with complaints. The idea behind the procedure is that it does provide a quick and relatively cheap method for people to have their disputes resolved by someone with expertise in the area. The limitations are that any ombudsman has limited jurisdiction and powers.

(c) Private arbitration. This occurs where the parties themselves have agreed that the dispute should be resolved outside the court system by an arbitrator who has the relevant expertise to determine the matter (see **12.4**).

(d) Court-ordered arbitration. This occurs where, although the parties have issued court proceedings, the court itself refers the matter to a less formal procedure. The general idea is that the simplified procedure and assistance of the arbitrator enables the parties to present their own cases.

(e) Mini-trials. This particular technique has been used in commercial cases where there is a dispute between two companies, whereby there is an oral presentation using supporting documents to a panel, who have the power to settle the dispute. Essentially, senior executives of the two companies sit, possibly with an independent assessor, and consider the case as presented by the two companies (who may use their in-house lawyers). Although a mini-trial is still relatively formal and expensive, the matter may be resolved more quickly and cheaply than through the litigation process. In addition, it is resolved in private. The process can be varied to meet the needs of the particular companies, and the particular dispute, and in fact amount to a high-level negotiation to settle the matter.

(f) Negotiation. As has been stated already, a large percentage of cases settle. Although many are done within the context of the litigation process, the outcome of the case is determined through negotiation, often by the lawyers. People are becoming much more conscious of the importance of negotiation skills in the overall resolution of civil disputes.

(g) Conciliation. This means of resolving a dispute is similar to negotiation in that it does not rely on a third party imposing a decision on the parties to the dispute. A third party is involved but, rather than being the decision-maker, he or she provides assistance in a variety of ways, e.g., information or acting as a channel through which the parties can communicate with each other, to facilitate the parties themselves reaching agreement on how the dispute should be settled.

(h) Mediation. This means of resolving a dispute is very similar to conciliation in that it does involve a third party, the mediator, whose main role is to facilitate a negotiation between the two parties in dispute. The mediator takes a more active role as facilitator and may, e.g., identify areas of dispute, assist the parties to discuss their differences, and suggest possible solutions for the parties to consider. Exactly how interventionist the mediator is will depend on the matter in dispute, e.g., whether it is a commercial dispute or a neighbourhood disagreement, and the particular philosophy or practice of the mediator.

The above methods differ in a variety of ways from court or tribunal procedure. The first two, although similar to courts and tribunals in that the parties look to a third party to make the decision, have more circumscribed jurisdiction and powers than courts or tribunals. Arbitration, which also relies on a third party to make the decision, has been an alternative to litigation for some years now and has developed rules almost as complex as those used in litigation.

The final three differ from court or tribunal proceedings in that they all rely on the parties themselves reaching an agreement. Conciliation and mediation do involve a third party but only to facilitate the decision by the disputing parties. Negotiation has no third party. Although lawyers may actually do the negotiating on behalf of the parties, they are still very much representing their own individual clients.

12.4 Arbitration

12.4.1 WHAT IT IS

Generally private arbitration will be an option chosen by the parties themselves (by agreement) although certain statutes provide for reference of particular types of dispute to arbitration. Commercial contracts often contain clauses providing for reference of disputes to arbitration. These clauses may be specifically agreed by the parties, or incorporated as a result of codes of practice of trade associations, national or international. The role and conduct of such arbitrations will be governed by what is agreed and by the current statutory framework (the Arbitration Acts are being revised).

12.4.2 HOW IT WORKS

An arbitration is like a trial, in that both parties present their case to an arbitrator who makes an award, i.e., he or she fulfils a role very similar to that of a judge in deciding the case. The award is final and binding on the parties unless the agreement provides otherwise. There is limited right of appeal of the decision to the High Court.

The differences from a trial are in the way in which the arbitrator is appointed and the procedure followed. The arbitrator may be named in the agreement or the agreement may provide for the appointment, either by later agreement of the parties or by an outside body, e.g., Royal Institute of Chartered Surveyors. The person selected need not have special qualifications. However, he or she will usually be qualified in the relevant field and the agreement may require the person appointed to have specific qualifications. The parties may also draw up the terms of reference for the arbitrator.

The agreement may set out the procedure to be followed or this may be left to the arbitrator to decide. There are no set rules, although the rules of natural justice must be followed (i.e., each party to be given a fair opportunity to be heard and the arbitrator must be independent of the parties). In very broad terms, an arbitration can follow a procedure similar to a court case, in that each side prepares its own case and then presents it to the arbitrator. However, an arbitration is not subject to all the detailed procedural rules of civil litigation and there are, for example, no provisions for payment into court. It is, however, frequently possible to imitate procedural rules if this would be useful. Thus, for example, it is possible to make a written 'without prejudice' offer that may be referred to in connection with costs if the offer is not accepted.

12.4.3 AREAS IN WHICH IT IS USED

Arbitration is most commonly used where commercial or specialist knowledge is particularly important. The attractions of arbitration are that: the parties retain more control over the procedure, e.g., the date of the hearing can be fixed to suit their needs as opposed to having to be fit into court lists; the hearings are in private; and the arbitrator is selected usually for his or her expertise or experience in the area disputed. In theory, arbitration should also be more informal, cheaper and speedier than court proceedings. However, this is not always so.

12.4.4 BARRISTERS' ROLE

A barrister preparing a case for arbitration would do much the same as he or she would in preparing a case for trial. He or she would also have to be aware of the different procedure to be followed and what, if any, his or her involvement would be in selecting the arbitrator or determining the terms of reference. A barrister may also train to be an arbitrator through the Chartered Institute of Arbitrators.

APPROPRIATE DISPUTE RESOLUTION

12.5 Mediation

12.5.1 WHAT IT IS

Mediation is a form of voluntary non-binding 'without prejudice' negotiation assisted by a neutral third party. The third party, the 'mediator', does not have power to make a decision nor to give individuals legal advice. The mediator's role is to attempt to bring the two parties to a dispute closer together to assist them in reaching agreement. The method by which the mediator does this, and the range of techniques used, will vary depending on the type of dispute and the philosophy of the mediator or the organisation to which the mediator belongs. A large number of people are forming a variety of associations and/or businesses to do mediation. Mediators range from being quite interventionist and/or 'evaluative' to being purely 'facilitative'. On the interventionist/ evaluative end of the range, the mediator takes an active part in seeking settlement both suggesting and commenting on solutions. At the truly facilitative end of the range, mediators see their role as enabling the parties to find and agree their own solution. There are therefore, strong prohibitions on the mediator either suggesting or commenting on solutions. There is some discussion in the literature on mediation as to whether 'evaluative' mediation is really mediation at all because of the interventionist role played by the mediator.

As yet there is no specific qualification to be a mediator. Many different groups are becoming involved in the development of mediation, partially by setting up services themselves and partially by trying to influence the way in which the whole area in being formalised (and taken over by professionals!). Some argue strongly that lawyers are not the ideal people to be mediators, given their training and adversarial mindsets, and that mediators should be chosen from those in the 'caring/ facilitating' professions whose training is more akin to what is required in mediation. Although there are as yet no set qualifications to act as a mediator, many organisations now do require people who act as mediators for them to have undergone a training programme of some type. Formal qualifications and professionalisation of this area of work is definitely on the horizon (which has its advantages and disadvantages). Codes of conduct and ethical rules are not far behind.

12.5.2 AREAS IN WHICH IT IS USED

Mediation is used in a broad range of areas from commercial disputes worth very large sums of money to disputes between neighbours about the level of noise. Family and divorce mediation is also growing. Because mediation is a rapidly developing field of work and therefore changing, it is difficult to set out all the areas in which it is becoming a realistic and used method of resolving disputes. However, one could differentiate between three basic types of mediation:

- Family and divorce. In the past few years, mediation has been used increasingly in divorce and family matters. The government intend to run a pilot project over a two-year period to precede the implementation of more definite requirements for mediation within the litigation process. A variety of associations deal with this type of mediation, in particular the Family Mediators Association (FMA) and the National Family Mediation (NFM). In addition to offering mediation services, they train people to act as mediators.

- Commercial disputes. Large commercial concerns are turning to mediation to resolve disputes which might otherwise take a lot of time and money to resolve through the courts. The RSC rules require a statement setting out what alternative methods have been considered to resolve the matter prior to setting down in High Court. The Centre for Dispute Resolution (CEDR) is the biggest provider of this type of mediation in the UK. It was launched in November 1990 and has as its members over 150 of Europe's leading companies and professional firms.

NEGOTIATION

- Community disputes. This type of mediation covers a fairly broad range of disputes which are matters of concern to a community. Thus it could cover neighbour disputes, problems in school, environmental issues, etc. There are also victim/offender mediation services. With the development of mediation, each of these areas will probably itself develop as quite a distinct area. Mediation UK acts as a coordinator of information about groups who provide mediation services, generally within this type of mediation.

12.5.3 HOW IT WORKS

Agreement by both parties that they will use mediation to attempt to resolve the dispute is essential (without agreement of BOTH parties it will not proceed). There is no set procedure for the conduct of a mediation. Again, different organisations have developed their own procedures which may vary depending on the type of dispute. Most however, will have an opening session with the mediator and both parties. The mediator will set out the purpose of the mediation and his or her role, emphasising that it is for the parties to reach agreement, not for him or her to impose one. Each party may then be given an opportunity to explain how he or she sees the case. This enables the parties and the mediator to get some idea of the extent of the dispute and the positions of each party.

One of the most significant differences in the methods used is whether the mediation takes place with the parties present in the same room or is conducted with the parties in different rooms with the mediator moving back and forth (or shuttling) between them:

(a) In the first method there are likely to be some formalities such as an opening session, each party being given an opportunity to explain how he or she sees the dispute after which discussion becomes more general with the mediator encouraging the parties to address each other rather than the mediator. The underlying principle of this method, used by many community mediators, is that the parties must communicate with each other and unless they can do that any agreement is unlikely to last.

(b) In the second method, used more in commercial mediations, after the opening session, the parties are located in separate rooms and the mediator sees them separately to discuss the dispute from their individual points of view (Americans call this part of the process 'caucusing'). Having discussed the case with the individual parties, the mediator can take information, which each party permits the mediator to take, to the other side. The mediator 'shuttles' back and forth between the parties trying to get them to reach agreement. In the sessions with the individual parties, the mediator will be doing two things principally, first, giving information that he or she is permitted to give to the other side and secondly, getting the party with whom he or she is discussing the case to really think about realistic possibilities for settlement. The mediator may also be making suggestions of ways in which settlement may be reached. A concluding session will be held jointly, to confirm what has been agreed between the parties, or that there is no agreement.

If agreement is reached, it can be treated as a contract.

12.5.4 BARRISTERS' ROLE

Barristers' potential role in mediation is threefold. First, knowing when to consider mediation as an alternative to litigation, and ensuring that the client is aware of the possibility and the advantages and disadvantages of it. Secondly, representing clients at mediations. Legal aid is not available for mediation. However, in large commercial mediations, the parties may be represented by counsel. Finally, some barristers are themselves acting as mediators in a variety of disputes.

12.5.5 DIFFERENCE BETWEEN NEGOTIATION AND MEDIATION

Lawyers in a negotiation may fulfil some of the functions of a mediator or conciliator in that they bring a more objective view to what is possible. In both negotiation within the litigation context, and in mediation, the parties are seeking an agreement which is acceptable to both parties and may do so by using objective criteria or a 'fairness standard'. The real difference between the two is the control by the parties over the standard used to gauge the settlement and how the lawyer uses the court's assessment of the merits of the case.

Where the lawyer acts as mediator, he or she must adopt the ethos of mediation and shake off both the adversarial mindset of the litigation lawyer and the decision-maker mindset of the judge. The mediator is not arguing for either party, nor does he or she determine the outcome.

Where a lawyer accompanies a client to a mediation, his or her role is more akin to the usual role of the lawyer in litigation, i.e., to assist his or her client. The difference here is that mediation seeks to resolve disputes by standards of fairness largely chosen by the parties to the mediation. There is no obligation to consider, and no particular emphasis given, to the strengths of the competing legal rights of the parties. In litigation, the standard against which the parties judge any settlement is the likely assessment of the merits of the case by the court. Lawyers acting in mediation will have to learn not to be wedded to the merits in considering the settlement.

THIRTEEN

ASSESSING NEGOTIATION SKILLS

13.1 Learning Lawyers' Negotiation Skills

13.1.1 NEGOTIATION SKILLS FOR BARRISTERS

Learning how to adapt and expand existing negotiation skills for use as a lawyer entails performing and observing the skills in appropriate contexts and being reflective about what you do, see and hear. Most barristers will use their negotiation skills, at least in the early years of practice, primarily in the context of resolving disputes within the litigation process, generally at the court door.

The BVC negotiation course covers a range of cases and types of negotiation (see **2.2**) but concentrates on situations in which settlement is sought at some stage in the litigation process, generally using scenarios where negotiations are done at the court door. The course focuses on teaching the skills necessary to conduct such negotiations within the limitations imposed (see **Chapter 3**, in particular **3.3**). It includes the theoretical and behavioural aspects of negotiation and you are expected to understand and recognise the different strategies and tactics and use those that are appropriate in the circumstances. The main thrust of the course, however, is ensuring that you understand and can control the content of the discussion in a negotiation.

13.1.2 LEARNING SKILLS USING PERFORMANCE CRITERIA

Negotiation is a complex skill. It requires intellectual and presentation skills. It also involves emotional and behavioural aspects, some of which operate on an unconscious or semi-conscious level. Although recognising a good settlement is relatively straightforward, it takes a solid understanding of negotiation to analyse a performance and identify precisely how this particular settlement was achieved and what was and was not effective. To be able to analyse a performance and use that analysis to improve your own skills, you must be able to identify those aspects of the negotiation that were well done and those that were badly done. You must also be able to understand how you can reinforce those aspects of the skill that you already do well and recognise those aspects of the skill that you need to and can improve. Although you cannot change your personality and it is very difficult to alter long-standing behaviour patterns, you can develop the ability to control the substance of the negotiation discussion and to present and respond effectively. However, there is a limit to the number of factors to which you can attend in observing or critiquing a negotiation performance. The performance criteria highlight those aspects that will influence the content and outcome of the negotiation and which you can change or reinforce as appropriate. They identify the aspects of negotiation on which you should be concentrating in learning the skill.

The criteria are used throughout the course. The tutor relates his or her feedback on performances to the criteria. You are also expected to assess and give criteria based feedback on your own and colleagues' performances.

NEGOTIATION

13.2 The Negotiation Course

13.2.1 THE TASKS

During the negotiation course and in the assessment you will be required to undertake the following tasks:

(a) prepare to negotiate by carrying out the appropriate analysis, evaluation and planning;

(b) write a plan setting out your analysis, evaluation and proposals for the conduct and structure of the negotiation;

(c) conduct a negotiation involving one or more items on which agreement is required to reach an overall settlement including determining the appropriate method of recording the settlement to ensure that it is enforceable and effective;

(d) draft an agreement which accurately reflects the settlement reached ensuring that all matters are included in sufficient detail and in an appropriate form.

13.2.2 THE ASPECTS BEING ASSESSED

The course has a very practical focus. Although it requires an understanding of some theoretical aspects, the course is designed to teach you how to prepare for and conduct a negotiation effectively by being able to control the content of the discussion in the negotiation and focus the discussion on seeking a good settlement. The performance criteria are therefore focused on assessing these practical skills, i.e., how well you have identified and evaluated the matters which will form the content of the discussion and how effectively you use this analysis and evaluation in presenting your case and responding to your opponent in the negotiation to reach a good settlement for your client. Thus, the criteria are used to assess ability in two distinct areas. First, they assess the intellectual skills of analysis and judgement which you will use both preparing for and conducting the negotiation. Secondly, they assess presentation skills used in controlling what you say and how you say it in the negotiation.

Some skills can be broken down into identifiable aspects that can be considered discretely, e.g., questioning and advising in conference skills. However, a negotiation is a dynamic interactive process without identifiable discrete phases. The behaviour patterns that have been identified are very general and involve a multiplicity of aspects with overlapping phases which are frequently repeated. Not all negotiations exhibit the same phases and, in any one negotiation, neither negotiator has more control than the other over how it is conducted. It is therefore not possible to break a negotiation performance into identifiable stages and assess the effectiveness of each stage.

The performance criteria therefore focus on the following aspects:

(a) identifying and pursuing objectives and using concessions to move to settlement;

(b) doing relevant analysis and evaluation and using that appropriately in the negotiation;

(c) presenting your client's case;

(d) responding to your opponent;

(e) observing the rules of professional conduct.

13.2.3 THE PERFORMANCE AND ROLE OF THE PLAN

Negotiation is a skill that involves moving to a compromise that reflects both what the parties want and what can be argued on their behalf. Although your preparation should identify the strengths and weaknesses of your case and the arguments that can be used for and against you, what you actually say in the negotiation will be circumscribed. Getting the best for your client means revealing information that assists in reaching a good settlement and using arguments that will persuade your opponent to move towards you. Although much of your analysis will inform what you say in the negotiation, much of it will not be expressly stated or revealed to your opponent. Thus, for example, you may have an opponent who has not seen some of the weaknesses of your case or arguments that could be put on his or her client's behalf. It would be counter-productive to set them out in the negotiation. Alternatively, your opponent may offer something by way of compromise that is a very good deal. It would be fruitless and counter-productive to respond by explaining why you are accepting the offer. You just accept it.

The plan therefore serves two purposes. First, it is an 'aide-memoire' for you to assist you to be 'on top of the case' in the negotiation; clear about the arguments and compromises that can or should be made in the negotiation. Secondly, it assists anyone watching the performance to understand your rationale for what you say in the negotiation and the proposals you put to or accept from your opponent.

13.3 The Negotiation Criteria

13.3.1 OBJECTIVES AND CONCESSIONS AND MOVING TO SETTLEMENT

This criterion assesses how well you have identified what you wish to achieve in the negotiation and planned how you are going to move from what your client ideally wants to something which is acceptable to the other side without sacrificing more than is necessary of what your client wants. It also covers how effectively you then pursue this in the performance. Thus it assesses your ability both to analyse the case and to put that analysis into practice in the negotiation. It breaks down into a number of overlapping aspects.

13.3.1.1 Identifying the objectives of both parties

Consideration of this aspect includes looking at how thoroughly and precisely you have identified what your client wants. Have you identified all of the client's relevant wishes extending your analysis to both legal and non-legal objectives? Have you looked beyond the client's stated goals at the underlying needs, interests and reasons which may influence those goals and considered the context of negotiation, for example, whether or not the parties have/wish to have an ongoing relationship? It also includes consideration of how effectively you have prioritised the objectives by reference to the value placed on them by the client. Have you clearly identified and differentiated between what the client must have (the point beyond which the client will not settle), what the client would like to have and what he or she is prepared to forego to get the more valued items? Full consideration of what the other side might be seeking from the negotiation is another aspect of this criterion. How well have you identified what the other side may want and the reasons he or she may have to settle? It also includes assessing the extent to which you have differentiated between those objectives on which the parties are in direct conflict, i.e., satisfying one party will be at the expense of what the other party wants, and those on which the parties' objectives may be more compatible and where there may be scope for creating solutions which partially or wholly satisfy both sides.

13.3.1.2 Identifying the 'items' to be negotiated

Not all of the parties' objectives or areas of disagreement between them are matters that will be negotiated and identifying the items which are likely to be negotiated is an essential aspect of this criterion. This includes consideration of whether you have differentiated between matters which must be negotiated to reach settlement, e.g., precisely how much money changes hands or whether a boundary line will or will not be moved, and other matters which will not necessarily be negotiated because they are about the parties' positions (e.g., determining whether or not a contract was breached) or matters which are not really negotiable (e.g., maintaining a friendship). Thus the

NEGOTIATION

'items' to be negotiated should include all those matters on which reaching settlement is both necessary and realistic in the circumstances. In addition to the specific negotiable objectives of the parties, this should include the method by which any settlement is recorded, ensuring that it is the most appropriate method given the terms of the settlement, any procedural requirements and the wishes of the parties.

13.3.1.3 Planning the concessions

This criterion also assesses how well you have planned the concessions you will seek and make. Concessions are proposals for moving to settlement on items which are subject to negotiation and must be distinguished from matters which are not concessions, e.g., admissions of fact or agreement on the law (see **9.4.2**). Effective concession planning involves identifying both what concessions you will seek from your opponent and what concessions you will offer. These should be based on a combination of your client's wishes and priorities, your evaluation of the case and the best overall settlement achievable for your client. You should identify the most achievable settlement for your client and plan so that the offers you make are staged, starting with the most achievable and working towards compromise gradually, each proposal sacrificing as little of what your client wishes as possible. Concessions should also be planned so that you are trading items of lower value to your client to get those that are more valued. Finally, concessions should build on what the other party appears to be seeking.

13.3.1.4 Planning how to conduct the negotiation

One of the objectives of a court door negotiation is to attempt to reach settlement in the time available. That means using the time efficiently. This includes identifying the areas on which discussion would be useful and those on which it would not; identifying what information exchange would assist and how much testing of the case would assist to determine an appropriate settlement standard. It also includes consideration of how to structure the negotiation to ensure that all relevant matters are covered as efficiently as possible and in an order which will enable you to obtain the best for your client. Finally, it covers consideration of how to start the negotiation in a way which is conducive to the structure you would like to adopt.

13.3.1.5 Pursuing a good settlement

This aspect of the criterion assesses how well you put your analysis into practice in the negotiation. It includes assessing your ability to conduct the negotiation in a way which gives your client the best possible overall outcome given the wishes of both parties, the arguments advanced on both sides and the approach taken by the opponent. It assesses your ability to re-appraise issues in light of information exchanged, arguments put by the opponent and assessment of what the opponent is likely to be prepared to do to move to settlement. It also assesses your ability to make rational judgements on what is a reasonable compromise based on the client's priorities, the merits of the case and the practicalities of what is suggested and to resist succumbing to behavioural strategy and tactics and either becoming too positional or giving away too much. This is judged on the basis of the concessions sought and made, e.g., not making any unnecessary concessions or not refusing to make reasonable ones, and the reasoning for what is proposed and agreed.

13.3.1.6 The settlement

Finally, under this criterion any settlement reached is considered to see whether it is as close to your client's objectives as possible, covers all the relevant matters in sufficient detail and is recorded in an appropriate form given the context in which the negotiation took place. This includes consideration of both the overall agreement and the individual terms agreed to see whether they are within the client's objectives and are clear, practical and enforceable.

13.3.2 ANALYSIS AND EVALUATION

This criterion assesses your ability to analyse the case, evaluate it on the basis of that analysis and then use that analysis and evaluation in preparing for and conducting the negotiation. It also breaks down into a number of overlapping aspects that divide into two main categories of analysis and evaluation.

13.3.2.1 Analysis

This includes identifying the issues underlying the dispute, using the law and facts to formulate arguments that can be used for and against you in the negotiation and identifying the information which is likely to be exchanged in the negotiation. The main component parts of analysis are:

(a) The issues in dispute. It is important to understand the issues that will form the negotiation. This involves clearly identifying the underlying legal and factual issues and differentiating between those that are disputed and those that are not. Thus a claim may be based on a breach of contract in which breach is admitted but loss is denied.

(b) The facts. A fluent grasp of the facts is essential for effective negotiation. This includes clear identification of the relevant facts and any gaps or ambiguities and differentiation between those facts that are agreed and those that are disputed. Being on top of the figures is also important as is being able to do the necessary calculations in the negotiation.

(c) The law. A solid understanding of the relevant substantive, procedural and evidential law is essential as is a sound application of the law to the facts of the case to reach a well-reasoned view of the merits of the arguments on both sides.

(d) Evidence and information. Identifying the evidential basis of the parties' allegations is important as is distinguishing between solid and weak evidence and determining how this can be used in the negotiation. Equally important is identifying the information you should seek from your opponent and the information that might be sought by your opponent and planning how you will deal with this in the negotiation.

(e) Argument formulation. This involves putting all of the above analysis together to construct legal, factual and practical arguments that you can use to support your case. Equally it includes identifying those arguments that your opponent might use against you in the negotiation so that you are prepared to deal with points raised by him or her. It also involves relating these arguments to the issues in dispute and the items to be negotiated so that you are clear how the arguments can be used in seeking settlement.

13.3.2.2 Evaluation

On the basis of the analysis done, you must evaluate the case considering your client's claims and your opponent's claims both overall and on individual items. This involves being clear where your strengths and your opponent's weaknesses lie and planning how you can use them effectively in the negotiation. Equally it involves being clear where your weaknesses and your opponent's strengths lie and planning how to counter them. Evaluation of the arguments available to both parties and how these arguments would influence a court judgment is clearly an important aspect. However, strengths and weaknesses may also stem from the availability of information to the parties, the evidential basis of allegations or interpretation of legal principles. Identifying how the merits of the case may influence the negotiation, in particular in determining any standard against which to judge whether or not any offer made or settlement suggested is reasonable and/or fair, is also an important part of evaluation. It is also essential to relate this evaluation and assessment of an appropriate settlement standard to your analysis of the client's objectives and concession planning to determine what is achievable and how best to use it to seek settlement. Finally, consideration of what strategy is appropriate given the context of the negotiation and the client's objectives should be based on the analysis and evaluation.

13.3.3 PRESENTING YOUR CLIENT'S CASE EFFECTIVELY

This criterion assesses your ability to present your client's case in a way that enables you to achieve the best settlement; your ability to use persuasive argument and proposals for compromise to move to a settlement which is the most favourable one

NEGOTIATION

achievable for your client in the circumstances. Aspects considered under this criterion include the following.

13.3.3.1 Clear, concise and coherent presentation at an appropriate pace

As with good advocacy, speaking clearly and concisely is important as is having a coherent approach, in particular in respect to what you are seeking and the arguments you use. Your presentation should take into account that you are negotiating with a fellow lawyer and terminology and explanations of concepts should be tailored accordingly. In addition, your presentation should take on board the time frame in which you are working and the need to deal with the matters at an appropriate pace.

13.3.3.2 Presenting your client's case in the best light

This includes setting out what your client is seeking from the negotiation clearly and precisely. It also includes presenting your client's case in the best possible light, where appropriate, using the strengths and marginalising weaknesses or not unnecessarily revealing those that may not be known to the opponent.

13.3.3.3 Persuasion through argument and proposals

Your ability to persuade your opponent to move towards you in reaching settlement is an important aspect of this criterion. This involves presenting cogent, relevant argument clearly, confidently and concisely. This involves more than just repeating what is in your brief or asserting facts or law. It means giving your opponent justifiable reasons why your client's point of view should prevail. It also involves using argument appropriately, i.e., in a way that is likely to achieve the desired settlement. Thus, argument can be used to test the opponent and the case where such testing is useful. Alternatively it can be used to justify or explain a proposal or concession being sought from your opponent. Persuasive techniques also include initiating proposals for settlement. In presenting your client's case, you also need to be able to make or seek concessions appropriately. Deciding exactly when and how to do this is one of the most difficult aspects of negotiation. You need to be flexible and 'make the running' where it would assist in moving the negotiation on. You also need to make judgements 'on the hoof' taking into account what you are seeking to achieve, your view of the case given the discussion which has taken place, the time available to reach settlement and how far the negotiation discussion has progressed.

13.3.3.4 Seeking or offering information appropriately

Seeking and offering information is part of negotiation. In presenting your client's case, you need to ensure that you seek information from your opponent or offer it when this would be beneficial to the negotiation or to you in assessing how you will work towards compromise. However, just seeking information for the sake of it can be counter-productive and a waste of time.

13.3.3.5 Using appropriate strategy/language/manner

The strategy, language and manner you adopt in presenting your client's case will have an effect on the negotiation. Being too adversarial is counter-productive where it increases the confrontational nature of the negotiation unnecessarily and pushes both negotiators away from seeking settlement and into purely justifying their client's positions and not seeking ways to move to settlement. Being too conciliatory and co-operative can also be counter-productive where there is a failure to recognise that the negotiators, while attempting to seek settlement, are also representing parties with potentially opposing interests. The result may be that the client's objectives are not properly pursued and the settlement reached is less good than it might have been.

13.3.3.6 Being flexible/taking control where appropriate

A negotiation will rarely go exactly as you planned and you will have to adapt to the approach and style of your opponent. There are no rules about the order in which the negotiators should conduct the negotiation nor how the time should be divided between the negotiators in discussion. Sometimes both negotiators have a similar and compatible approach to the negotiation. However, sometimes the two negotiators have different approaches or styles which means that one does more of the talking than the other. There is nothing wrong with this provided the discussion is productive and moving the negotiation towards a settlement which will be a good one for your client. However, when this is not the case, you must be prepared to step in and steer the negotiation back to a more productive discussion.

13.3.4 RESPONDING TO YOUR OPPONENT

This criterion assesses your ability to listen to what your opponent says and respond to it in a way which progresses the negotiation, protects your client's position as far as possible and increases the prospects of reaching a good settlement for your client. This means being flexible, maintaining your cool and ensuring that you have your eye on the ball (i.e., seeking settlement) and not getting side-tracked into discussions that are counter-productive or irrelevant. It also means responding confidently, clearly and persuasively. Aspects considered under this criterion include the following.

13.3.4.1 Listening carefully

A very important aspect of responding to your opponent is listening carefully to what is said, ensuring that you do understand the points he or she is making. You need to ensure that thinking about your response or the points you want to make does not interfere and result in you not hearing what is said, hearing inaccurately or misunderstanding what is being said. Even when you do listen carefully, you may not understand what your opponent means and may need to check the meaning of what was said.

13.3.4.2 Responding quickly, accurately, coherently and moving to settlement

Responding to your opponent effectively includes responding efficiently, replying quickly and being very clear and accurate in what you say. It also includes ensuring that you keep a clear focus on your client's objectives and your view of the case and that this is reflected in your responses. You also need to ensure that your response is one that will assist in moving to settlement and is not taking the discussion off course into irrelevant or peripheral matters.

13.3.4.3 Responding to argument

Your ability to respond appropriately to arguments put by your opponent includes consideration of whether or not your response assists in reaching a good settlement for your client. Arguing for the sake of it is counter-productive as it can make the negotiation more confrontational than necessary and wastes valuable time. Your responses need to be reasoned ones which have a purpose, e.g., useful testing of the case or your opponent to assist you to gauge what compromise would be reasonable in the circumstances. Continuing to respond to an opponent's argument with further argument long after the merits of the case or issue under discussion are clear is inappropriate where it serves no useful purpose. You must use your judgement and be ready to respond in some way other than just continuing the arguments on the merits. Thus, for example, you could, on the basis of the testing already done, put a proposal for settlement to your opponent, either seeking a concession from him or her or offering a concession.

13.3.4.4 Responding to weaknesses revealed by your opponent

In court door negotiations, particularly those at interim stages, neither negotiator will have full information about the case. Your opponent may have information that you do not which weakens your case and reveals this at some point in the negotiation. Although you may absorb the information and readjust your assessment of the case and the settlement which is achievable on behalf of your client, your response to your opponent should be measured and protect your client's position as far as possible. Conversely, your opponent may reveal a weakness in his or her case of which you were unaware. You need to be able to factor this information in to your assessment of the case in much the same way. You also need to gauge how this information can be used appropriately in the negotiation discussion to reinforce its impact on any settlement standard.

13.3.4.5 Information exchange

Your opponent may seek information from you. You need to be able to gauge whether or not the revealing of the information sought weakens or strengthens your client's

NEGOTIATION

case or is neutral. You also need to be able to gauge whether or not you should reveal it and, if so, how best to frame your response. In providing information you also need to ensure that you do not mislead your opponent as this is unprofessional behaviour (see **13.3.5** below). Your opponent may also present you with information which is not contained in your brief (e.g., expert evidence of the value of an item) and you need to respond appropriately, e.g., asking for the source, validity of this and/or asking to see any documents held by your opponent.

13.3.4.6 Concessions

If and when your opponent makes proposals to you either on individual items or as to overall settlement, you need to respond appropriately ensuring that your response is based on rational judgement and not just a reaction to any offer having been made or to your opponent. Your response should take into account your analysis and evaluation of the case and any changes to that evaluation as a result of what has been revealed or discussed in the negotiation. If you require time to consider proposals, take it, but bearing in mind the need to use time efficiently. Similarly you may be tempted to respond to an opponent's argument by making concessions yourself. If so ensure that this response is appropriate and based on proper evaluation of the case and that you are not just reacting to your opponent and succumbing unnecessarily.

13.3.5 PROFESSIONAL CONDUCT

As a barrister you are bound by the Code of Conduct and must act within it at all times. The principles in the Code apply equally to conducting a negotiation at the court door as they do to conducting a case in the courtroom. This criterion assesses your observance of the Code of Conduct and ethical behaviour. It includes consideration of your ability to identify ethical issues in your preparation and act appropriately both in presenting and responding in the negotiation. Matters that fall within this criterion include ensuring that you are acting within instructions, seeking settlement in accordance with your client's wishes and not misleading your opponent. It also includes acting professionally towards your opponent, being polite and courteous at all times.

13.3.5.1 Acting within your instructions

This covers several aspects. You must ensure that you do not exceed the authority given to you by your clients. This means ensuring that you are clear about the extent of your authority and any specific limits that have been put on it. You must also ensure that you do not actively mislead or deceive your opponent, e.g., not inventing facts, overstating your case, stating that you have evidence to support a particular allegation which you do not have. In addition, you must not knowingly conceal matters that ought properly to have been disclosed, e.g., a document which should be included in the disclosure process and you must give full and frank disclosure where appropriate.

13.3.5.2 Acting professionally towards your opponent

As a barrister you must always act professionally, treating all those with whom you deal with courtesy. This includes your opponent in a negotiation. You must be polite and avoid bullying or unseemly aggressive behaviour. Adopting a competitive strategy or style does not give you a licence to be rude. You can state your case assertively but politely. When negotiating against an opponent who has over-stepped the boundary of professional behaviour, you must resist the temptation to respond in kind. You must remain professional and polite. In addition, if you have said something you regret having said, e.g., you have made a mistake or accepted a proposal that you should not have, you must not pretend that the words were not spoken. You must accept that they were spoken and deal with the result ethically.

FOURTEEN

SAMPLE EXERCISE

IN THE TAUNTON COUNTY COURT   Claim No. TA501001

BETWEEN:

                    MEGADELL FOODS LIMITED   Claimant

                            and

           ANGUS WARLEY (t/a CHOC FOLIE)   Defendant

INSTRUCTIONS TO COUNSEL FOR THE CLAIMANT

£150

QUENTIN ROGER & OWLBY
1 Dover Sweep
Southampton
Hants
SO22 4YP

Solicitors for the Claimant

NEGOTIATION

INSTRUCTIONS TO COUNSEL

Counsel is instructed on behalf of the Claimant in this matter, Megadell Foods Limited, which is resisting the application to set aside the judgment in default obtained on 16th February 2000.

This firm was instructed to commence proceedings at the beginning of December 1999. Counsel will note the nature of the claim from the Particulars of Claim enclosed with these papers. Judgment was regularly obtained on 16th February 2000. On 6th March 2000 the Defendant applied to have the judgment set aside and Counsel will see from the witness statement in support enclosed with these papers that Mr Warley is claiming that he was in hospital and he did not know of proceedings. He is attempting to set aside the judgment on the merits.

The view of the Claimant company is a commercial one in that if the judgment is to be set aside they are interested in a settlement that disposes of the entire matter without recourse to further delay and costs. The chocolate retained has not yet been sold on and the company is keen to get the Defendant to buy this from them provided the original terms as to payment can be met. Counsel is directed to the enclosed statement of Rupert Bryson for full details of the company's position and the full background to this action. The company is not however willing to settle at any cost as it is of the view that the Defendant has been the author of the problems.

This firm contacted solicitors for the Defendant upon being served with the application. They are instructing Counsel and we have suggested a meeting prior to the hearing to see whether this matter can be resolved to the interest of both sides. They are agreeable and Counsel is therefore instructed to attend early and speak to the other side with the purpose of coming to terms if possible. Counsel is entrusted to examine the issues fully and reach the best acceptable settlement for the Claimant. Failing acceptable compromise Counsel is instructed to resist the setting aside of the judgment obtained.

Costs to date excluding Counsel's fee are approximately £400.

SAMPLE EXERCISE

STATEMENT OF RUPERT BRYSON

I am the managing director of Megadell Foods Limited. We are a company importing various foodstuffs from the continent. One of our lines is premium grade chocolate which is the subject of this dispute.

The company employs various representatives who visit retail outlets and set up deals with them and supply aftercare. One of our representatives was a Mr Leon Haalen who left us in September last year. He appears to have set up the contract with Choc Folie. As is usual he set up a deal whereby we contracted to provide a year's supply of the product. The other terms were our standard ones, to supply the product to the customer's premises, and payment to be made 30 days after invoice (which was on delivery) with an interest clause for late payment. I see that Mr Haalen arranged for delivery to be between 10th and 15th of the month.

Of course it is our policy to provide foodstuffs of high quality and to keep the customer happy at all times. It is correct to say that we train our representatives to keep in touch with the customer and tell the customer to address any queries to the representative. Unfortunately in this case, due to Mr Haalen's departure, there was a slight hiatus with customer care in the West Country as we were unable to replace Mr Haalen until the end of November.

To fulfil our side of the contract, we contracted with Luglian Chocolate of Ghent, Belgium to supply us with the chocolate at a total cost of £9,000. Our storage, delivery and operating costs can be assessed at £200 per month (I can get full details from our accounts department if necessary). They contracted to deliver to us in two cargoes, the first six months' supply in August and the second six months' supply in January. The profit we were due to make on the deal was £14,920 in total.

The first record I have of any complaint from Choc Folie is a fax sent on 25th October 1999 (the one exhibited to Mr Warley's affidavit). That seems very late in the day if the product was not up to standard when delivered on 9th October. I note that the fax does not say what the problem is. I have to accept however that we did have a West Country customer care problem at the time. I am suspicious when Mr Warley says in his affidavit that he telephoned us many times as we have an efficient system and <u>all</u> telephone messages are recorded. I have investigated and not found any messages recorded from him at that time. I cannot say whether messages were left on Mr Haalen's mobile.

When the fax was brought to my attention I took personal action and telephoned the customer. My records show that this was on 27th October 1999. I pride myself in being of an equable disposition but found the customer most unreasonable. I said that the foodstuffs would be examined when delivery of the November order was made. I said this could take place a little early on 4th November just a few days after the conversation. This seemed to me the most sensible course to take. As I recall it was very difficult to make sensible headway with the customer who kept complaining about our poor service. The conversation was lengthy but not very productive.

I had checked the customer records before telephoning and noted that the customer had not made any payment for the September delivery and enquired of the customer what the position regarding this was. Again the response was confusing and negative. I pointed out the customer's obligations and the customer reacted in an almost hysterical fashion.

After about twenty minutes of conversation when little I was saying was accepted, the customer told me that as far as he was concerned he was not interested in our product and would not be paying for anything else delivered. He told us not to bother coming to look at the October chocolate delivery as he was going to bin it. I find it hard to believe that he would have said that if there had been anything wrong with the chocolate and I then took the view that he was just trying to avoid payment for the goods already received.

NEGOTIATION

After the conversation I made a note for the orders department to hold back the November delivery to the customer. I have checked with the department and there is no record of further contact from Mr Warley or from Choc Folie. In November the accounts department referred the matter to our action department and a warning letter was sent (copy attached). No communication or payment was received from the customer. The matter was put in the hands of our solicitor.

The company was able to sell on the remaining product from the first cargo delivered in August 1999 (2,000 kilogrames). However, although we did try to cancel the January cargo, the terms of the Luglian contract made this impossible. We therefore have six months' supply left, i.e., 3,000 kilogrames. It is a specialised product which has proved difficult to sell on. The chocolate is still in good condition having an 18 month shelf life from the date of the delivery to us.

I see from Mr Warley's affidavit that he is claiming half the October delivery was defective. I can only say that it is a great shame that he did not let us investigate the position thoroughly at the time. I am still rather suspicious about the whole thing. However, I can concede that our after sales service in the West Country was not up to scratch during the relevant period last year. We now have a thoroughly efficient West Country representative, Mr Knox, who I have been personally overseeing since he started with us. We have received good reports about him from our West Country customers.

I cannot really comment about Mr Warley being in hospital at the time although again it seems rather dubious. It is just raised as if that decides the whole thing. If there had been some proper communication at the time then this contract might have continued without a hitch. Indeed we still have the product and would be willing to re-supply if the customer is absolutely clear that the full contract terms regarding payment must be complied with. Of course payment for the chocolate already supplied must be made at once. Having said that, Choc Folie clearly could be a good continuing customer for us and if this matter can be resolved so that relations might continue in the future then we would be satisfied. I am willing to be advised on what would be a satisfactory settlement as continuing this matter is not commercially attractive to us.

SAMPLE EXERCISE

MEGADELL FOODS LIMITED

15, THE ESTATE, CHEAM HILL, SOUTHAMPTON, SO33 7JM

our ref 99/GHCF0001

18th November 1999

Choc Folie Angus Warley,
17, Lebbell Spring Way,
Bridgewater,
Somerset.

OUTSTANDING AMOUNT £2,520

Our records show that the above amount remains outstanding on the following invoices:

1. ch99/0001 date 11.09.1999
2. ch99/0002 date 9.10.1999

UNLESS PAYMENT IS MADE IN FULL WITHIN THE NEXT 14 DAYS WE WILL HAVE NO ALTERNATIVE BUT TO SEEK THE FULL SUM BY LEGAL ACTION

If payment has been made already please accept our apologies for this demand for payment.

ACCOUNTS DEPARTMENT,
MEGADELL FOODS LIMITED

NEGOTIATION

IN THE TAUNTON COUNTY COURT											Claim No. TA501001

BETWEEN

MEGADELL FOODS LIMITED					<u>Claimant</u>

and

ANGUS WARLEY (t/a CHOC FOLIE)				<u>Defendant</u>

PARTICULARS OF CLAIM

---

1. At all material times the Claimant was a company engaged in the import and sale of foodstuffs to retail outlets and the Defendant was a sole trader engaged in the manufacture and retail sale of chocolate confectionery to the general public.

2. By a written agreement dated 16th July 1999 between the Claimant and the Defendant, the Claimant agreed to sell to the Defendant 6,000 kilogrammes of premium grade Belgian chocolate. The chocolate was to be delivered in 12 monthly instalments of 500 kilogrammes per instalment at a total price of £15,120.

3. There were express terms of the contract that:

    (i) Deliveries would be between 10th and 15th of each month, commencing in September 1999;

    (ii) Payment would be made monthly against invoices drawn by the Claimant;

    (iii) Payment would be made to the Claimant by the Defendant 30 days after delivery of the invoice and interest was payable thereafter at a rate of 12.75% per annum.

4. Pursuant to the contract the Claimant delivered to the Defendant 500 kilogrammes of chocolate on 11th September 1999 and 500 kilogrammes of chocolate on 9th October 1999.

5. The Defendant has failed and refused to pay the sum of £2,520 or any part thereof under invoices drawn by the Claimant for the deliveries.

6. By a telephone conversation on 27th October 1999 the Defendant purported to terminate the contract. Further by his conduct in failing and/or refusing to pay the sums due as set out in paragraph 5 above the Defendant evinced an intention no longer to be bound by the contract and therefore repudiated the contract.

7. By reason of the matters set out above the Claimant has lost the benefit of the contract and has thereby suffered loss and damage.

PARTICULARS OF LOSS AND DAMAGE

Loss of profit on the sale of 5,000 kilogrammes of chocolate @ £0.82 per kilogramme .... £4,100.

8. The Claimant claims interest pursuant to the terms of the contract on the sum claimed in paragraph 5 above from 30 days after the delivery of the invoices at the contractual rate of 12.75% per annum amounting to £47.52 to the date of the issue of the summons in this action and at a daily rate thereafter of £0.88 per day.

9. Further the Claimant claims interest pursuant to section 69 of the County Courts Act 1984 on the sums claimed in paragraph 7 above at such rate and for such period as the Court thinks fit.

AND the Claimant claims:

(1) Under paragraph 5 above the sum of £2,520;

(2) Under paragraph 7 above damages for breach of contract;

(3) Under paragraph 8 above contractual interest;

(4) Under paragraph 9 above interest pursuant to section 69 of the County Courts Act 1984.

STATEMENT OF TRUTH

DATED 20th December 1999

NEGOTIATION

Defendant: A. Warley:
1st Statement of Witness
Dated: 6.3.2000

IN THE TAUNTON COUNTY COURT   Claim No. TA501001

BETWEEN

MEGADELL FOODS LIMITED   Claimant

and

ANGUS WARLEY (t/a CHOC FOLIE)   Defendant

WITNESS STATEMENT OF ANGUS WARLEY
IN SUPPORT OF APPLICATION
TO SET ASIDE JUDGMENT IN DEFAULT

---

1. I live at 10, The Close, Swainton, Bridgewater, Somerset, and I am the proprieter of an unincorporated business called Choc Folie and make this statement in support of my application to set aside judgment in default which was entered on 16th February 2000. In so far as the content of this statement is within my personal knowledge it is true, and in so far as it is not within my personal knowledge it is true to the best of my knowledge, information or belief.

2. I became aware of the Claimant's claim only on 25th February 2000 when the judgment was served upon me at my business address. Regrettably, on 17th December 1999 I crashed my car sustaining a broken leg and other injuries. I was taken to hospital and remained there until 24th February 2000. In fact from October onwards I had been finding it difficult to keep up with all the demands running your own business entails. I know I overlooked the paperwork, I simply didn't have the energy to cope with administrative matters. In all the circumstances I believe I have a valid reason for not replying to the summons as well as a good defence to the Claimant's claim.

3. I accept there was a contract as stated in the Particulars of Claim and the terms stated in that contract. The contract was in the Claimant's standard terms and was agreed by myself and Mr Haalen, a sales representative on behalf of the Claimant. However there were further terms of the contract that the Claimant company were responsible for the chocolate until acceptance by the purchaser and that any complaint about quality could be investigated at once. Further, as this was a business contract I am advised by my solicitor and believe there was an implied term as to the chocolate being of satisfactory quality.

4. The chocolate supplied on 9th October was of poor quality in that approximately one half had a whitish residue on the surface and was not usable. Attempts were made to reach Mr Haalen by telephone and messages were left on his mobile telephone and at the Claimant's offices. There was no response to these messages. A fax sent to the Claimant on 25th October 1999 in a last attempt to get the chocolate resupplied is marked exhibit 'AW1'.

5. I spoke to a Mr Bryson of the Claimant company around the end of October who said that the problem would be sorted out when the next delivery was made. This was not sufficient as we were suffering losses due to the non-supply. The accounts for our 3 shops show a loss of £1,500 profit when compared to the same month last year. We did not have enough chocolate to make up chocolate items to sell in the 3 shops. I told Mr Bryson that if we were not resupplied at once then we did

not wish to be supplied further. The shops were losing approximately £50 per day, not to mention customers long-term, so I believe this was reasonable. We could not wait another week or two.

6. Because of the supply of defective chocolate we had to obtain further supplies. This could not be arranged until 28th October 1999. We were due to supply goods for a 'Chocaganza' weekend on 30th to 31st October 1999. In the event the goods could not be completed to the ornate style ordered because of the limited time and the organisers have only paid two-thirds of the contract price, cutting our anticipated profit by £2,000.

7. I did not pay for the September chocolate (which was satisfactory) because I considered that the Claimant should sort out the problems with the October chocolate first.

8. I dispute that I ended the contract either impliedly or expressly. I assert that it was the Claimant who ended the contract by failing to resupply Choc Folie with chocolate of merchantable/satisfactory quality. If I am found to have ended the contract I assert I was entitled to do so because of the Claimant's own breach of contract. In any event I dispute the Claimant's loss of profit as stated; the Claimant should have made good its losses. I further believe we have a claim for the loss of profits caused by the supply of defective chocolate both for loss of sales and loss of profits on the 'Chocaganza' contract.

9. In the circumstances I believe I have a valid defence to the Claimant's claim and am entitled to set off my counterclaim against the claim made by the Claimant, and I ask this Honourable Court to set aside the judgment in default obtained by the Claimant on 16th February 2000.

STATEMENT OF TRUTH

Signed: Angus Warley

Dated etc.

NEGOTIATION

Exhibit AW1

CHOC FOLIE

Offices:

17, Lebbell Spring Way, Bridgewater, Somerset,
tel 0446 234883   fax 0446 234881

also at

BRIDGEWATER	TAUNTON	MINEHEAD
17, Garnet Way, Bridgewater	134, High Street, Taunton	94, Long Street, Minehead

25th October 1999

TO THE MANAGING DIRECTOR, MEGADELL FOODS LIMITED
15, THE ESTATE, CHEAM HILL, SOUTHAMPTON, SO33 7JM

URGENT

I NEED A RESPONSE. PLEASE CONTACT WITHOUT DELAY. CHOCOGANZA WEEKEND THREATENED/SHOP LOSSES MOUNTING.

ANGUS WARLEY, CHOC FOLIE

SAMPLE EXERCISE

IN THE TAUNTON COUNTY COURT   Claim No. TA501001

BETWEEN

                    MEGADELL FOODS LIMITED   Claimant

                                and

                    ANGUS WARLEY (t/a CHOC FOLIE)   Defendant

---

INSTRUCTIONS TO COUNSEL FOR THE DEFENDANT

                                                              £175

HOGGSLEY, BRYANT & CHAMLEY
175 Hele Ascent,
Bridgewater,
Somerset

Solicitors for the Defendant

NEGOTIATION

INSTRUCTIONS TO COUNSEL

Instructing Solicitors act for Angus Warley who trades as Choc Folie, and is the Defendant in this matter. Counsel is instructed in a hearing in which the Defendant seeks to set aside judgment in default obtained by the Claimant, Megadell Foods Limited, on 16th February 2000.

Counsel will see the claim made against Choc Folie from the enclosed Particulars of Claim. The Defendant's position is set out in the statement of Mr Angus Warley.

Mr Warley is the sole proprietor of Choc Folie. Mr Angus Warley consulted us a short while ago when he was served with judgment in default (which was regularly obtained). Mr Warley says that he had not known of the proceedings as he had been in hospital following a car accident although unfortunately there is no documentary evidence of this as yet.

Mr Warley has made a witness statement in support of setting aside judgment in default which is enclosed. As Counsel will see he is seeking to set judgment aside on the merits.

Judgment in default was entered on 16th February 2000 for the amount claimed plus interest. Counsel will see that the Defendant not only contests the merits of this judgment but is raising a counterclaim. However, Mr Warley is most anxious that this matter be settled if at all possible as he is struggling to keep the business going. He was happy with the original quality of the chocolate supplied and would like to resolve matters with a view to contracting with the Claimant in the future.

We have spoken to Solicitors for the Claimant and have the impression that their client is keen to settle this matter if mutually agreeable terms can be reached. We agreed that it would be profitable for Counsel to discuss possible resolution of the action prior to the hearing although the Claimant is still formally opposing setting the judgment aside. Would Counsel therefore attend in good time to discuss terms with Counsel for the Claimant. If settlement is not reached Counsel should seek to have the judgment set aside.

Our costs to date are £250 plus Counsel's fee.

SAMPLE EXERCISE

STATEMENT OF ANGUS WARLEY

1. About four years ago I opened the shop 'Folie de Chocolat' in Bridgewater, Somerset. The shop sells all kinds of chocolate, specialising in high-quality home made chocolates, truffles and other chocolate items. In 1997 I opened two other branches 'Choc Around the Clock' in Minehead and 'Choc Til You Drop' in Taunton. I set up trading as 'Choc Folie' which employs staff. However, I am a sole trader.

2. I obtained chocolate supplies from various wholesalers and I employed a couple of workers to make up chocolate products in the kitchens in Bridgewater. About half of the sales were from made up products; the other half were bought-in. About three-quarters of the profits came from the made-up products — things like chocolate truffles, animals and Christmas and Easter products.

3. In June 1999 I was introduced to a particularly fine Belgian chocolate by Mr Leon Haalen, a representative of a company called Megadell Foods of Southampton. I was so impressed I invited him to visit our Bridgewater shop in July (1999). At that meeting I explained to Mr Haalen that I would like to contract on a monthly basis although I reassured him I would probably continue to place orders for several months. Mr Haalen said that Megadell would only supply on a yearly contract, as their suppliers in Belgium traded on that basis, but that it was the policy of the company that if the buyer was unhappy with the product at any time then they would do anything in their power to satisfy the customer and he hadn't known a dissatisfied customer yet. He quoted the company's slogan (which I later saw on its delivery vans) 'The finest foods to your order'. He said that any problems with quality would be investigated at once. I stressed that it was essential that I had a constant supply of good quality chocolate as I depended on good quality to make up the products such as animals and truffles etc. which were my real profit makers. I also explained that several times a year I participated in events to promote chocolate sales, particularly at the fancier end of the market, and that one such event was coming up in the late autumn which was particularly important as it was a country-wide fair or 'chocoganza weekend'. He seemed to take my concerns on board so I signed on the dotted line there and then agreeing that I would be supplied on a monthly basis but with an overall contract for a year's supply.

4. When I signed the contract at that meeting I knew that it was for a year but I believed Mr Haalen when he said quality was assured and I believed that meant I could end the contract if unhappy. There were further terms that Megadell would deliver to our Bridgewater base and be responsible for the product until accepted by us and would investigate any problems with quality immediately on receiving a complaint. Delivery and payment were as in the Claimant's claim. The price per kilogramme was 10p more than that of our usual supplier, but we were happy to pay it as the chocolate was of a better quality.

5. The first delivery was made on 11th September 1999 (together with an invoice for £1,260). The chocolate was of superb quality. We were extremely impressed. However, when the October delivery arrived on 9th October (invoiced as before) we discovered on unpacking that about a half of the delivery had deteriorated so that there was a whitish layer on it. It was not usable. We endeavoured to contact Mr Haalen who had told us that he was the first port of call for any complaints. Between 10th and 15th October several messages were left for him both at the factory number and on his mobile phone which he did not seem to switch on. Because of the problems I decided not to pay for the September chocolate until everything was sorted out. Mr Haalen had been so reassuring that I was sure it would all soon be resolved.

6. By 19th October we were running very low on usable chocolate supplies. This was particularly worrying as we had a contract to supply the Chocaganza weekend at the Royal Taunton Hotel on 30th and 31st October. I had specifically set aside the

Megadell chocolate for use as it was a better quality than other supplies I already had and now I was running out entirely. I left an urgent message for Mr Haalen at the factory number, sure that he would sort out the matter. However we had heard nothing by 25th October and I therefore sent a fax for the attention of the managing director of the company with my concerns.

7. On 27th October I spoke to Mr Rupert Bryson of Megadel. I'm afraid my temper frayed when he seemed to know nothing about the problem and was very casual about the whole matter, saying the problem would be investigated when the November delivery was made. I exploded and told him what to do with his chocolate. He then had the cheek to say that we should pay for the September supply immediately. At this I told him there was no way he would get a penny and neither would I pay for anything else delivered, a comment I regretted as soon as I put the phone down but which felt good at the time.

8. Thereafter I phoned around for other supplies and was re-supplied by my usual supplier on 28th October. We then worked through night and day on the Chocaganza contract to get everything ready but there was simply not enough time to make the more ornate designs ordered. The organisers refused to pay the full fee for supply of the products and I can't say I blame them. We accepted a lesser fee which cut our profit by £2,000. I fear they will not use us next year.

9. During October the three shops' profits were down £1,500 in total compared to the previous year as we did not have enough chocolate items to supply them. I have accounts for the two periods that show this and can produce them if asked. I still have the mouldy chocolate if Megadell care to see it.

10. As far as I was concerned the matter ended in October. I must say I was regretful at losing such a quality supply of chocolate but forgot about the episode being far too preoccupied with keeping the business going and fulfilling contracts with customers. Shortly after this in early November, I began to feel increasingly unwell, always tired and lethargic which I put down to heavy work commitments. Regrettably I let the paperwork slip and have only just come across Megadell's final demand dated 18th November 1999. On the 17th December I was injured in a car crash and was rushed to hospital. I remained in hospital until 24th February. I was dumbstuck to receive the judgment a few weeks ago. It seems very harsh that Megadell are seeking to claim from me for ending the contract. In my view I was totally justified in doing so.

11. I do feel this matter has got totally out of hand. Perhaps if I had known about Megadell's claim earlier I could have sorted this out. I'm aware that I will have to accept some responsibility for letting things get this far. I really need this whole matter sorted out as quickly as possible and at maximum benefit to me.

12. The funny thing is that even after all this hassle I would consider being resupplied by Megadell if I can be clear about the terms. The chocolate that was properly supplied was of a better quality than my original supplier — people buying from the shops actually mentioned it and I haven't found anything else as good. I would be interested in ordering about 500 kilogrammes per month from them. I'd want a personal assurance from their managing director that I would have no more problems and prompt attention if I had any more complaints though.

SAMPLE EXERCISE

MEGADELL FOODS LIMITED

5, THE ESTATE, CHEAM HILL, SOUTHAMPTON, SO33 7JM

Our ref 99/GHCF0001

18th November 1999

Choc Folie Limited,
7, Lebbell Spring Way,
Bridgewater,
Somerset.

OUTSTANDING AMOUNT £2,520

Our records show that the above amount remains outstanding on the following invoices:

1. ch99/0001 date 11.09.1999
2. ch99/0002 date 9.10.1999

UNLESS PAYMENT IS MADE IN FULL WITHIN THE NEXT 14 DAYS WE WILL HAVE NO ALTERNATIVE BUT TO SEEK THE FULL SUM BY LEGAL ACTION

If payment has been made already please accept our apologies for this demand for payment.

ACCOUNTS DEPARTMENT,
MEGADELL FOODS LIMITED

NEGOTIATION

IN THE TAUNTON COUNTY COURT Claim No. TA501001

BETWEEN

MEGADELL FOODS LIMITED Claimant

and

ANGUS WARLEY (t/a CHOC FOLIE) Defendant

PARTICULARS OF CLAIM

1. At all material times the Claimant was a company engaged in the import and sale of foodstuffs to retail outlets and the Defendant was a sole trader engaged in the manufacture and retail sale of chocolate confectionery to the general public.

2. By a written agreement dated 16th July 1999 between the Claimant and the Defendant, the Claimant agreed to sell to the Defendant 6,000 kilogrammes of premium grade Belgian chocolate. The chocolate was to be delivered in 12 monthly instalments of 500 kilogrammes per instalment at a total price of £15,120.

3. There were express terms of the contract that:

    (i) Deliveries would be between 10th and 15th of each month, commencing in September 1999;

    (ii) Payment would be made monthly against invoices drawn by the Claimant;

    (iii) Payment would be made to the Claimant by the Defendant 30 days after delivery of the invoice and interest was payable thereafter at a rate of 12.75% per annum.

4. Pursuant to the contract the Claimant delivered to the Defendant 500 kilogrammes of chocolate on 11th September 1999 and 500 kilogrammes of chocolate on 9th October 1999.

5. The Defendant has failed and refused to pay the sum of £2,520 or any part thereof under invoices drawn by the Claimant for the deliveries.

6. By a telephone conversation on 27th October 1999 the Defendant purported to terminate the contract. Further by his conduct in failing and/or refusing to pay the sums due as set out in paragraph 5 above the Defendant evinced an intention no longer to be bound by the contract and therefore repudiated the contract.

7. By reason of the matters set out above the Claimant has lost the benefit of the contract and has thereby suffered loss and damage.

PARTICULARS OF LOSS AND DAMAGE

Loss of profit on the sale of 5,000 kilogrammes of chocolate @ £0.82 per kilogramme .... £4,100.

8. The Claimant claims interest pursuant to the terms of the contract on the sum claimed in paragraph 5 above from 30 days after the delivery of the invoices at the contractual rate of 12.75% per annum amounting to £47.52 to the date of the issue of the summons in this action and at a daily rate thereafter of £0.88 per day.

SAMPLE EXERCISE

9. Further the Claimant claims interest pursuant to section 69 of the County Courts Act 1984 on the sums claimed in paragraph 7 above at such rate and for such period as the Court thinks fit.

AND the Claimant claims:

(1) Under paragraph 5 above the sum of £2,520;

(2) Under paragraph 7 above damages for breach of contract;

(3) Under paragraph 8 above contractual interest;

(4) Under paragraph 9 above interest pursuant to section 69 of the County Courts Act 1984.

STATEMENT OF TRUTH

DATED 20th December 1999

NEGOTIATION

Defendant: A. Warley:
1st Statement of Witness
Dated: 6.3.2000

IN THE TAUNTON COUNTY COURT

Claim No. TA501001

BETWEEN

MEGADELL FOODS LIMITED   Claimant

and

ANGUS WARLEY (t/a CHOC FOLIE)   Defendant

WITNESS STATEMENT OF ANGUS WARLEY
IN SUPPORT OF APPLICATION
TO SET ASIDE JUDGMENT IN DEFAULT

---

1. I live at 10, The Close, Swainton, Bridgewater, Somerset, and I am the proprieter of an unincorporated business called Choc Folie and make this statement in support of my application to set aside judgment in default which was entered on 16th February 2000. In so far as the content of this statement is within my personal knowledge it is true, and in so far as it is not within my personal knowledge it is true to the best of my knowledge, information or belief.

2. I became aware of the Claimant's claim only on 24th February 2000 when the judgment was served upon me at my business address. Regrettably, on 17th December 1999 I crashed my car sustaining a broken leg and other injuries. I was taken to hospital and remained there until 24th February 2000. In fact from October onwards I had been finding it difficult to keep up with all the demands running your own business entails. I know I overlooked the paperwork, I simply didn't have the energy to cope with administrative matters. In all the circumstances I believe I have a valid reason for not replying to the summons as well as a good defence to the Claimant's claim.

3. I accept there was a contract as stated in the Particulars of Claim and the terms stated in that contract. The contract was in the Claimant's standard terms and was agreed by myself and Mr Haalen, a sales representative on behalf of the Claimant. However, there were further terms of the contract that the Claimant company were responsible for the chocolate until acceptance by the purchaser and that any complaint about quality could be investigated at once. Further, as this was a business contract I am advised by my solicitor and believe there was an implied term as to the chocolate being of satisfactory quality.

4. The chocolate supplied on 9th October was of poor quality in that approximately one half had a whitish residue on the surface and was not usable. Attempts were made to reach Mr Haalen by telephone and messages were left on his mobile telephone and at the Claimant's offices. There was no response to these messages. A fax sent to the Claimant on 25th October 1999 in a last attempt to get the chocolate resupplied is marked exhibit 'AW1'.

5. I spoke to a Mr Bryson of the Claimant company around the end of October who said that the problem would be sorted out when the next delivery was made. This was not sufficient as we were suffering losses due to the non-supply. The accounts for our 3 shops show a loss of £1,500 profit when compared to the same month last year. We did not have enough chocolate to make up chocolate items to sell in the 3 shops. I told Mr Bryson that if we were not resupplied at once then we did

not wish to be supplied further. The shops were losing approximately £50 per day, not to mention customers long-term, so I believe this was reasonable. We could not wait another week or two.

6. Because of the supply of defective chocolate we had to obtain further supplies. This could not be arranged until 28th October 1999. We were due to supply goods for a 'Chocaganza' weekend on 30th to 31st October 1999. In the event the goods could not be completed to the ornate style ordered because of the limited time and the organisers have only paid two-thirds of the contract price, cutting our anticipated profit by £2,000.

7. I did not pay for the September chocolate (which was satisfactory) because I considered that the Claimant should sort out the problems with the October chocolate first.

8. I dispute that I ended the contract either impliedly or expressly. I assert that it was the Claimant who ended the contract by failing to resupply Choc Folie with chocolate of merchantable/satisfactory quality. If I am found to have ended the contract I assert I was entitled to do so because of the Claimant's own breach of contract. In any event I dispute the Claimant's loss of profit as stated; the Claimant should have made good its losses. I further believe we have a claim for the loss of profits caused by the supply of defective chocolate both for loss of sales and loss of profits on the 'Chocaganza' contract.

9. In the circumstances I believe I have a valid defence to the Claimant's claim and am entitled to set off my counterclaim against the claim made by the Claimant, and I ask this Honourable Court to set aside the judgment in default obtained by the Claimant on 16th February 2000.

STATEMENT OF TRUTH

Signed: Angus Warley

Dated etc.

NEGOTIATION

Exhibit AW1

CHOC FOLIE LIMITED

Offices:

17, Lebbell Spring Way, Bridgewater, Somerset,
tel 0446 234883   fax 0446 234881

also at

BRIDGEWATER	TAUNTON	MINEHEAD
17, Garnet Way,	134, High Street,	94, Long Street,
Bridgewater	Taunton	Minehead

25th October 1999

TO THE MANAGING DIRECTOR, MEGADEL FOODS LIMITED
15, THE ESTATE, CHEAM HILL, SOUTHAMPTON, SO33 7JM

URGENT

I NEED A RESPONSE. PLEASE CONTACT WITHOUT DELAY. CHOCOGANZA WEEKEND THREATENED. SHOP LOSSES MOUNTING.

ANGUS WARLEY, CHOC FOLIE

FIFTEEN

SUGGESTED READING

Books

Gifford, D. G., *Legal Negotiation: Theory and Applications*, 1989, St Paul, Min, West Publishing Co.

Fisher, R. and Ury, W., Patton, B., *Getting to Yes — Negotiating Agreement Without Giving In*, (2nd ed), 1991, Penguin Books.

Ury, W., *Getting Past No: Negotiating Your Way from Confrontation to Cooperation*, 1991, Business Books Ltd

Williams, G. R., *Legal Negotiation and Settlement*, St Paul, Min, West Publishing Co.

Articles

Bergman, P., 'Is that a fact? Arguments in problem-solving negotiations' (1994) IJLP 1(1) pp. 81–85.

Condlin, R., 'Cases on Both Sides: Patterns of Argument in Legal Dispute Resolution' 1985 *Maryland Law Review* 44, pp. 64–136.

Condlin, R., 'Bargaining in the Dark: The Normative Incoherence of Lawyer Dispute Bargaining Role' 1992 *Maryland Law Review* 51, pp. 1–104.

Goodpaster, G., 'Lawsuits as Negotiations' 1992 *Negotiation Journal*, July issue, pp. 222–239.

Menkel-Meadow, C., 'Legal Negotiation: A Study of Strategies in Search of a Theory' 1983 *American Bar Foundation Research Journal* No. 4, p. 903.

Menkel-Meadow, C., 'Toward another View of Legal Negotiation: The Structure of Problem Solving' 1984 *UCLA Law Review* 31 N4, pp. 754–832.

Menkel-Meadow, C., 'Lawyer Negotiations: Theories & Realities — What We Learn From Mediation' 1993 *Maryland Law Review* 56(2), pp. 361–379.

Priest, G. L. and Klein, B. 'The Selection of Disputes for Litigation' (1984) 13 *Journal of Legal Studies* 1.

Taylor, M., 'Teaching Negotiation: Changing the Focus from Strategy to Substance' (1999) 16:1 *Journal of Professional Legal Education*, pp. 23–52.

INDEX

Accommodation 29
Additional terms, unilateral addition 57
Adversarial language 57
Advice 23
  ethics 89
Advocacy
  court behaviour 2–3
  negotiation compared 1–2
Agenda 12
  'moving on' 56
  setting 48–9, 132
  tactics 56
Aggressive behaviour 36, 130
Aggressive tactics 58, 63–4
Agreements *see* Convergence; Negotiated agreement; Settlement
Alternative dispute resolution 157
  arbitration 159, 160
  complaints procedures 158
  conciliation 159
  mediation 159, 161–3
  mini-trials 159
  negotiation 159
  ombudsman procedures 158–9
Anchoring 60
Appeals 19, 155
Appropriate dispute resolution 157
Arbitration
  areas in which used 160
  barrister's role 160
  court-ordered 159
  meaning 160
  private 159
Argument
  bargaining strategies 82–3
  case preparation 81–2, 102–3
  deal-making negotiations 80–1, 82
  dispute resolution 79–80, 81–2
  factual 78–9, 81
  legal 78–9, 81
  persuasion by 8, 50, 77–83, 134–5
  preparation and planning 81–2, 102–3
  presentation skills 82
  for sake of arguing 83
Assessment of proposals, settlement standards 12–13, 102
Assessment of skills
  criteria 167–72
  learning skills 165
  tasks 166

Authority of client
  acting within 22, 96, 127, 143
  ethics and 22, 89, 96, 127, 143
  lack or limited 58
  preparation and planning 96
Avoidance 29

Backtracking 56
Bargaining 8, 14, 132, 135–6
  collaborative negotiator 83
  competitive bargainer 82
  cooperative negotiator 83
  persuasion by argument 82–3
  plea bargaining 15
  strategic bargaining theory 17
Barristers
  court-door negotiations 19–21, 95
  division of functions 90
  limited access to information 20
  relationship with client 20
  role 18–22
    in arbitration 160
    in mediation 162
Best Alternative to a Negotiated Settlement (BATNA) 44, 47, 51, 64, 103
Bidding 131
Bluffing 60, 88
Body language 84–5
Bottom line *see* Walkout
Boulwarism 55
Breakdown 14, 132
  see also Deadlock
'Brer Rabbit' technique 54
Brief
  analysis in preparation 95–6
  endorsement on 146–7
Brinkmanship 62
Bunching, concessions or demands 50, 54

Calderbank offer 88
Civil dispute stages
  appeal 19
  enforcement 19
  initiating proceedings 18
  interlocutory 18
  pre-action 18
  trial 18
Client
  acceptance of settlement 143–4
  advising 23, 89
  authority

Client — *continued*
    acting within 22, 96, 127, 143
    ethics and 22, 89, 96, 127, 143
    lack or limited 58
    preparation and planning 96
  benefits of settlement 17–18
  decisions taken by 23
  lawyer as representative 23
  objectives 8, 22, 39, 98
    financial 96
    hidden 97
    legal 96
    matching 27
    meeting 141–2
      evaluation 104
    personal 96–7
    practical 96
    preparation and planning 26, 96–7, 108–9
    presentation of 49
    several 97
    working to achieve 127
    written list 108–9
  relationship with
    barristers 20
    competitive strategy and 36
    cooperative strategy and 38
    solicitors 19
  separation of negotiator from 58
Code of Conduct 87
Cognitive influences 69–75
  communication skills
    listening skills 74, 84
    observation skills 73–4
    verbal skills 74–5
  concessions 71–2
  distractions 72
  emotions 69
  expectations 69–70
  failure to cope 73
  mirroring behaviour 72–3
  perceptions 69–70, 71
  persuasion *see* Persuasion
  reciprocal behaviour 72–3
  selective perception 71
  self-fulfilling prophecy 70
Collaborative strategy 29, 31
  advantages 46
  bargaining strategy 83
  limitations 46–7
  principled 31, 33, 40–5
    BATNA development 44, 47, 51
    focus on interests not positions 41–2
    limitations 46–7
    objective criteria 44
    options for mutual gain 43–4
    other party not principled 44–5
    separate people from problem 41
  problem-solving 29, 31, 33, 40, 45–6
    fair or just solution 46
    intellectual approach 45
    limitations 47
    reasoned interchange 45
    shared interests 45
Communication skills
  body language 84–5
  listening skills 74, 84
  non-verbal communication 84–5

Communication skills — *continued*
  observation skills 73–4
  verbal skills 74–5
Competition, apparent increase as tactic 61
Competitive behaviour 14
Competitive strategy 29, 31
  advantages 35
  bargaining strategy 82
  concessions/offers 33–4
  cooperative distinguished from 32–3
  cooperative similarities with 31–2
  as cover for lack of preparation 36
  deadline 34
  dealing with competitive negotiators 36–7
  distrust 34, 35
  information exchange 34
  limitations 36
  matching style 35–6
  measuring success 35
  on-going relationships and 36
  opening demands 33
  risks 35–6
  stance 34
  underlying assumptions and ethos 33
  walkout 34, 51
Complaints procedures 158
Compromise 7, 29, 55
  see also Cooperative strategy
Concessions 7
  backtracking 56
  based on analysis and evaluation 105–6
  Boulwarism 55
  bunching 50, 54
  competitive strategy 33–4
  compromise 55
  conditional statements 50
  consideration of 135–6
  cooperative strategy 38, 39
  dividing issues up into smaller issues 55
  early 54
  false demands 50, 54
  how to make 50
  importance 104
  logrolling 55–6
  making and seeking distinguished 104
  misleading concession pattern 56
  moving to settlement 50
  preparation and planning 27–8, 64, 106–7, 109
  procedure for making 135
  provisional 135
  psychological influences 71–2
  reopening 56
  self-fulfilling prophecy 70
  single offer approach 55
  split the difference 55
  strategic planning role 107
  tactics 54–6
  trade-offs 55–6
  use of 50
  see also Demands; Offers
Conciliation 159
Conciliatory language 57
Conditional statements 50
Conduct of negotiation
  acting within authority 22, 96, 127, 143
  agenda setting 48–9, 132
  convergence 14, 130, 138–9

INDEX

Conduct of negotiation — *continued*
    agreement on formula 139
    agreement on overall deal 139
    agreements on individual issues 139
  deadlock *see* Deadlock
  dealing with opponent 130
    aggressive or entrenched 130
    refusing to agree 130
    weak or ill prepared 130
  ethics 128
  gathering information 134
  objectives of client *see* Objectives of client
  overall structure 142
  presentation *see* Presentation
  progress definition 136
  responding 57–8, 129, 142
  review 141–2
  strategy review 142
  tactics 136
    review of 142
  see also Process of negotiation; Setting up negotiation; Settlement; Starting negotiations
Context
  factual 98–9
  general 98
  legal 99–100
  of negotiated agreement 144
  practical 98
  in preparation and planning 94–5, 97–100
Contract, negotiated agreement 150–1
Control, maintenance of 64
Convergence 14, 132, 138–9
  agreement on formula 139
  agreement on overall deal 139
  agreements on individual issues 139
Cooperative behaviour 14
Cooperative strategy 29, 31
  advantages 38
  bargaining strategy 83
  competitive distinguished from 32–3
  competitive similarities with 31–2
  concessions 38, 39
  conciliatory stance 38
  continuing relationships 38
  information exchange 37, 39
  limitations 39
  matching style 38
  offers 38
  opening demands 37
  risks 39
  underlying assumptions and ethos 37
Court
  behaviour 2–3
  officials 22
  return to court
    commencement of new action 155
    enforcement of order 155
    existing action 155
Court orders
  final 152–4
  interim 151–2
Court-door negotiations 19–21, 98, 131
  entrenched attitudes 20–1
  lack of facilities 21
  preparation and planning 95
Court-ordered arbitration 159

Cross-cultural negotiation 11
Deadlines 62
  competitive strategy 34
Deadlock 72
  advantages of agreement 65
  bogged down 137
  common ground 65
  conduct of negotiation 136–8
  dead-ends 138
  dealing with 64–5
  disadvantages 65
  emotions 137–8
  going round in circles 137
  lack of cooperation 137
  lack of information 136–7
  move to hypothetical 65
  occurrence of 64
  reaching 138
  reasons for 64–5
  review of progress 64
  tactics 64–5
  take of break 65
Deal-making negotiations 80–1, 82
Deed, negotiated agreement 150–1
Defusing emotions 66–7
Demands
  bunching 50, 54
  competitive strategy 33
  cooperative strategy 37
  dividing issues up into smaller issues 55
  escalating 54–5
  extreme opening demand 54
  false 50, 54
  new, at end of negotiations 57
  precondition 54
  seeking proposals and 57
  tactics 54–6
  see also Concessions; Offers
Discussion 14, 131, 134
Dispute resolution 9
  alternative 157
    arbitration 159, 160
    complaints procedures 158
    conciliation 159
    mediation 159, 161–3
    mini-trials 159
    negotiation 159
    ombudsman procedures 158–9
  appropriate 157
  litigation, disadvantages of 157–8
  persuasion by argument 79–80, 81–2
Distributive negotiation 9–10
Draft agreement
  persons preparing after negotiation 145–6
  preparation as tactic 59

Effectiveness
  preparation and planning 25–8
  presentation 128–9
  recognition of 24–5
  theory and practice 25
  traits 25
Emotions 59, 69
  causing deadlock 137–8
  defusing 66–7
Endorsement on brief 146–7

197

NEGOTIATION

Enforcement 19
  appeals 155
  commencement of new action 155
  by court 155
  grudging acceptance and 144
  oral agreement 154
  provisions in agreement 145, 155
Equality of power 12
Escalating demands 54–5
Ethics 87–91, 128
  advising client 89
  authority of client 22, 89, 96, 127, 143
  between counsel discussions 88
  Code of Conduct 87
  court 90
  dubious tactics 63–4
  information untrue and calculated to mislead 60, 88–9
  instructions, importance of 89
  lay client 89
  problems 90–1
  professional client 90
  'without prejudice' negotiations 87–8
Evidence, analysis 100–1
Exchange of information 7–8, 12
  bluffing 60, 88
  competitive strategy 34
  cooperative strategy 37, 39
  ethics 60, 88–9
  failure to give 61
  flow of information 60–1
  method 51
  tactic 60–1
  untrue and calculated to mislead 60, 63, 88–9
Exercise 169–88
'Expanding the pie/cake' 43, 105
Expectations 69–70
Exploration 14, 131, 134
Extreme opening demands 54

Face to face discussions 11, 12
False demands 50, 54
Fax, negotiation by 11, 12
Final court orders 152–4
Final offers 62

Hypothetical questions 65

Impersonal matters 10
Inexperience 65
Information
  gathering 134
  lack of 136–7
  see also Exchange of information; Issues, factual
Initiating proceedings stage 18
Instructions
  acting within 96, 127
  importance of 89
Integrative negotiation 9–10
Interactive process 8
Interim court order 151–2
Interlocutory stage 18
International negotiation 11, 12
Interpretations 12
Issues 11–13
  analysis 100–1
  factual

Issues — *continued*
  agreement of 99
  analysis 101
  analysis of evidence 100–1
  available to both sides 98–9
  context 98–9
  familiarity with 98
  figures 99
  gaps in information 99
  identification 97, 100
  presentation 102–3
  strengths and weaknesses 101
  in final agreement 144
  identification 97, 100
  impersonal matters 10
  integrative 43
  legal
    analysis 101
    context 99–100
    identification 100
    presentation 103
    procedure and practice 100
    remedies 100
    strengths and weaknesses 102
    substantive law 100
    summary of 109
  multiple 9, 43
  personal matters 10, 97
  preparation and planning 27, 97–100, 108–9
  single 9, 43
  written list of 108–9
  'zero-sum' 9–10, 43

Judge, negotiations with 21, 90

Labour relations 11
Language
  adversarial 57
  body language 84–5
  conciliatory 57
  presentation and 129
Learning skills 2–5
Letters
  negotiation by 131
  setting up negotiation 11, 12, 131
Listening skills 74
  persuasion 84
  responding 129
Litigation
  benefits of settlement 17–18
  disadvantages 157–8
  reasons for 16
  reasons for going to trial 18
  settlement after issue of process 16–17
  uncertainties 79
  variables 17
Logrolling 55–6

Maintenance of control 64
Mediation 159
  areas in which used 161–2
  barrister's role 162
  meaning 161
  mediator 161
  negotiation compared 163
  procedure 162
Mini-trials 159

INDEX

Mirroring behaviour 72–3
'Moving on' 56
Multiple issue negotiation 9, 43

Negotiated agreement
  choice of form 144
  context 144
  contract or deed 150–1
  detail to include 144–5
  draft preparation 145–6
  endorsement on brief 146–7
  enforcement *see* Enforcement
  exchange of letters as record of terms 147–50
  final court order 152–4
  interim court order 151–2
  issues to be covered 144
  terms 147–50
  Tomlin order 153, 154
Negotiation
  advocacy compared 1–2
  agenda *see* Agenda
  alternative dispute resolution 159
  conduct *see* Conduct of negotiation
  court behaviour 2–3
  court-door negotiations 19–21, 95, 98, 131
  exchange of information *see* Exchange of information
  face to face discussions 11, 12
  fax 11, 12
  importance of skills 1–2
  issues *see* Issues
  learning skills 2–5
    literature 4
    by observation 3–4
    unconscious learning 3
  letters 11, 12, 131
  meaning 7–8
  opening *see* Starting negotiations
  parties or players *see* Parties
  preparation and planning *see* Preparation and planning
  process *see* Process of negotiation
  setting up *see* Setting up negotiation
  telephone 11, 21, 131
  types 8–11
New action, enforcement failure and 155
Non-verbal communication 84–5

Objective standards 60
Objectives of client 8, 22, 39, 98
  financial 96
  hidden 97
  legal 96
  matching 27
  meeting 141–2
    evaluation 104
  personal 96–7
  practical 96
  preparation and planning 26, 96–7, 108–9
  presentation of 49
  several 97
  working to achieve 127
  written list 108–9
Objectives of opponent 26
  identification of 97
  written list of 108

Observation skills 73–4
Offers
  Boulwarism 55
  consideration of 135–6
  final offer as tactic 62
  making 135
  provisional 135
  single offer approach 55
  strategic planning role 107
  see also Concessions; Demands
Ombudsman procedures 158–9
Opening positions *see* Setting up negotiation; Starting negotiations
Opponent
  aggressive or entrenched 130
  dealing with 130
  finding out about case 133
  objectives 26, 97, 108
  personal knowledge of 97
  refusing to agree 130
  weak or ill prepared 130
Options
  'expanding the pie/cake' 43, 105
  for mutual gain 43–4
Orientation 13, 131
Outcome of negotiation 104–5
Overall structure 56–7, 109, 131–3, 142
  planning 103–4, 107–8

Pace of presentation 129
Parties
  judges 21, 90
  lawyers for other side 21
  litigants in person 10–11, 21
  multiple parties 11
  one-off players 10
  presence at negotiation 131
  repeat players 10
    lawyers as 23
  representatives 10–11
  two parties 11
  see also Client; Opponent
Perceptions 69–70
  selective perception 71
Personal matters 10, 97
Personality clash 65–6
Persuasion 2, 77–85
  argument 8, 50, 77–83, 134–5
    bargaining strategies 82–3
    case preparation 81–2
    deal-making negotiations 80–1, 82
    dispute resolution 79–80, 81–2
    factual 78–9, 81
    legal 78–9, 81
    presentation skills 82
    for sake of arguing 83
  body language 84–5
  listening skills 84
  non-verbal communication 84–5
  questioning 85
  reframing approach 57–8, 67
Place of negotiation 131
  court-door negotiations 19–21, 98, 131
Planning *see* Preparation and planning
Plea bargaining 15
Positioning 13, 131

NEGOTIATION

Pre-action negotiation 18
  preparation and planning 94
Preconditions 54
Preparation and planning
  analysis of brief 95–6
  analysis of papers 26
  authority of client 96
  BATNA 44, 103
  checklist 124–5
  client objectives 26, 96–7
    list of 108–9
  competitive strategy as cover for lack 36
  concessions 27–8, 64, 104–7, 109
  context of negotiation 94–5, 97–100
  court-door negotiations 95
  coverage 93–4
  effectiveness and 25–8
  evaluation 104
    concessions based on 105–6
    factual issues 101, 102–3
    legal issues 102, 103
    objectives of client 104
  failure to cope and 73
  instructions 96
  issues 27
    factual
      agreement of 99
      analysis of evidence 100–1
      available to both sides 98–9
      context 98–9
      figures 99
      gaps in information 99
      identification 97, 100
      presentation 102–3
      strengths and weaknesses 101
    identification 97, 100
    legal
      context 99–100
      identification 100
      presentation 103
      strengths and weaknesses 102
      substantive law 100
  legal and factual argument 81–2, 102–3
  matching objectives 27
  negotiation structure 28, 109
  objectives of client 27, 96–7
  opponent's objectives 26
  outcome of negotiation 104–5
  overall structure 103–4, 107–8
  pre-action 94
  preparation coverage 93–4
  presentation 101–4
  strategic planning 107–8
    coverage 94
    in written plan 109
  tactics 64
  written plan 108–9
    list of client's objectives 108–9
    list of opponent's objectives 108
    sample 109, 110–23
    strategic planning and tactics 109
    structure of negotiation 109
    summary of issues 109
Presentation
  clarity 128
  coherence 128
  effective 128–9

Presentation — *continued*
  factual issues 102–3
  flexibility 129
  language use 129
  legal issues 103
  of objectives 49
  pace 129
  persuasion by argument 82
  preparation and planning 101–4
  review of 142
Private arbitration 159
Problem-solving *see* Collaborative strategy
Process of negotiation
  appeals 19, 155
  bargaining 14, 132, 135–6
  bidding 131
  breakdown 14, 132
  commencement of new action 155
  conclusion *see* Settlement
  convergence 14, 132, 138–9
  discussion 14, 131, 134
  exchange of information 51
  exploration 14, 131, 134
  moving to settlement 49–50
  opening 13, 131
  orientation 13, 131
  overall structure 131–3
  positioning 13, 131
  presentation of objectives 49
  proposals 131, 135–6
  see also Conduct of negotiation; Settlement; Starting negotiations
Progress definition 136
Proposals 131, 135–6
Provisional concessions 135
Psychological influences, concessions 71–2
Psychological tactics 58–9

Questioning 2
  persuasion by 85

Reactions 30
Reciprocal behaviour 72–3
Reframing approach 57–8, 67
Rejection 67
Renegotiation 56
  after client refusal to accept 143–4
Representatives 23
Reservation point 51
Responding 58, 129
  listening skills 129
  review of 142
Retaliation 36

Sample exercise 173–92
Saving face 68, 71
Seating arrangements 131
Selection theory 16–17
Selective perception 71
Self-fulfilling prophecy 70
Setting up negotiation
  face-to face 131
  letters 131
  papers 131
  persons present 131
  place 131
  seating 131

Setting up negotiation — *continued*
  telephone 131
  see also Starting negotiation
Settlement 14, 132
  adding condition after 57
  after issue of proceedings 16–17
  appropriateness 140
  assessment standard 12–13, 102
  benefits for client 17–18
  checklist 140–1
  client acceptance 143–4
  conclusion of process 139–41
  convergence 14, 132, 138–9
  form of *see* Negotiated agreement
  moving to 49–50
  not all issues 141
  persuasion by argument 79–80
  predictability of outcomes 17
  reasons for 15–18
  selection theory 16–17
  shaking hands 143
  strategic bargaining theory 17
  variables 17
Shaking hands 143
Silence, as tactic 59
Single issue negotiation 9, 43
Solicitors
  division of functions 90
  relationship with client 19
  role 18–22
Split the difference concessions 55
Starting negotiations
  agenda setting 48–9, 132
  atmosphere 48
  first offer 49
  mutually agreed start 133
  opening positions 13
    competitive strategy 33
    cooperative strategy 37
    planning 107
  opponent to start 134
  setting up *see* Setting up negotiation
Strategic bargaining theory 17
Strategic planning 107–8
  coverage 94
  opening 107
  overall structure 107–8
  roles of offers and concessions 107
  structure and tactic use 107–8
  written list 109
  in written plan 109
Strategy 30–3
  accommodation 29
  avoidance 29
  choice 47–8
  collaborative 29, 31
    advantages 46
    bargaining strategy 83
    limitations 46–7
    principled 31, 33, 40–5
      BATNA development 44, 47, 51
      focus on interests not positions 41–2
      limitations 46–7
      objective criteria 44
      options for mutual gain 43–4
      other party not principled 44–5
      separate people from problem 41

Strategy — *continued*
  problem-solving 29, 31, 33, 40, 45–6
    fair or just solution 46
    intellectual approach 45
    limitations 47
    reasoned interchange 45
    shared interests 45
  competitive 29, 31
    advantages 35
    bargaining strategy 82
    concessions/offers 33–4
    cooperative distinguished from 32–3
    cooperative similarities with 31–2
    as cover for lack of preparation 36
    deadline 34
    dealing with competitive negotiators 36–7
    distrust 34, 35
    information exchange 34
    limitations 36
    matching style 35–6
    measuring success 35
    on-going relationships and 36
    opening demands 33
    risks 35–6
    stance 34
    underlying assumptions and ethos 33
    walkout 34, 51
  compromise 29
  cooperative 29, 31
    advantages 38
    bargaining strategy 83
    competitive distinguished from 32–3
    competitive similarities with 31–2
    concessions 38, 39
    conciliatory stance 38
    continuing relationships 38
    information exchange 37, 39
    limitations 39
    matching style 38
    offers 38
    opening demands 37
    risks 39
    underlying assumptions and ethos 37
  planning use 107–8
  review of 142
  style distinguished 30
  written plan 109
Strengths
  factual issues 101
  legal issues 102
Style
  matching competitive strategy 35
  matching cooperative strategy 38
  strategy distinguished 30

Tactics
  agenda 56
  aggression 58, 63–4
  anchoring 60
  concessions 54–6
  conduct of negotiation 136
  deadlock
    advantages of agreement 65
    common ground 65
    dealing with 64–5
    disadvantages 65
    move to hypothetical 65

NEGOTIATION

Tactics — *continued*
   occurrence of 64
   reasons for 64–5
   review of progress 64
   take of break 65
 demands 54–6
 draft agreements 59
 dubious 63–4
 exchange of information
   accuracy 60
   bluffing 60
   failure to give 61
   flow of information 60–1
   untrue and calculated to mislead 60
 forcing the issue 62
 increasing competition 61
 inexperience 65
 'moving on' 56
 objective standard 60
 offers 54–6
 order 56–7
 personality clash 65–6
 planning use 107–8
 preparation 64
 psychological 58–9
   aggressive 58
   positive emotions 59
   silence 59
   strokes 59
   tit-for-tat 59
 reframing approach 57–8
 responding 57–8
 review of 142
 separation from client 58
 setting parameters 59–60
 specific 53–62
 structure 56–7, 107–8
 team working 62
 threats 63–4
 time use 61–2
 tit-for-tat 59, 73
 unforeseen problems 65
 walkout 62
 in written plan 109
 written plan 109
 see also Techniques
'Take it or leave it' approach 55
Team working 62
Techniques
 defusing emotions 66–7
 educating 68

Techniques — *continued*
 reactions 66
 reframing position 67
 rejection 67
 saving face 68
 time to think 66
 see also Tactics
Telephone
 negotiation by 11, 21, 131
 setting up negotiation 131
Termination of existing action 155
Thinking time 66
Threats 63–4
Time
 brinkmanship 62
 court-door negotiations 19–20
 deadlines 62
 thinking time 66
 use as tactic 61–2
Tit-for-tat tactic 59, 73
Tomlin order 153, 154
Trade-offs 55–6
Transactional negotiation 9
Trial 18

Unilateral addition of additional terms 57

Verbal skills 74–5
 hesitations 75

Walkout 64
 competitive strategy 34, 51
 reservation point 51
 tactic 62
Weaknesses
 preparation and planning
   factual issues 101
   legal issues 102
'Without prejudice' negotiations 23–4
 ethics 87–8
Witnesses 22
Written plan 108–9
 list of client's objectives 108–9
 list of opponent's objectives 108
 sample 110–23
 samples 109
 strategic planning and tactics 109
 structure of negotiation 109

'Zero-sum' negotiations 9–10, 43